Black neighbors

Black neighbors:
Negroes
in a northern
rural
community
Second Edition

George K. Hesslink
Pomona College:
The Claremont Colleges

Second Edition

with the Contribution of
Joanne M. Hesslink
Claremont Graduate School

The Bobbs-Merrill Company, Inc., Publishers
Indianapolis • New York

Library of Congress Cataloging in Publication Data

Hesslink, George K.
  Black neighbors.

  Bibliography: p.
  1. Negroes—Cass Co., Mich. 2. Cass Co., Mich.—
Race question. I. Title.
F572.C3H4 1973   301.45'19'6073077412
ISBN 0-672-61237-2   73-8915

301.4519
H46b
96313
man. 1976

*The author is indebted to the following for permission to quote: Everett
Claspy; Robert J. Kundtz; Jack M. Ryder; Western Michigan University for
A Survey of Cassopolis Public Schools; The Geographical Review (from
Vol. 58, 1968, and Vol. 59, 1969; copyrighted by the American Geographical
Society of New York).*

To George John and his Misty.

Foreword to the First Edition

Cases of stable and egalitarian communities of whites and Negroes in the United States are so rare that the discovery of a clear-cut instance is like finding a gold mine. George Hesslink has written a fascinating historical and sociological account of the development, persistence, and problems of a rural northern community that has remained bi-racial in character for more than a century. Frank F. Lee's *Negro and White in Connecticut Town*[1] gives us a description of race relations in a small northern community, but a town in which racial patterns were largely in the more standard superior-inferior mold. Professor Hesslink's book provides the important contrasting case.

The major power of *Black Neighbors* is an analysis of the forces which have formed the character of a particular community—one located in southwestern Michigan—Cass County. Thus Hesslink studies the contribution of the farmer-entrepreneurial social structure, and examines such specific factors as the nineteenth-century efforts of the Quakers to settle freedmen and ex-slaves on the nearby farm land. He analyzes the normative order which has developed in the community and which has contributed heavily to its character in the present day. In so doing, he provides a strong empirical sense of the possible in American race relations and addresses relevant theoretical and policy issues as well.

One of Hesslink's most important contributions is the aid he gives us in developing concepts less vague than "integration." He helps, principally, by providing a careful analysis of the relationships and differences between whites and Negroes in each sector of the community's life. As the reader will see, the author underwent a process of disenchantment, and came to recognize that even this community, where whites and blacks had lived in cooperation since before the Civil War, was further from full and true integration than he had initially perceived.

While the two races had more or less equal access to the market-

[1]Frank F. Lee, *Negro and White in Connecticut Town* (New Haven, Conn.: College and University Press, 1961).

place and the polling booth, they were not equals in voluntary associations or informal relations. Sharp income differences persisted,
and in many aspects of life the whites and Negroes constituted two
largely separate groups. The ordinarily amicable relations between
them carried an undertone that the Negroes were present on their
good behavior—at the sufferance of the whites. The established
Negro farmers by and large accepted and internalized this view.
Like the characters in E. Franklin Frazier's *Black Bourgeoisie*,[2] these
"old-time" Negroes were extremely protective of the status quo and
eager to disassociate themselves from Negro newcomers who came
on weekends to resorts in the area or who, since the thirties, had
begun to settle locally.

Yet the author does not become jaundiced, and the long-established
Negroes do not become Uncle Toms. Hesslink recognizes that while
the situation is far from ideal, it offers a context for Negro economic
accomplishment, self-respect, and community pride. The Negro
farmers are free to be just as uninteresting politically, socially, and
personally as their white neighbors. Despite the elements of accommodation to the whites, there is a true and mutually respected sense
of autonomy in the Negro community. The system really is a stable
bi-racial one—and it is this concept which may have much more
utility as a standard for evaluating structures of race relations than
the present integrated system does. This especially seems to be the
case in light of the general failure of large-scale efforts to encourage
a change in attitude and other attempts to alter the ghettoized and
deprived situation of Negroes in the city. For the body of these
people, the bi-racial situation of Cass County, whatever its seamy
aspects, would constitute a definite and significant social advance.

If this analysis implies bi-racialism as a realistic policy goal, it
should be clear that this is not the same as accepting separatism or
black power as ends. In my view, bi-racialism is seen, hopefully, as
a transitional condition which can lead to greater integration. Although it assumes that the Negro neighborhoods are to be largely
self-contained and must develop their own capacity for solving
their own problems, it recognizes that the system must operate,

---

[2]E. Franklin Frazier, *Black Bourgeoisie* (Glencoe, Ill.: The Free Press, 1962).

with the entire community—Negro and white—in mind, in a context of non-discrimination, mutual respect, and cooperation. As Hesslink found in Cass County, racial polarization on the national scene can threaten the stability and assumptions of the local bi-racial system. Moreover, when the author speaks of practical policy implications, he again recognizes the need for a cooperative context for bi-racialism. Although not blind to the many difficulties inherent in attempting to "transport" the more favorable aspects of community life, he talks of possible experiments in decentralizing ghetto populations into new planned smaller communities—but with racial balance and interracial cooperation and equity assured.

This book is a tribute to individual scholarship and drive, and to the continuing viability of the community study method prominent in the old Chicago school. Observations, unstructured interviews, analysis of documents, and other techniques are convincingly mustered here. This community has merited study for decades, but it took a person operating first on curiosity rather than financial support, and acting not as a member of a research team but as an individual—in this case affiliated with the Center for Social Organization Studies of the University of Chicago—to discover it and actually do the work. I understand that the author has continued his investigation in several other Negro communities elsewhere in North America. Let us hope he continues, for the accumulation of such studies may yield a comparative community sociology of race relations that is more precise about variations in the phenomena and about conditions under which these variations occur; and becomes, because of its freshness of implications, a more stimulating contribution than what we have had to date.

David Street
University of Chicago
July 1967

Acknowledgments to the First Edition

In a community study it would be deceptive to assume that the results accurately reflect the efforts made only by the researcher. In a very meaningful sense, the productivity of research ultimately depends upon the character of the data collected. In a community study the role of the respondent is critical. Therefore, whatever merit this study may possess stands as a tribute to both the graciousness of many individuals who gave freely of their time, information, and patience, and the relative lack of tension in which discussions of race relations could be conducted. It would indeed be appropriate to thank each of the many respondents individually. However, every possible step consistent with ethical scientific practice and sound scholarship has been taken to retain anonymity of respondents. Thus, all that can remain is a citation to those who, collectively, made this research possible.

Many individuals besides respondents have substantially contributed to the research. In particular, I would like to thank Mr. Loren Shahin, a former student of mine, whose perceptive analysis and insight during the many hours of his assistance made the project even more of a fascinating intellectual experience.

I would like to express my appreciation to Raymond W. Mack who, in addition to criticizing the present manuscript, excited my interest in sociology so that I became an undergraduate major. I also owe a most significant debt of gratitude to David Street who carefully examined an earlier draft of the manuscript and offered many helpful and constructive criticisms.

Finally, I thank my wife, a sociologist-by-osmosis, for her field observations, capable transcription of interim notes, editing, and typing of the manuscript. Of course, I must take full responsibility for errors of omission or commission in the research.

George K. Hesslink
Rutgers University
New Brunswick, New Jersey
March 1967

Acknowledgments to
the Second Edition

Community studies have never been a very efficient method for an individual to use in performing research. Such investigations are costly in terms of both time and money. A number of persons have freely given of their time, which in a very real sense is the more costly of the two. In addition to the many students who have offered suggestions or nudged the mind, I also owe a debt of gratitude to David P. Street, Director of Graduate Studies at the State University of New York, Stony Brook, for his critical reading of the second edition. Corinne Bybee has plodded through the hen scratches which I maintain constitute an approximation of writing, but perhaps they do not. Additionally, both Pomona College and The Bobbs-Merrill Company have provided generous fellowship assistance. Robert A. Burton has drawn on his creative abilities to expand the usual editorial role in a most challenging and helpful manner.

The Census Data Service of the University of Michigan, working with John Runcie, was able to extract meaningful tabulations from the 1970 United States Census tapes. The late Everett Claspy, a resident of the research area, made available data which he had collected over many years. Finally, my respondents, informants, and contacts established over the years in Cass County have again given of their time, perspectives, and patience. I mean much more than the usual routine gesture when I state that they are too numerous to thank individually.

George K. Hesslink
Claremont, California

Contents

part five: "Five years later"–replication and reflection

Tables

*Tables 16, 17, and 18 appear in the Appendix to the First Edition.

Figures

Note to the reader

The materials which you will be reading represent a relatively unusual effort in community studies research. They begin with a report of the results of a field study undertaken in the middle 1960's. This analysis is contained in Chapters One through Nine, which are identical to the corresponding chapters of the first edition. No changes other than the correcting of typographical errors have been made in these chapters.

In 1970 and 1971, we had the opportunity to return to the same community and to observe the alterations which had taken place. The process of return and restudy provided a vantage point from which to consider a number of important methodological issues. In addition, we found that the community had changed in several somewhat unanticipated ways. These changes are examined in Chapters Ten, Eleven, and Twelve.

Preliminary observations

part one

one:

A framework

for research

Introduction

While it is certainly true that the South has been undergoing what is perhaps its greatest social upheaval since Reconstruction days, it would be insufficient to assume that the racial problem is merely a regional or sectional issue. Sociologists have long observed that northern urban areas have been racked by widespread racial discrimination, disturbance, disorder, and more than occasional violence throughout the twentieth century. However, just as it is insufficient to conceptualize racial instability as a regional issue only, it may also be shortsighted to view it as simply one of the many concomitants of northern urbanization. Nevertheless, the sociological literature concerned with Negro-white relations reflects a basic pattern that seems to imply that racial instability is characteristically found only in the South and urban North. What about the rural North?

The lack of sociological research on patterns of Negro-white relations in the rural North could be justified only if one of two conditions prevailed: first, if there are no northern rural Negroes; or second, if they do exist, that they are of no significant sociological concern. As E. Franklin Frazier pointed out, only a small proportion of Negroes has ever settled in the rural North.[1] He also commented that "the rural Negro population has always consisted of widely scattered individuals and small groups in the various Northern states."[2] It is in this same vein that Myrdal observed, "Negroes are almost absent, not only from the large rural areas of the North, but also from most of the smaller cities."[3]

From the preceding comments, it would appear that few Negroes are found in the rural North and fewer still in one particular area, but the point still remains that although it might be a difficult search to locate a substantial number of these people, they *do* exist. Indeed, the 1960 census data for the five Midwestern states of Illinois, Indiana, Michigan, Ohio, and Wisconsin record 99,176 rural Negroes—90,248 of these living outside an incorporated area.[4] Although these numbers may be comparatively modest, they are not so unassertive as to be conveniently forgotten.

Prevalent assumptions

The sociological literature reflects several basic but often unstated assumptions concerning the nature and origins of racial tension and instability in the United States. Although these assumptions are interwoven and meshed together, they can be separated and explicitly stated:

1. The intense degree of racial prejudice found particularly in the deep South is not necessarily dependent on contemporary social

[1]E. Franklin Frazier, *The Negro in the United States* (New York: The Macmillan Company, 1949), p. 197.

[2]*Ibid.*

[3]Gunnar Myrdal, *An American Dilemma* (New York: Harper and Bros., 1944), p. 386.

[4]Throughout this research, unless otherwise stated, statistical comparisons of Negroes and whites will be drawn from U.S., Bureau of the Census, *U.S. Census of the Population: 1960. Characteristics of the Population*, Vol. I.

fact, but rather is a traditional part of a culture that is grounded primarily in the past. Myth, legend, and mental reconstruction of the meaning of social tradition bolster up the historical definitions of "place" assigned to Negroes.

2. Although the original source of prejudicial attitudes may lie in a conception of the past, it is soon reinforced by definitions of "social fact," such as the ideology of Negroes' inherent biological inferiority, the moral wrongness of integration, the sexual danger of Negroes' insatiable desires, and so on.

3. Prejudice, as an attitude or as a psychological predisposition to behave, becomes manifest in discrimination when this behavior is culturally legitimated and based on the likelihood of economic, political, social, or sexual profits. Thus, an ideology of inherent racial differences is likely to arise out of what is already pragmatic social policy. If the pragmatism becomes general, in the absence of long-standing and firmly held value commitments to the contrary, overt discrimination can graduate from the status of folk practices to be incorporated into the official normative standards of a culture. Thus, discrimination is not only legitimated in a formal way—it is also necessitated because its denial would constitute rejection of the major tenets of one's own culture.

4. Areas not previously known for traditional legitimation of racial prejudice and discrimination can evolve such beliefs and actions if faced by the large-scale migration of the visible racial minority. The influx of newcomers can be regarded as a socially threatening event if the migrant becomes an effective competitor in the acquisition of scarce resources such as housing, jobs, power, or social prestige. When the migrant's cultural attributes are dissimilar from those held central by the host culture, visible racial differences can become symbolic not only of a different group, but also of a group which might not be bound by the same cultural traditions and might, therefore, call these into question. Thus, racial *and* cultural differences can combine to provide a basic correlation which is only one mental step from an assertion of the causative role of race in social behavior (the same circumstance found in areas with long-standing cultural traditions of animosity).

5. If the migration of the racial minority is of a sizable magnitude and if their new home is one which could be characterized by heterogeneous composition marked by impersonal social contacts, the migrants are likely to be perceived as a monolithic threat with little or no internal differentiation. Thus, the visibility of race becomes a justifiable basis for legitimating the assessment of their "place" in the social structure with its attendant notions of expected behavior.

By accepting the above assumptions, one can begin with two quite variant social situations (the deep South, with traditional beliefs about Negroes, and the urban North, experiencing an influx of Negroes) and arrive, by different routes, at similar racial situations. These assumptions, then, can account for discrimination in both the North and South: (1) in the South, Negro and white exist in a social structure permeated with a tradition of a mutually bitter past perceptually brought on by actions of the other; and (2) in the North, discrimination is generated by the forces of friction in an impersonal urban environment faced with large-scale migration of a racially and culturally different people. However, in a northern area that has Negro residents but is rural, we might expect to find something different, for it would be less affected by traditions of animosity or the concomitant effects of urbanization.

One ultimate purpose of an analysis of a northern bi-racial rural area is to learn more about the social structure and processes involved in the society as a whole. The implications of examining deviant cases have attracted little attention or research in the study of intergroup relations. A notable exception to the general dearth of concern with the racial situation in the nonurban North is found in Morton Grodzins' essay, *The Metropolitan Area as a Racial Problem*.[5] He seems quite aware of at least the *theoretical* possibility of attempting to institute emigration from the northern urban centers to suburbs or small towns and villages. Everett Hughes recently commented on this problem:

[5]Morton Grodzins, *The Metropolitan Area as a Racial Problem* (Pittsburgh: University of Pittsburgh Press, 1958).

*Perhaps we [sociologists] failed to foresee present racial
movements because our whole inward frame is adapted to
study of the middle range of behavior, with occasional
conducted tours toward, but not dangerously near,
the extremes.*[6]

The issues

A study of a northern, rural, bi-racial area will allow us to address
a number of issues related to the gradual formation of a contemporary social structure: If the current order appears unique or
"subcultural," why is this so? If the dead hand of the past weighs
so heavily on the present, what are its contours? If contemporary
racial relations take a certain form, how might this form be related
to the original value commitment of a people prior to interracial
contact? How did the migration of a racially different group proceed? Where did they come from, how many came, and why? What
were their characteristics? More importantly, what were the perceptions and social definitions of the nature and meaning of this migration? Could the migrant assume a defined place in the new social
structure which was mutually regarded as acceptable, or was the
contact fraught with bi-racial friction and struggles? Was the migration ultimately perceived as an economic, social, and political
asset or liability to the host area?

Although it is necessary to evaluate social process over a period of
time, it is also required that one describe how a bi-racial community
operates as an on-going system of social relations. What forms of
behavior are found and how do these patterns fit into a systematic
analysis of "what goes on"? How does the community operate as
an economic machine to produce, distribute, and consume the many
necessary goods and services? What role does racial identification
play in economic decisions? What are the blunt realities of power
and subtle distinctions of influence utilized in the community? Is the

[6]Everett C. Hughes, "Race Relations and the Sociological Imagination," Presidential Address, *American Sociological Review*, 28 (December 1963), 890.

distribution of power organized in such a way as to incorporate
Negroes; or are they ignored and disenfranchised? Do Negroes have
full, partial, or nonexistent access to institutions of public services
in the community? Finally and crucially, is social interaction structured along racial lines so as to exclude Negroes from full participation? Are enduring interracial friendships and marriages found in
the community? If not, why not? If so, what might this tell about
the role of racial identity?

Two final areas of concern are raised with the recognition that a
stable social structure develops patterns of interrelations over a
length of time and, that concurrently, a community is subjected to
changes generated by the larger society. *First,* what internal understandings, definitions, and perceptions have evolved from the nature
of the institutional structure of the community? In this context, it
becomes appropriate to ask: What is a "Negro"? What social definitions do whites apply to this word, and what actions might be expected to flow from these definitions? What characterizes the self-
definition of Negroes—racial pride, unconcern, self-hate? How does
this perception structure their role relationships with other Negroes? Do they perceive "Negro" as a valid and meaningful cate-
gorizing variable? In short, is there a semidetached "Negro" subcommunity with definable properties and boundaries?

The *second* concern focuses upon the broad question of contemporary change. What forces external to the community imply the
necessity or desirability of internal adaptation? How does the community view itself? Is there a "we-they" distinction drawn on a community level so that the "outside world" is perceived as a hostile
"mass society"? When change enters the community, what form
does it assume—economic dislocation, political alteration, or social
restructuring? Is the migrant, as a carrier of at least some aspects of
the external society, perceived as an asset or liability?

The preceding is, then, a series of research questions that will serve
as a guide for the investigations to follow. Their explicit formulation, at this point, is intended to focus attention on those variables,
relationships, and processes which must be drawn out of the analysis of this unique community.

Delimitation of the study

In an effort to delimit the field of possible investigation, the five East-North-Central states (Illinois, Indiana, Michigan, Ohio, and Wisconsin) were chosen as the area of initial examination. For reasons of methodological advantage (concerning the form and adequacy of existing census data), the county has been used as the unit of analysis. As previously stated, in this broad area there are approximately 100,000 rural Negroes.

An inspection of the data presented in Table 1 reveals that a substantial majority of the 436 counties in these five states record 1 per cent or less of their population as Negro while only 22 exhibit a

Table 1: East-North-Central-state counties tabulated by percentage Negro[a]

Percentage Negro	Number of counties in state					Total ENC-state counties
	Ill.	Ind.	Mich.	Ohio	Wis.	
Less than 1	63	63	56	26	68	276
1	10	12	8	23	1	54
2	7	3	4	13	0	27
3	5	2	4	4	1	16
4	4	5	0	3	0	12
5	5	5	1	8	0	19
6	2	0	2	2	1	7
7	1	0	1	1	0	3
8	1	0	2	1	0	4
9	0	0	2	2	0	4
10 or more	4	2	3	5	0	14
Total Number	102	92	83	88	71	436

[a]*Census of the Population: 1960*, Vol. I, Pts. XV, XVI, XXIV, XXXVII, LI; Tables 28, 29.

Table 2: *East-North-Central-state counties with Negro population at or above five-state average of 8 per cent, ranked by percentage urban*[a]

Code[b]	County and state	Principal city	SMSA No.	Per cent urban	Per cent Negro
A	Pulaski. Ill.	None	...	0.0	36.2
B	Lake, Mich.	None	...	0.0	26.4
C	Cass, Mich.	Dowagiac	...	19.5	10.0
D	Kankakee, Ill.	Kankakee	...	49.1	8.7
E	Berrien, Mich.	Benton Harbor	...	49.6	8.5
F	Alexander, Ill.	Cairo	...	58.2	33.0
G	Muskegan, Mich.	Muskegan	122	67.0	8.4
H	Saginaw, Mich.	Saginaw	160	69.2	9.8
I	Clark, O.	Springfield	181	71.7	9.3
J	Genesee, Mich.	Flint	060	77.9	9.8
K	St. Clair, Ill.	E. St. Louis	162	81.8	18.2
L	Mahoning, O.	Youngstown	212	83.7	11.6
M	Summit, O.	Akron	002	86.8	8.0
N	Montgomery, O.	Dayton	045	90.2	11.7
O	Marion, Ind.	Indianapolis	081	91.2	14.3
P	Franklin, O.	Columbus	041	92.2	11.7
Q	Lucas, O.	Toledo	191	92.6	9.4
R	Lake, Ind.	Gary	068	93.6	17.0
S	Hamilton, O.	Cincinnati	036	94.6	14.3
T	Wayne, Mich.	Detroit	049	97.5	19.9
U	Cook, Ill.	Chicago	035	99.0	16.8
V	Cuyahoga, O.	Cleveland	037	99.6	15.5

[a]Same source as Table 1.
[b]These letters are used in Figure 1 to indicate location of the counties.

proportion Negro at or exceeding the East-North-Central state average of 8 per cent.

Table 2 examines these 22 counties in more detail. It is immediately apparent that only six of the counties are *not* subsumed by a Standard Metropolitan Statistical Area.[7] Furthermore, of these six counties, four are either at least half urban, border on Kentucky (and thus are not really "northern"), or both. Thus, only two of the 436 counties that show an above average proportion Negro are located outside of an SMSA, and are not contiguous with southern or border states.[8]

Investigation of the remaining two counties, Lake County (see B, Figure 1) and Cass County, Michigan (see C, Figure 1), shows that although they appear similar in initial demographic profile, they are actually quite different. In Lake County, located in the northwestern section of *lower* Michigan, 26 per cent of the population is Negro. Despite this high percentage, there are about 1,300 Negroes living in the county. In 1920, the Negro population of Lake County amounted to only 13 people. However, during the 1920's, real estate promotion rapidly increased the Negro population. At that time, Lake County was in a region that has been generally referred to as "cutover land."[9] In recent years, however, it has played an increas-

---

[7]The Standard Metropolitan Statistical Area (SMSA) "is a county or group of contiguous counties which contains at least one city of 50,000 inhabitants or more or 'twin cities' with a combined population of at least 50,000. In addition to the county, or counties, containing such a city or cities, contiguous counties are included in an SMSA if, according to certain criteria, they are essentially metropolitan in character and are socially and economically integrated with the central city." U.S., Bureau of the Census, *Census of the Population: 1960. U.S. Summary, Number of Inhabitants*, p. xxiv.

[8]A computation of the rural unincorporated areas *within* Standard Metropolitan Statistical Areas reveals that in the majority of the reported 22 counties the proportion of the rural population that is Negro rarely exceeds 2 per cent, and that the highest proportion is 6.5 per cent in Wayne County (Detroit), Michigan. The process of computing data on a county basis could possibly conceal smaller enclaves of rural Negroes. These settlements would become evident only upon computation of the racial composition for minor civil divisions (townships) in each of the 414 original counties that revealed less than 8 per cent Negroes in the East-North-Central states. Of the approximately 6,000 townships in this category, only 1 per cent of them exhibited a Negro population reaching 10 per cent or more. Finally, in a great majority of this remaining 1 per cent, the Negroes are once again found in urban or incorporated areas.

[9]Land that has been left relatively barren because of previous intensive removal of salable lumber.

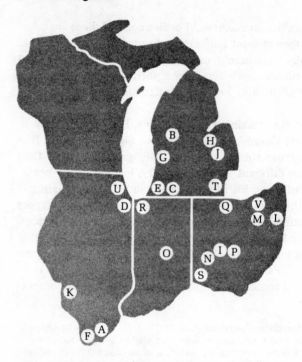

Figure 1: East-North-Central-state counties
with Negro population at or above five-state
average of 8 per cent

ingly prominent role as a Negro recreation center.[10] Thus, although
the census indicates that Lake County is heavily settled by Negroes,
an overwhelming proportion of this population is of recent migration and tends to be somewhat transient, reaching a high point in
summer. Therefore, the area does not assume the character of a
stable, bi-racial year-around social structure.

In Cass County, located in southwestern lower Michigan and bordering Indiana, are found more than 3,600 Negro residents. Like
Lake County, the area is predominantly rural. However, essentially
all of the Negroes in Cass County live as year-around residents, work

[10]*Michigan: A Guide to the Wolverine State,* compiled by workers of the
Writers' Program of the Works Projects Administration in the State of Michigan (New York: Oxford University Press, 1941), p. 433.

either there or in adjoining counties, send their children to local schools, and spend or invest their resources in that area. They are part of the permanently established nontransient population base. Therefore, Cass County, Michigan, would seem to fulfill best the previously stated criteria. This county, then, will provide the field data for an examination of a bi-racial northern rural area.

Data collection

To enable a comprehensive analysis of the community, I moved from Chicago to South Bend, Indiana, located approximately 15 miles from Cass County. From this vantage point, I was able to institute observations in the area over a two- and one-half year period, ending in 1965.

Data were examined from the official county records such as birth, death, and marriage statistics, church ledgers, school records, current and historical census materials, and agricultural records. Copies of newspapers, especially from the county but also from Chicago and Detroit, were examined and "clip files" constructed and maintained. Local libraries were searched for histories, clippings, photographs, narratives, and other items of interest.[11] Both current and historical plat books were obtained, and real estate transfers were examined. Additional information on Cass County was extracted from such diverse sources as Civil War records, Canadian newspapers, Underground Railroad[12] documents, and the *Congressional Record*. Some older respondents remembered enough local history to fill in much information the printed accounts lacked.

If one wished to regard every conversational contact with a resident of Cass County as an interview, the number of interviews conducted would literally run into the hundreds. However, a more restricted definition has been employed in this study so that 71

[11]Several histories written on various aspects of Cass County are found in local libraries. These include: Howard S. Rogers, *History of Cass County from 1825 to 1875* (Cassopolis, Mich.: W. H. Mansfield, Vigilant Book and Job Printer, 1875); Alfred Mathews, *A History of Cass County, Michigan* (Chicago: Waterman, Watkins and Co., 1882); and Mae R. Schoelzow, *A Brief History of Cass County* (Marcellus, Mich.: The Marcellus News, 1935).

[12]The pre-Civil War systematic means of flight for Negroes, predominantly slaves, from the Confederate states.

intensive and lengthy discussions of conditions in Cass County are presented as interviews.[13] These discussions were usually conducted in a respondent's home or place of business at his discretion and convenience. The length of these sessions ranged between thirty minutes and sixteen hours. An average interview lasted three to four hours. Contact in some of the longer interviews was discontinuous. The decision to conclude with 71 interviews was based on the recognition that I had passed the point of diminishing returns.

The basis upon which respondents were drawn tended to vary as a function of the "stage" of the research.[14] As an opening gambit, old-timers, who were known to be interested in reflecting upon community life, its past, changes over the years, and such, were contacted. From this type of interview, a second stage was generated—namely tracking down leads and utilizing entrees. (In retrospect, this was a particularly dangerous stage of the research because a beautifully idyllic, unified, untattered, and harmonious image of community relations had emerged. Obviously, leads are given and entrees arranged, consciously or not, that tend to document, not modify, a respondent's perception of the situation.) In the third stage, individuals were sought out because they occupied roles (official or otherwise) that would put them in access to the specific types of information that I desired. Individuals of the fourth stage were interviewed who, according to stages one, two, and three, would "really confuse things in your study," "would not want to be talked to," or "were really not part of the community." I found it interesting that only one of these allegedly "hostile" individuals refused to be interviewed and the others were generally perceptive, though occasion-

[13]The Appendix contains a complete list of respondents by number, including biographical information which will allow an individual's comments to be placed in context without revealing the respondent's identity. Information or commentary attributed to a respondent is indicated in textual materials by the use of "WR" for a white respondent and "NR" for a Negro. The number refers to the respondent's code identification.

[14]The term "stage" does not mean to imply a frozen system of priorities. No particular purpose would have been served by rigid adherence to the laws of cleanliness. Opportunities that opened unexpectedly were seized. Those official role individuals that I had anticipated might be other than receptive were shelved pending legitimate access. Finally, "trouble-makers" were interviewed whenever they wanted to "straighten me out."

ally uncomplimentary, in their observations. Finally, individuals mentioned by stages one and four were confronted with "what is the story now? I have heard this and that and really don't know what to make of it."

I used what Williams has called the "focused" type of interview in which the interviewer attempts to channel the unstructured discussion along productive lines.[15] The focused interview, as opposed to the "questionnaire or nondirective" type, proved to be the most successful method for gaining the largest amount of information and, at the same time, keeping the respondent from feeling that he was being "cross-examined." The use of direct questioning was scrupulously avoided whenever possible because so much of the desired information depended upon a respondent's willingness to discuss social situations in *his* terms, thereby revealing *his* conceptions.

The observer's role

Ultimately, only a small number of people were directly informed of my purposes and interests because neither my presence nor my behavior seemed to disturb them. Introductions to the respondent were accompanied by stating that "I live in South Bend, am at Indiana University, and am interested in the past and present conditions of Negroes in Cass County." General demeanor and dress (such as slacks or jeans and a sport shirt) were adopted to resemble the prevailing standards of dress as closely as possible. No regional or accent barriers between the respondent and investigator existed in this research.

Generally, the introductory remarks and appearance were sufficiently informative to quell any curiosity or doubts. If a respondent queried or appeared to want more information regarding either my identity or purposes, these were forthrightly stated. That is, "I teach sociology and race relations and am particularly interested in the

[15]Robin M. Williams, Jr., *The Reduction of Intergroup Tensions: A Survey of Research on Problems of Ethnic, Racial, and Religious Group Relations,* Bulletin 57 (New York: Social Science Research Council, 1947), p. 118.

history of this area," and "I am doing research and writing about the area."

Interviewing respondents in an interracial situation concerning race relations raises the question of the effects of the interviewer's race. While I am white, I was helped by a student of mine of Lebanese extraction (previously mentioned in the Acknowledgments). He was assumed to be white by white respondents and often taken as Negro by Negro respondents. This became obvious when I was told several times by Negro respondents, "I think I told that real light Negro the same thing a while back." The information he received and that which I gained was substantially the same—regardless of who made the first contact—even though repeated interviews were timed as much as six months apart. Another less obvious but quite important effect of the interview situation is the possibility that a researcher, by inadvertently raising awareness of a previously unimportant topic, could ultimately force respondents to fabricate observations. It is often observed that respondents attempt to "satisfy" an observer by reporting what they think he wants to hear. A relative lack of success with the nondirective form of interview suggested that racial relations were not an object of immediate and burning concern to many respondents. Occasionally, for example, a conversation would drift from the characteristics of a Negro farmer down the road, to the condition of his soil, and on to the weather, never to return to the farmer without gentle prods. If it was obvious that a respondent knew very little about racial conditions in the county, no effort was made to "push him." Because a lack of knowledge or an unwillingness to respond can be manifested in like behavior, a record was kept of unproductive contacts (of which there were four —one Negro and three whites).[16]

Although I have retained the immediate flavor and local color of the area, deliberate clouding of biographical identities in the study of a small community is desirable to protect the anonymity and privacy of respondents.

[16]The Negro was a recent migrant to the area, as was one of the whites. Of the other two whites, one was more interested in trying to sell me something; the other, because of a business position of high visibility, took a version of the Fifth Amendment.

two:

The community:

an overview

Physical appearance and population characteristics

Although Cass County may be demographically unusual, the "first trip" appearance of the area is singularly uninspiring. Upon entering the county after driving north from Indiana (see Figure 2), the only visible boundary symbols are a routine marker informing the traveler that he has just entered Michigan, a sign pointing out that he has simultaneously entered the Cass County Soil Conservation District, and a small clustering of modern but modest ranch houses huddled just out of the reach of Indiana's extensive taxation powers.

As in most rural or semirural Midwestern areas, one sees, in the distance, men operating tractors, women hanging wash or working in small garden plots, and children playing too close to the road. Passing through the small villages, one encounters a variety of parked vehicles ranging from mud-covered broken-down farm trucks to current model sports cars. The downtown buildings project an almost garish assemblage of old, worn facades next to new aluminum and glass "Sunday-best" efforts resembling the "clean-up,

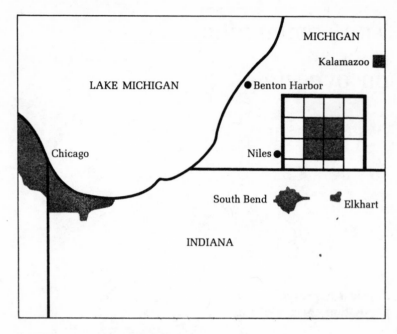

*Figure 2: Geographical location of Cass County,
Michigan, including surrounding urban centers*

fix-up, paint-up" campaigns of recent years. Most homes look
weathered and somewhat obsolete. In Cassopolis, the county seat,
rests a quaint but deteriorating courthouse that appears to stagger
under the weight of an imposing clock tower.

Although everything seems typically characteristic of a Midwestern farm area, one is suddenly impressed by the realization that a
high proportion of the residents are Negroes. Dorson, in a recent
work analyzing the nature of Negro folklore in Michigan, comments:

*Outwardly the rectangular farms, red barns, and dumps of
cattle suggested a typical community of husbandrymen.
But in one startling respect Calvin [a township] differed from
her neighbors; most of her thousand souls were Negroes.*[1]

[1]Richard M. Dorson, *Negro Folk Tales in Michigan* (Cambridge: Harvard University Press, 1956), p. 1.

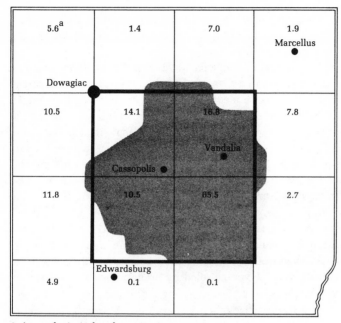

● Areas of principal settlement
▩ Cassopolis school district (approximate)

Figure 3: Cass County, Michigan

ᵃPercentage of township population that was Negro in 1960 census.

The accuracy of these impressions is confirmed when it is remembered that one tenth of the 36,932 residents of Cass County are indeed Negroes.[2] Out of a total of 3,706 Negroes, 2,825 (76 per cent) are classified as rural by the census (80 per cent of the county's total population is rural).

The preceding map of Cass County (Figure 3) illustrates: (1) the principal settlements in the county, consisting of one city and four

[2]It might be noted that the feeling exists in a number of respondents that the proportion of Negro residents has been severely underestimated by the census. Because of the strong possibility that this feeling indicates only the character of perception and not social fact, the lack of concrete proof to suggest non-reporting, and because no feasible way of deriving separate and possibly different statistics exists, census reports will be employed with the reservation that they may be underestimating the number of Negroes in the population.

villages; (2) the location of the 15 township units, including the proportion Negro in each; and (3) the approximate boundaries of the
Cassopolis school district.

Although the general area of investigation is Cass County, it must
be recognized that a county, as a political unit, does not necessarily
or automatically reflect a meaningful entity of social relationships.
The primary focus of investigation is the area roughly delimited by
the boundaries of the Cassopolis school system. It is noted from
Figure 3 that this area includes the majority of four townships—one
of which (Calvin) is 66 per cent Negro, and three others that contain
a more modest proportion of Negroes (17, 14, and 10 per cent respectively). In this area are located Cassopolis (population 2,027), the
county seat, and the village of Vandalia (population 360), both of
which serve as political, economic, retail trade, and service centers
for the Calvin Township area. The only operating high school in the
area is established in Cassopolis. Nearby is a nationally advertised
"Negro resort" and a lake encircled by predominantly finer homes
owned by whites.

The village of Cassopolis is 19 per cent Negro. Vandalia, five miles
to the east, is approximately 70 per cent Negro.[3] The proportion
Negro in the four-township area is 22 per cent. In addition to the
concentration of Negroes in the immediate research area, Dowagiac,
in the northwestern portion of the county, has 880 Negroes in a
population of 7,200 (12 per cent). It can be noted, therefore, that
Negroes have congregated in two principal areas in the county:
Dowagiac and the four-township research area.

Contrary to what one might expect in a rural farm area, the county
has been experiencing a fairly rapid rate of population increase.
Between 1950 and 1960, the population of Cass County increased by
almost one third. This compares favorably to a 23 per cent rate of
increase for the state of Michigan during the same period.[4] An examination of the components of this increase reveals that the fer-

[3]The proportion Negro in Vandalia can only be estimated because census data
are not tabulated for unincorporated villages.
[4]Cass ranked tenth out of 83 Michigan counties in the rate of increase between
1950 and 1960, even though its character is rural. Allan Beegle et al., Michigan
Population: 1960. Selected Characteristics and Changes, Special Bulletin 438
(East Lansing: Michigan State University Agricultural Experimental Station,
1962), p. 16.

tility ratio for the county is less than average for the state,[5] so that the important source of gain has been in-migration rather than natural increase. Only one other Michigan county experienced as large a proportionate increase because of migration. Also, only one other county in Michigan has a lower proportion of its population in the "native" category (that is, born in Michigan). The average for the state is 72 per cent native born; for Cass County it is 59 per cent. Although the county borders Indiana, these data are not an ecological artifact of this situation. A total of 11 Michigan counties border a different state, yet the proportion of native-born in these counties is identical to the state average.[6] Between 1955 and 1960, more than 50 per cent of the migrants to Cass County were from another state.[7] The precise reasons for these increases will be examined later. However, it should be pointed out here that the racial composition of the increase favors Negroes.

The economic base

To a significant extent, the county's economic base is directly related to agricultural pursuits and the necessary activities that support farming, such as implement dealers, livestock exchanges, construction trades, and cooperative associations.

Of the total 312,000 land acres in the county, 259,000 are in farm land, of which 197,000 are tillable. The typical farm is slightly over 100 acres in size and the value of the land is about $200 per acre. One third of all farms are operated on a part-time basis. Nine times out of ten, the operator of a farm unit also owns the property that he manages.[8] General farming is the predominant form of agricul-

[5]The number of children under five years of age per 1,000 women aged 15 to 49 (fertility ratio) equals 531 for Cass County. The Michigan average is 580. Ibid., p. 35.

[6]Census of the Population: 1960, I, 184.

[7]Ibid., p. 294.

[8]When compared to state averages, none of the above figures deviates significantly with one exception: 72 per cent of all land in Cass County is in farms compared to 40 per cent for Michigan. Figures in this section were obtained from U.S., Bureau of the Census, County and City Data Book: 1962, pp. 180–181, 190–191; and "Program of Cass County: Soil Conservation District, State of Michigan, December 1947" (revised), p. 3.

tural pursuit in the county. Livestock, grain, and dairy production all play important roles.[9] Relatively conducive climatic conditions prevail for fruit orchards which are common along the shore of Lake Michigan. Thus, in the western portion of the county, apples, peaches, grapes, and other fruits are produced.

In addition to the predominantly agriculturally based economy, recreation and resort facilities are assuming greater economic importance. One finds 250 lakes and ponds within the county. A survey, conducted in 1958, showed that the county possessed 5,500 cottages, primarily clustered around the many small lakes. During the summer months, the area population swells by one third as vacationers flock to the lakes from the relatively more populated surrounding areas.[10]

"Lakism" is having a significant economic effect on the county. Although the price of farm land is relatively modest, desirable lakefront property brings approximately $50 per running foot.[11] At present there are at least eight private camps in the county owned by such organizations as church and scout groups. "Weekending" in Cass County adds an additional boost to the economy because of its accessible location to both Chicago and Detroit. The advantages of the recreational resources can be emphasized by the realization that the additional revenue flows into the county without the necessity of constructing a comparable capital structure to produce wealth. Both white and Negro vacationers purchase goods and services in Cass County with income generated elsewhere.

The area is primarily agricultural, and a sound industrial base and accompanying skills have lagged but are not totally absent. It will be remembered that approximately one third of the farm units are classified as part-time operations. This information, and the fact that 42 per cent (compared to the Michigan average of 14 per cent) of employed persons work outside of the county, would imply more

[9]*Directory of Cass County: Issue of 1963-1964*, Compiled and Arranged by Kenneth M. Poe, County Clerk, for the Cass County Board of Supervisors.
[10]*Ibid.*
[11]WR–13. This figure was related to me in 1964. Obviously, land prices are volatile and subject to fluctuation so that this figure is undoubtedly a serious underestimation.

industrial employment (as opposed to industrial production) than one would first imagine. In a sense, then, many of the residents present to the area the same advantageous circumstances as the vacationers do—they spend their earnings, but the county does not need to construct a productive system to justify the level of consumption.

In the specific area of study—Cassopolis, Vandalia, and surrounding townships—there is one industrial plant (a mobile home manufacturer) employing slightly over 100 employees and a number of smaller operations with perhaps 10 to 15 employees each. However, the majority of local workers with marketable industrial skills work in the surrounding urban centers such as South Bend and Kalamazoo.

This situation has mixed blessings. On one hand, the consumption level of the area is higher than the productivity, *but,* the level of economic prosperity is largely controlled by forces and economies in other regions beyond local control. For example, when the Studebaker Corporation relocated in Canada in December 1963, the majority of its automotive facilities in South Bend were closed down. As a result, 128 Cass County residents, both whites and Negroes, were unemployed.[12] Because of relatively meager employment possibilities in the county, most of these men faced the necessity of either attempting to secure reemployment outside the research area or remaining unemployed.

If it is difficult to find employment opportunities in the immediate area, why do people maintain their residences there and accept the rigors of a five to 30 mile daily commutation? One explanation is that the general cost of living is lower in Cass County than in surrounding industrial centers, and discussions with respondents constantly point to a high level of local pride and a strong sense of area identification. A comment like "I couldn't move because my parents are buried here and I was educated here" was not uncommon. An individual tends to be seen—and thus sees himself—not only as an individual *but also* as a temporary recipient of a family tradition. In the interviewing, it was not unusual to hear a 60 or 70 year old man referred to as someone's son. Pride in family, in area, and in

[12]*South Bend Tribune,* January 1, 1964.

tradition are powerful centripetal motivations. Numerous respondents indicated that the centrifugal pull of greater economic prosperity elsewhere was felt, but was not so powerful as to dislodge them from their life in a comfortable and meaningful "community." This attitude is primarily characteristic of the older residents. Younger people are more likely to tip the equation in favor of what they see as greater prosperity and opportunity rather than the narrow boundaries dictated by tradition. However, even the young tend to be influenced by a certain amount of tradition.

The level of economic prosperity in the county is low-average for the Midwest. The median income of families in 1959 was $5,400 compared to a state average of $6,250. Surrounding counties, with the exception of one, range between $200 and $500 a year higher. Houses are modestly priced so that one may purchase a home in either of the two villages for around $5,000 to $7,000. Most residences appear to be clean and well kept but the houses are fairly old. Vandalia has no municipal facilities for water supply or sewage treatment. Thus, as previously proposed, the general physical appearance of the area is calm, not broken down, but weathered.

Social contact

Much of the visible social contact in the area can be charted at the mid-morning coffee break. In the several small village cafés one can find many of the local businessmen discussing an issue over coffee and a sweetroll. Farmers who have "come to town" for supplies (or talk) join in. Weather generally commands top billing, and is followed closely by politics. Although most of the field work took place prior to the impending 1964 presidential election, heated political discussions were still much in evidence in the summer of 1965. Often, the "socialistic drift" of Franklin D. Roosevelt and his followers is bemoaned, the virtues of Goldwater's policies extolled, and the latest "commie-front organization" exposed.

The villages function not only as service centers in an economic sense, but also as gossip centers. One does not have to tarry long before overhearing who said what to whom and under what conditions. A variety of associational and special interest groups are sustained in this manner. Talk is a plentiful commodity and the ability to listen to spontaneous conversation saved much effort in the initial stages of data collection. It was thus possible to get the general "feel" of the area before searching out respondents.

At first glance, one cannot detect any particular excitement generated by the existence of racial differences in the communities. Throughout this deliberately brief overview of Cass County's external appearance one does not detect any "race related" issues other than that Negroes are there—they are neither ignored nor courted. Rather, they appear to be normally interwoven into community life. They go about their business in the same fashion as the whites, are about as prosperous, seem to live throughout the area, and interact with their neighbors in a mutually satisfactory fashion. When a Negro and white meet in a café or on the street, greetings are usually on a *reciprocal* first name basis.

First impressions are not necessarily an accurate reflection of the complexities and understandings of community life. We must look more closely, therefore, to establish whether or not Cass County portrays the situation described by Killian and Grigg:

When sociologists have taken the trouble to study the place of the Negro in smaller cities and towns in the North, not in the densely populated urban "jungles," they have found the white man's sense of group position to be just as strong as it is in the South, although more subtly manifested.[13]

---

[13]Lewis Killian and Charles Grigg, *Racial Crisis in America: Leadership in Conflict* (Englewood Cliffs, N.J.: Prentice-Hall, 1964), p. 111.

Historical antecedents

part two

three:

The Quaker

and the

Negro

Introduction

*In Negro communities, as in communities anywhere in the
United States, the economy, regional-cultural features,
demography, and history interplay to quality life and to
condition the relationships of institutions and persons to the
larger community. The precise effect of these factors taken
separately or in the many possible combinations is still
inadequately understood or measured.*[1]

The importance of the variables cited by Lewis and Hill is emphasized when one examines the basic relationships between the contemporary character of a culture and its own traditions. It has been
proposed that Cass County is a deviant case. But deviant from
what? Presumably, the implication is not deviant from its own

[1]Hylan Lewis and Mozell Hill, "Desegregation, Integration, and the Negro Community," *The Annals of the American Academy of Political and Social Science*,
304 (March 1956), 116.

historical origins, but rather, deviant from external contemporary normative standards. If this be the case, then it must be recognized that a likely source of this contemporary deviance is to be found in the slow evolution of this community.

The current sociological literature is replete with examples of ways the contemporary social structure can and often does mirror a series of historical events that could be called tradition. For example, Simpson and Yinger observe:

Contemporary whites still react to the Negro in a given way,
to a certain extent because he once was a slave. Attitudes
were then formed which have become part of the culture,
to some degree living an independent and autonomous life and
to some degree continually reinforced by the actual present
status of the Negro, which is partly a result of those
very attitudes.[2]

They then proceed to comment that "where this historical background was different, a different pattern of relationships has become fixed in the traditions and passed onto the contemporary people."[3]

Basing their argumentation on similar proposals concerning the nature of the relationship between the contemporary social structure and long-standing unwritten "understandings," several authors find the generation and maintenance of group prejudice to be imbedded in the conceptions of traditional social relationships.[4] But why should a series of events, possibly giving initial credence to prejudicial attitudes, have such salience?

[2]George E. Simpson and J. Milton Yinger, *Racial and Cultural Minorities: An Analysis of Prejudice and Discrimination* (New York: Harper and Row, 1958), p. 154.

[3]*Ibid.*

[4]See, for example, Edwin R. Embree, *Brown Americans: The Story of a Tenth of the Nation* (New York: Viking Press, 1945), p. 160; Gordon Allport, *The Nature of Prejudice* (Garden City, N.Y.: Doubleday & Co., 1958), p. 204; and Herbert Blumer, "Race Prejudice as a Sense of Group Position," *Race Relations: Problems and Theory,* Jitsuichi Masuoko and Preston Valien, ed. (Chapel Hill: The University of North Carolina Press, 1961), p. 223.

Indeed, perhaps the answer becomes the solution to the continuity of any social system through time. The maintenance of some definition of the status quo need not and often is not justified on rational reasons or contemporary fact. Rather, sentiments and folk beliefs carry considerable weight in the determination of current social behavior. The possibility of group conflict provides the basis of a further entrenchment of the sources of friction and leads to more pervasive statements of group position. In these terms, then, an examination of the historical evolution of Cass County, as a deviant case, becomes the process of searching out the nature and evolution of definitions of group position.

Prevailing conditions and value commitments prior to Negro settlement in Cass County

Until the 1820's, southwestern Michigan was part of the wilderness that comprised the Northwest Territory. In 1825 (the same year the Erie Canal opened, thereby promoting westward migration) what is now Cass County received its first non-Indian settler. Shortly afterward it became the first permanently settled area in southwestern Michigan.[5]

These isolated lands, which offered a refuge for persecuted peoples, appealed to the various settlements of Friends (now commonly called Quakers—a name which then conveyed a significant amount of sarcasm and rejection) then located in the eastern and southern United States. The persecution of ethnic and religious minorities is not an unknown lesson of American history and Quakers were harshly treated for what their "more conventional" neighbors regarded as strange beliefs and practices.[6] Thus, the "early settlers [of Cass County] were nearly all Quakers or Friends who came from the South, leaving that locality on account of slavery."[7]

The distaste that most Quakers exhibited for the institution of

[5]*Cass County, Michigan,* a pamphlet of historical information compiled by the Cass County Historical Society, 1960.

[6]One of these "strange beliefs" was the inherent equality of man before his Creator.

[7]Rogers, p. 209.

slavery is the subject of continued and extensive historical documentation. As Aptheker observed, "with the end of the eighteenth century it may be said that the institution of Negro slavery had practically ceased to exist among accepted Quakers."[8] Quakers became the first well-known organized source of support to the fugitive slave from the plantation South.[9] The fame of the Quakers' position spread to such an extent that Furnas remarks that George Washington, at one time, was reported to have been quite pessimistic about the chances of recovering his lost slave property because of the aid and assistance Quakers proffered.[10]

As northern opposition to "the southern institution" became more solidified, the plantation South became more defensive about what it considered to be an economically advantageous system—basing the production of "King Cotton" on slavery and bondage. In addition to the presumed advantages of a plentiful and controllable labor force, literally hundreds of millions of dollars were "invested" in the slaves. What could be a more logical defense than to assert that Negro slaves were biologically inferior, and then imply that the southern plantation system had done them a favor by uprooting them from one continent and offering them a shack and slavery in another?[11]

Although Quakers had objected to the institution of slavery before the advent of the doctrines of racial inferiority, these propositions could be categorized as the proverbial last straw.[12] When the belief in free will, equality of man before God, and an observance of the

[8]Herbert Aptheker, "The Quaker and Negro Slavery," *Journal of Negro History,* 25 (1940), 355.

[9]Frazier, p. 96.

[10]J. C. Furnas, *Goodbye to Uncle Tom* (New York: William Sloane Associates, 1956), p. 207.

[11]For a more extensive discussion of this issue, see Peter I. Rose, *They and We: Racial and Ethnic Relations in the United States* (New York: Random House, 1964), p. 27.

[12]Although, for many years, the Quakers had been a prime force in the abolition of slavery, it must be remembered that this position was not always accepted. Aptheker observes, for instance, that "Friends were forbidden, in 1676, to allow their slaves to attend their meetings. The penalty for failure to comply was the confiscation of half the value of every slave at a meeting," p. 334. Later, the opposition to bondage and slavery was not a uniformly accepted policy of

brotherhood of man confronted the realities of the southern economic system, their continued existence in the social structure became a profound contradiction to the Quakers—they could not prosper without slavery in a system so oriented to the utilization of slave labor, nor could they live with their consciences in it. In this sense, Quakers were one of the first victims of the "American dilemma."[13] The presence of a dissident and vocal Quaker minority created a severe threat to the maintenance of the status quo. A parting of the ways was indicated. In an ironic sense then, some of the first "cast-offs" of the slave system were white men.

The departure of Quakers did not, however, imply the absence of trouble—only the physical departure of "the trouble-makers." For, as Quakers migrated northward, their abolitionist tendencies became more and more pronounced. Finally, the significant step was taken—the active subversion of that which they considered to be an evil system. This subversion was ultimately accomplished in three ways: first, by the establishment of communities in the North that could be characterized as quasi-religious settlements where Negroes usually found a welcome; second, by actively supporting and staffing the operation which became known as the Underground Railroad;[14] and finally, by the creation of "free labor societies" to avoid having to consume, transport, or otherwise handle goods which were produced by bonded labor in the slave states.

The Quaker communities became havens for the oppressed and homeless fugitive slaves. Of course, these communities could function most effectively only in areas where state or territorial law, and

---

all Quaker factions. Furnas reminds us that the "Undergrounders were 'read out of meeting' " by groups of orthodox Friends, p. 209. Aptheker also remarks that not until just before the Civil War were Quakers able to offer a particularly articulate opposition to slavery, p. 331.

[13]The metaphoric use of Myrdal's famous title should not be taken lightly. The dilemma which the Quakers faced more than a century ago is nearly the same as the one Myrdal discusses. The difference is, however, that the Quakers were able to solve their dilemma, while contemporary America has not!

[14]Furnas, p. 208, states that "certain slave hunters who frequently lost track of their quarry near the Quaker-dominated town of Richmond, Indiana, where Coffin was settled, complained, he said, that 'they never could get the slightest intelligence of their slaves after they reached my house . . . there must be an Underground Railroad of which I was president.' "

especially local sympathy, permitted. The original charter of the Northwest Territory explicitly stated:

*There shall be neither slavery nor involuntary servitude in
said territory otherwise than in the punishment of crimes
whereof the party shall have been duly convicted; provided
always that any person escaping into the same, from whom
labor or service is lawfully claimed in any one of the original
states, such fugitive may be lawfully reclaimed and conveyed
to the person claiming his or her labor or services aforesaid.*[15]

It should be noted that even though the territorial ordinances prohibited slavery as an institution, it did not condone such migration operations as the Underground Railroad. In effect, if enforced, provisions of the law effectively ruled out the Northwest Territory as a haven for the fugitive. It is, however, true that various states effectively nullified some of the latter provisions of the territorial document.

In *Uncle Tom's Cabin*, Harriet Beecher Stowe's emotion-filled novel, the dramatization of Eliza escaping across the Ohio River on ice floes mentions a kindly white gentleman who helped her to safety and dry clothing on the Cincinnati side. Many suspect that the gentleman was drawn after Levi Coffin, an extremely active abolitionist and reputed "president" of the Underground Railroad. In his book, *Reminiscences*, Coffin mentions that:

*I was well acquainted at Young's Prairie [in Cass County],
Michigan. There was a settlement of Friends there, . . . and
[they] were among the early settlers of that neighborhood.
Some had formerly been my neighbors in Indiana. I had been
at Young's Prairie, and visited several of the families of
fugitives in that settlement.*[16]

[15]*Michigan in Books* (Lansing, Mich.: The State Library), 5, No. 3 (Winter 1963), 127–128.

[16]Levi Coffin, *Reminiscences of Levi Coffin* (Cincinnati: Western Tract Society, 1876), p. 368.

In Cass County, Quakers had found a refuge where both their convictions regarding personal behavior and their usually unpopular attitudes concerning abolition could be given free reign.

Once the Quakers had settled, concern for their "black brothers" began to acquire a missionary zeal. Even if the interest in fostering Negro fugitive in-migration emanated from a value commitment, it certainly did not conflict with economic realities. Here, in the Michigan wilderness, was almost unlimited room for settlement and expansion. Therefore, an "ideal" situation prevailed—the Cass County Quakers could be true to their Christian commitments without paying the sacrificial price of economic competition and social upheaval. Soon after the initial settlement of Quakers, economics, social conditions, and beliefs *all* indicated the validity of the previous commitments to human equality.

The northward migration of Negroes

Existing records on the migration of Negroes do not suggest that the purpose of fleeing was to reach Young's Prairie (Cass County) specifically, but rather, to gain safety wherever it might be found. Although some fugitives did find a degree of protection in southern and central Ohio and Indiana, many plodded on to Michigan, and in numerous cases, they strove to reach the "North Star"—Canada. The primary motivating force influencing the continued northward migration was, of course, fear of recapture, not the desirability or attractiveness of the particular area for potential or actual settlement.[17]

Figure 4 indicates that Cass County was a culmination or terminal point of the Indiana and Ohio operations—called the Quaker or Ohio line—of the Underground Railroad. It was also a junction with

[17]Fear of the horrors of recapture should not be underestimated. Even if the Negro had run from a kindly master who additionally offered freedom from reprisal, the folk beliefs of the fugitives were that capture meant a return not to northern Kentucky, but to the deep South—an area which was desperately feared.

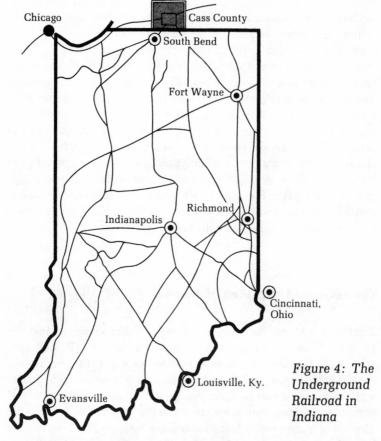

Figure 4: The
Underground
Railroad in
Indiana

the Illinois line. At this point, where the two lines joined, a common course to Canada was pursued by those who felt it necessary
to push further on.[18] Schoelzow's history of Cass County estimates
that at least 15,000 fugitive slaves passed through Cass County—
most of them on their final journey to Canada.[19] The comparison of
the number of Negroes fleeing slavery by way of Cass County and
the total number having fled the South prior to the Civil War would

[18]Rogers, p. 131; and Schoelzow, p. 59.
[19]Schoelzow, p. 60.

indicate that approximately one out of every four fugitives may have passed through the county.[20]

Although the institution of slavery readily provided the motive for a *slave* to become a *fugitive*, not all Negroes migrating North in general, and then to Cass County in particular, were at that time slaves. Lomax reports that in 1848 there were almost 500,000 *free* Negroes in the United States.[21] Estimates of the regional location of these free Negroes before the Civil War indicate that about one half were in the slave-owning southern states.[22] The remainder gradually left the South, apparently by general agreement. Emancipated Negroes, although technically free men, were not particularly wanted in the South. To the slave-owning aristocracy, free Negroes were a constant source of embarrassment to the system for they succeeded in purchasing land, practicing a craft, and thereby prospering. Furthermore, freed Negroes were not necessarily a source of inspiration to their brothers still in bondage. Rather, they were often despised —evidently because their freedom, which was often granted as a reward for "meritorious service" to the system, was gotten by the suppression of other slaves.[23] Regardless of the particular reason for the favored position, slaves' resentment toward freedmen ran deep and they in turn disassociated themselves from the masses. Thus, Booker T. Washington noted:

Under the conditions of slavery, the position of the free Negro was a very uncomfortable one. He was, in a certain sense, an anomaly, since he did not belong to either class. He was

[20]William H. Pease and Jane H. Pease state that "between 1830 and 1860 upwards of 60,000 Negroes fled the South to the North." *Black Utopia: Negro Communal Experiments in America* (Madison: The State Historical Society of Wisconsin, 1963), p. 4.

[21]Lewis E. Lomax, *The Negro Revolt* (New York: The New American Library, 1963), p. 27.

[22]Embree, p. 22.

[23]One could easily compare the resentment of the free Negro of the Antebellum South with the hostility generated 100 years later by a Negro "Uncle Tom-ing it." In a subtle way, the first "Uncle Toms" were these emancipated Negroes because ultimately the stability of their position depended on pleasing the distrustful and powerful white political and economic systems.

distrusted by the white people, and looked down upon by
the slaves.[24]

Ultimately then, migration to and through Cass County was not entirely a "fleeing-in-the-night" operation. Many Negroes left the South voluntarily with the full knowledge of their former masters and neighbors. Because of the attrition of free Negroes by migration, the South was gradually allowing itself to be bled of a skilled, educated, and productive labor force.[25]

A final group of migrating Negroes was emancipated upon the death of their masters and encouraged to seek their fortunes in free states. Freedom could mean disaster to plantation slaves who could demonstrate few particular skills or other resources. Often these Negroes had no family and little knowledge of how to protect their interests. They too had to flee to people they could trust.

Thus, all three of these categories—fugitive slave, freedman, and forcibly emancipated—became the "excess baggage" of a system they had helped to create and prosper. Especially in the middle South or border states, these "push" migration factors combined with the "pull" of northern abolitionist sentiments. Furnas comments on these issues:

The [Underground Railroad] railheads were so remote from
the Deep South that few Black Belt slaves were ever
passengers. A given field hand's chances of ever meeting an
Abolitionist "enticer" were practically nil.[26]

[24]Booker T. Washington, *The Story of the Negro: The Rise of the Race from Slavery* (New York: Doubleday, Page and Co., 1909), I, 193.

[25]One can, of course, propose that this situation is still occurring with both whites and Negroes who leave the South. The continual replacement of Negro labor by mechanized agricultural methods produces a tremendous number of dispossessed though technically free Negroes. The economic and political realities have reduced the exploitive profits in that the rural southern Negro is no longer wanted. For an excellent discussion of some of the pressures inducing out-migration from the South, particularly from Mississippi, see James W. Silver, *Mississippi: The Closed Society* (New York: Harcourt, Brace and World, 1964).

[26]Furnas, p. 231.

*Thus it can be assumed that the [Underground Railroad] agent
and the solicitous Abolitionist practically never saw the
typical Deep South field hands to unsettle their
preconceptions of what kind of human raw material slaves
were. Even black farm hands from the small plantations of
Virginia and Maryland would be several cuts above the
characteristic cotton chopper.*[27]

Sheer geographical limitations, or what might be termed the friction of space, operated as a selective mechanism so that the migrating Negroes usually did not originate from a strongly dissimilar
section of the country, but rather from states bordering the free
North. Other selective mechanisms that tended to decrease social
dissimilarity between many of the Negroes and their northern bene-
factors were color and cultural advantage or intellectual capacity.
While no one is likely to maintain that Negro fugitives were "passing for white," there does seem to be agreement that lightness of
skin color was a trait of many Negroes migrating northward. For
instance, Herskovits observes:

*It must be remembered also that the earliest freed slaves were
those of mixed-blood, very often the light colored ones, and it
is the descendants of these who have had the best chance to
make their way in a civilization the standards of which are
essentially white standards.*[28]

It can be noted, then, that the lighter strains of Negroes had a definite advantage.[29] Thus a second set of selective mechanisms was re-

[27]Ibid., p. 243.

[28]Melville J. Herskovits, *The Myth of the Negro Past* (Boston: Beacon Press,
1958), p. 60.

[29]Although long forgotten by the middle of the twentieth century, mixed bloods
were at one time regarded as superior in the South. Embree, p. 7, observes that
"these blood mixtures of slave days were often what the scientists today would
call eugenic. Often the best white blood, represented by the white planters and
their sons, joined with that of Negro girls chosen for their comeliness, intelligence, and attractive personalities. Patrick Henry was so impressed by the
superiority of the mixed breeds that, while speaker of the Virginia Assembly,

lated to northward migration. William Still, one of the few Underground Railroad "conductors" to keep records of "passengers," noted that "it scarcely needs be stated that, as a general rule, the passengers of the [Underground Railroad] were physically and intellectually above the average order of slaves."[30] Generally confirming Still's observations, Herskovits proposed that the most educated and intelligent Negroes were the ones who resented the bondage system most deeply.[31]

Finally, the attraction of the Underground Railroad or other means of northern migration influenced mainly the lighter, culturally or intellectually superior Negroes from the border states. As might be expected, the abolitionist cause was enhanced and strengthened by the existence of these Negroes as "case examples" of the "unjust horrors" of the slave South. Predictably then, migrating Negroes were not only the recipients of religiously-oriented generosity and brotherhood, but they also served to provoke what degenerated into a regional or factional battle between northern abolitionists and southern plantation owners.[32]

The Negro in Cass County: original settlement and adjustment

I [Booker T. Washington] have often been asked to what extent the Negro race has the ability for self-direction and government, and the power to initiate and to make continuous progress unaided.

---

he introduced a bill offering a state bonus to children of mixed parentage. The bill was carried to a second reading and might have been passed had not Henry at just that time been made governor and thus diverted from his unusual legislative campaign."

[30]William Still, *The Underground Rail Road* (Philadelphia: Porter & Coates, 1872), p. 2.

[31]Herskovits, p. 104.

[32]Although one would not wish to be too suspicious, the very existence of free Negroes in the North may have served as a pawn in the regional factionalism that developed. The Quakers and the northern sympathizers attempted to gain an eminently superior moral position as a result of the abolitionist activities.

I want to try to answer this question in part at least, not by abstract argument, but by telling the story of a self-governing community of colored people.

The group of negroes whose story I want to tell reside in Cass County, Michigan. Among the early settlers to that part of the state were several Quakers who had left their former homes in the South because they did not approve of slavery. In Michigan, as elsewhere, these Quakers soon let it be known that not only were they opposed to the institution of human slavery, and that runaway slaves would receive a friendly welcome among them, but that they would also receive physical protection if necessary. In addition to becoming an asylum for escaping slaves, this community of Quakers soon became a station on the "Underground Railroad."[33]

Local histories record the arrival of the first Negro in Cass County to have been in 1836 when a Quaker preacher settled in Calvin Township with a fugitive slave.[34] Here he remained permanently and farmed for a living. This man, and those that followed him shortly thereafter, formed "the nucleus for a settlement of free Negroes which was constantly . . . [increased] by fugitives from the other side of the Ohio River."[35] The formation of this original "nucleus" was perhaps one of the most critical junctures in the development of the Negro settlement in the Calvin Township area of Cass County.[36]

Communication may have been both slow and tedious in the 1840's, but news of a haven for the fugitive slave spread rapidly.

[33]Booker T. Washington, "Two Generations Under Freedom," *The Outlook*, 73 (February 7, 1903), 293.

[34]Schoelzow, p. 57.

[35]Washington, *Story of the Negro*, I, 245.

[36]In discussing the settlement of the Negro in Cass County, one must make explicitly clear what this term means and how it is used in the present volume. The term "Negro" is defined in the sociological sense: if a man is thought of as a member of a category of people defined as Negro, he is a Negro. However, when we have occasion to examine intraracial stratification in detail, the serviceability of this definition will be seriously called into question.

Information concerning this settlement of no more than a handful of Negroes seemed to produce two immediate results:

First, the actual presence of Negroes in an area lent credence to the belief that the Quakers were willing and able to offer assistance to the fugitive. Furnas states:

Practically every clump of Negro settlers in the free states
was an Underground depot by definition, for the runaway
considered a black skin an even more reliable promise of help
than a Quaker broadbrim.[37]

Second, that Quakers had settled with Negroes in a particular area seemed to offer a high degree of attraction to those Negroes who were already emancipated by their masters on an individual basis. Woodson states:

This settlement [Cass County—Calvin Township] had become
attractive to fugitive slaves and freedmen because the
Quakers settled there welcomed them on their way to freedom
in Canada and in some cases encouraged them to remain
among them.[38]

After the historical significance of the first Negro settler in Cass County was noted, accounts of further continuing migration become sketchy and incomplete. However, it is recorded that several small groups of free Negroes entered the Calvin Township area in 1845 or 1846 and purchased small farms. The names of these settlers are presently everyday words in the county and several of their descendants were interviewed as part of this study. One respondent offered:

The Chicago papers say that migration [to Calvin Township]
is due to the Underground Railroad. They are all wet. We were
here before that. My folks were never slaves. [NR-7.]

[37]Furnas, p. 214.

[38]Carter G. Woodson, A Century of Negro Migration (Washington: The Association for the Study of Negro Life and History, 1918), p. 28.

It is estimated that there were about 100 Negro settlers in Penn and Calvin Townships in 1846.[39] The Chain Lake Baptist Church, reportedly the oldest Negro church in Michigan, was established in the late 1840's.[40]

Negroes, attracted from a distance to Cass County by the promise of refuge in or near the Quaker settlement, did receive such assistance. Evidence that help was actually given to Negroes is indicated in the following statement:

Many slaves reached this vicinity and settled near Cassopolis, for, once here, they felt themselves quite safe. Much of Cass county was cleared by those slaves who were given five acres of land each, a cabin, and the right to grow their own crops. One of the queer settlements, called "Ramptown," was located on this farm [owned by a Quaker pioneer] and was composed of one hundred negro cabins whose occupants came largely from the "Carolinas."[41]

James Corrothers describes the original Calvin Township settlement (here referred to as "The Chain Lake Settlement") as follows:

Fugitive slaves and a few free Negroes who reached this part of Michigan in the early " '40's," liked "The Chain Lake Region" and settled there; and, defying capture or molestation, remained and prospered. They felled the forests, drained the swamps, laid out roads, and named the watercourses. They called their colony "The Chain Lake Settlement," and it is so known to-day [1916]. In the course of a few years they established schools, and imitated, as best they could, the government of white men. In a quiet way, this unique Negro colony in the North had become somewhat known even prior to the Civil War.[42]

[39]Schoelzow, p. 59; and Rogers, p. 133.
[40]*Michigan: A Guide to the Wolverine State*, p. 410.
[41]Helen Hibberd Windle, "The Underground Railroad in Northern Indiana, Based on Personal Narratives and Famous Incidents," Mimeograph (South Bend, Ind., 1939), p. 14.
[42]James D. Corrothers, *In Spite of the Handicap* (New York: George H. Doran, Co., 1916), pp. 17–18.

Constant support of the Negro settlement by such men as the son of the nationally known abolitionist preacher, Charles Osborn, enabled continued growth.[43] Not only were Negroes treated as free human beings, but, as Baker states, "At a time when the North was passionately concerned in the abolition of slavery the colour of his skin sometimes gave the Negro special advantages, even honours."[44]

A week before the close of the decade (1840's) of the original Negro settlement, a group of 41 ex-slaves arrived in the Calvin Township area of Cass County. They had been emancipated upon the death of their master in Cabell County, Virginia (now part of West Virginia). The slave holder willed $15,000, which was to be used to purchase land in a free state. The comparative wilderness of Cass County was selected. Each of the former slaves (men, women, and children) was provided with a tract of 18 acres of land, and a log cabin was constructed for each family. The total acquisition of land was approximately 700 acres.[45] The number of Negroes in the county rose to 389 with 158 of these clustered in Calvin Township. Thus, by 1850, 25.3 per cent of the population of that township was Negro.[46]

Conclusion

Writing about the Calvin Township area, Booker T. Washington stated:

In the story of this development there is nothing startling or remarkable. It is simply the story of the growth of a people when given the American chance to grow naturally and gradually.[47]

[43]Mathews, p. 383.

[44]Ray Stannard Baker, *Following the Color Line*, 2nd ed. rev. (New York: Harper and Row, 1964), p. 217.

[45]See Washington, *Story of the Negro*, I, 246; Corrothers, p. 18; and Pease and Pease, pp. 27–28.

[46]U.S., Bureau of the Census, *Seventh Census of the United States: 1850*, p. 888.

[47]Washington, *The Outlook*, 73, 305.

Although Washington may have lucidly touched upon some philosophical issues, he has glossed over the basically unique combination of events that promoted the original settlement of Negroes in several townships of Cass County:

1. The original migration by the Quakers was motivated by a desire to escape a system considered to be evil after finding it necessary to reject the social order from which they had come.

2. In the early 1840's Cass County was largely unsettled wilderness. Negroes could locate there without consuming scarce resources which might force the Quakers to pay a high price for their religious and moral commitments.

3. Through the operations of the Underground Railroad, staffed by Quakers, Cass County became known as a haven for the oppressed.

4. The major Underground Railroad lines in the Midwest, transporting substantial numbers of fugitive slaves, converged in Cass County.

5. The area was far enough removed from the South to make recapture of the Negroes by former masters very tedious and quite expensive.

6. In addition to attracting fugitives, the conditions in the county were desirable enough to encourage free Negroes with some resources of their own to settle in the area.

7. Awareness of the settlement ultimately made possible grants of land, monies, and homes by departed masters to their slaves.[48]

8. An agriculturally-based economy operating in sparsely settled but fertile land removed competition as a likely possibility and made cooperative efforts beneficial to all.

9. Negroes, escaping from one social order—or rejected by it— were basically the guests of the Quakers and, therefore, local histories record that they attempted to fit into the prevailing cultural patterns whenever possible—without, however, actually becoming Quakers.

[48]The researcher has been informed by county officials that a number of wills from southern plantation owners were probated in Cass County to insure that the Negro would receive what the will intended for him to have.

Thus, as Mathews observes:

*The history of the settlement of Calvin presents a marked
contrast when compared with the other townships of the
county, and shows what small circumstances sometimes tend
to shape the entire destiny of a community.*

*Little did the pioneers of this township, who were endowed by
nature with a love for the whole human race, suppose, when
they extended a helping hand to the trembling slaves fleeing
from a heartless taskmaster, that hundreds of this race would
eventually become their neighbors and co-workers in
subduing and cultivating the soil, and take an active part in
township affairs.*

*Many of these pioneers, in their integrity of character, their
kindness of heart, and their contempt of danger, and their
cheerful endurance of toil, privation and hardship, in an
isolated situation, and under the most discouraging
circumstances, rank with the men who have assumed a
national, if not world wide, reputation.*[49]

[49]Mathews, p. 380.

four:

The evolution
of a stable
social order

A decade of crisis: 1850–1860

The period of original settlement, described in Chapter Three, of
the Calvin Township region by Negroes must be seen as a time of
continuous fear of reprisal or capture by southerners. Although
these fears were quite real in the minds of the fugitives, recapturing
activities were typical only farther "down the line" in Indiana and
Ohio—not as far north as Michigan. Thus, the decision to remain in
Cass County depended on the tolerable balance of two *directly* related variables: distance and safety.

These estimations, which had to be made by the fugitives as well as
the Quakers, depended on the outcome of another series of cost-
reward equations. Namely, what magnitude of loss did the fleeing
human cargo represent to the slave holder and what price might he
be willing to pay to effect retrieval of his "property"? This could not
be easily estimated because, in addition to the obvious dollar value
loss, the constant drain of slave labor made the system of bondage
increasingly expensive and decreasingly dependable. Indeed, in
some areas, particularly in the border states, slave owners "voluntarily" forsook the employment of slave labor as the maintenance

of order became increasingly unpredictable. Generally, however, it could be assumed that if the losses became excessive, the slave holder's attempts to recapture the fugitive might be carried farther north, surmounting the many barriers craftily constructed by Negroes, Quakers, and their sympathizers.

In the winter of 1846–1847, an association of planters from a northern Kentucky county (Bourbon), suffering from the slow attrition of slave resources, banded together to more effectively pursue and recapture escaped slaves "stolen by the rascally abolitionists."[1] In 1848, this association formed a search party that left Kentucky and headed for Cass County with the intention of returning to their former masters many of the fugitives that had settled in Cass. The specific details of the raid are unimportant to comment on here. However, the historical significance is that the raid's *early stages* were successful. The Kentuckians, with their superior weaponry and the element of surprise, were in fact able to capture many of the Negroes. However, that was the extent of their success as the raid ended in failure.[2]

The Michigan raid holds particular significance when one considers the historical development of Cass County. Although the capture was ultimately aborted, it did point out that the increasing loss of slave labor in the southern and border states had begun to make Cass County more vulnerable. In addition, some of the fugitives in question had formerly belonged to personal friends of Henry Clay:

. . . and the pressure brought to bear by their owners had
much influence in shaping that great leader's course of action
on the Fugitive Slave Law in 1850, which in turn was among

[1]"Historic Calvin: A Cass County Village and a Township that Defied Kentucky Raiders," *Journal* (Detroit), January 6, 1896.

[2]Unknown to the raiders, a band of white residents had formed to frustrate their plans. A confrontation between the outraged residents and the southern raiders took place. The Quakers, presumably to prevent violence, suggested that the Kentuckians concerned walk the three or four miles to Cassopolis to present proof that the fugitives were indeed their property. However, as the raiders were unable to produce a copy of Kentucky's constitution demonstrating that it was a slave state, they were arrested by the sheriff for kidnapping and were summarily jailed. Several days later a sham trial was held and after paying the court costs, they were released. Meanwhile, the Negroes sought by the raiders fled to Canada where safety was certain.

*the chief inciting causes of our Civil War. The Michigan riot,
cited by him in detail in Congress, proved of such great service
in securing passage of the bill.*[3]

While northern areas already had various forms of "Black Laws"[4]
on the books, they were often unenforced. For instance, in 1829 the
territory of Michigan forbade any former slave to settle in the area
unless he was able to prove that he was self-supporting. The provisions of the Fugitive Slave Law, passed by Congress in September
1850, were much harsher because they greatly simplified the process
by which a plantation owner might prove a slave to be his "property." Fugitive slaves, indeed, all Negroes, were thus placed in
jeopardy. The resulting threat to the community in Calvin Township, and other areas of the North, became so severe that many fled
from there to Canada—the "North Star."

I visited one of the most historically famous of the original Negro
settlements in Canada—Buxton, Ontario—and observed Negro farmers and a small rural school primarily attended by Negro students.[5]
As in Calvin Township, many of the ancestors of these residents
had been quietly farming the land for more than 120 years. Some
of the same individuals whose names appear in the earliest history
of Calvin Township are also mentioned in the accounts of the early
settlement of Buxton.[6]

[3]"Historic Calvin: A Cass County Village and a Township that Defied Kentucky
Raiders," *Journal* (Detroit), January 6, 1896.

[4]"Black Laws" generally refer to statutes in which the intent and usually the
practice was to discourage the in-migration of fugitive slaves from southern
states.

[5]A small Negro child of about nine years old looked at the license plate on my
parked automobile which bore the phrase "Illinois—Land of Lincoln." He said
to one of his young friends, "Illinois! That's in America. Lincoln—he is the one
that freed us!"

[6]Some of the schools established in the Buxton settlement to educate both the
fugitive adults and children did not, by statute, exclude nearby white settlers.
It is, perhaps, ironic that the whites observed that the schools run by the
Negroes were so superior that they closed their own and enrolled their children
in the Negro school; Brion Gysin, *To Master—A Long Goodnight: The Story of
Uncle Tom, A Historical Narrative* (New York: Creative Age Press, 1946), p. 124.
In addition, "the Buxton Settlement actually raised the value of adjoining
farms. The Buxton settlers were spoken of by white people as good farmers,
good customers, and good neighbors"; Fred Landon, *Journal of Negro History*,
3, No. 3 (1918), 366.

The pre-Civil War era in Cass County

I have been unable to locate accurate information relating the exact
number of fugitives fleeing to Canada from Cass County following
the passage of the Fugitive Slave Law.[7] It is impossible to estimate
this accurately from the census data because return migration to
Cass County from Canada may well have taken place between the
censuses of 1850 and 1860. Moreover, the operations of the Underground Railroad not only continued but intensified between 1850
and 1860. Thus, Table 3 reveals a series of high proportionate increases in the Negro populations of several selected geographical
areas.

In addition to the surprising evidence that Cass County contained
more Negroes in the years 1850 and 1860 than did the city of

*Table 3: Negro population in 1850 and 1860, including
percentage increase, by selected geographical units*

Area	1850	1860	Per cent increase
Michigan	2,500	6,700	168
Cass County	389	1,368	252
Calvin Township	158	795	403
Chicago	323	955	196

[7]The Negro population of Canada grew rapidly in the years following the passage of the Fugitive Slave Law in 1850. It has been estimated that many thou-
sands fled the United States during those years. One aspect of the migration
provides striking documentation for my earlier contention that longer journeys
from slavery were motivated by fear—this is borne out in that Negroes began
a reverse migration to the United States even before the Civil War had ended.
Gysin, p. 184, reports that by 1870 the Negro population of Canada was half of
its level for the 1850's. The American Missionary Society estimated that the
Negro population of Canada at the outbreak of the Civil War was 40,000; Ontario History, No. 4 (1949), 195.

Chicago, it will be noted that the high level of danger of recapture for Negroes in the decade prior to the Civil War did not deplete the settlement founded in Cass County.

One might expect that the rapid increases in Negro population that Calvin Township experienced would probably produce outbursts of racial prejudice and, perhaps, even discrimination. Indeed, John Hope Franklin comments that such rapid increases in the Negro population in Michigan met with unpleasant reactions: "Northern whites had shown no usual hostility to Negroes who were already in their midst, but they did not welcome the crude, rough type which came from the South."[8] Although this situation may have been characteristic of other areas of Michigan, I have located absolutely nothing in the histories of Cass County which would indicate the presence of any racial prejudice, tension, or friction during these years. I would propose that the forces, postulated in Chapter Three, continued to contribute to the commitment of racial equality in the Calvin area: Negroes' and Quakers' mutual rejection of a prior social system, an abundance of farm lands, a growing national reputation that had to be "lived up to," and, of course, the deep religious conviction of the Quakers.

The percentage of Calvin Township population that was Negro in 1850 was 25.3. In ten years it had grown to 57.8 per cent of the population. Some of the lands supporting this settlement were purchased by the Negroes, during that decade, with funds derived from estates that had been filed in Cass County by various former masters who wanted to be certain that "their Negroes" would get the funds willed to them. Additional acreage was also gained by successfully farming progressively larger and larger plots of land. Perhaps the most revealing aspect of local value commitment is that the Quakers made available cabins and plots of farm land to those fugitives who arrived in destitute and abject poverty.[9]

[8]John Hope Franklin, *From Slavery to Freedom: A History of American Negroes* (New York: Alfred A. Knopf, 1948), p. 231.

[9]Although evidence of these plots is no longer visible on current plat maps and the cabins no longer stand, several older residents remembered both from their childhood.

The Civil War: participation and pride

Abolitionist sentiments in many northern areas reached a crescendo by the outbreak of the Civil War. To the northern abolitionist, the Civil War was a moral crusade—a battle of liberation. Despite the predominantly pacifistic orientation of the Quakers, the people of Cass County and of Michigan devoted themselves wholeheartedly to the war effort. The extent of this commitment is startling when one notes that Michigan sent one seventh of its *population* to the Civil War.[10]

   The Union took a somewhat ambiguous stance on the question of recruitment and enlistment of Negro soldiers. Although Negroes from Cass County and elsewhere did, in fact, serve in the Union armies early in the conflict, it was not until the Emancipation Proclamation (January 1, 1863) that the Union officially sanctioned the employment of Negro soldiers.[11] During—and before—this time, Calvin Township Negroes were recruited into a unit known as the First Michigan Colored Infantry. This unit later became known as the 102 U.S. Colored Infantry (102 U.S.C.I.).[12] There is evidence that the men enlisted in this regiment fought side by side with recruits from the Buxton settlement in Ontario.[13] In all, 1,446 men served in the 102 U.S.C.I. It was first organized in Detroit in the summer of

[10]Schoelzow, p. 72.

[11]Frazier, p. 106.

[12]A search was conducted in cemeteries in the Calvin Township area. The experience was essentially a recitation of the current family names, but the process revealed that 22 men had served in the 102 U.S. Colored Infantry, three in other units of the U.S. Colored Infantry, and two Negroes (determined by family name) had been enrolled in "non-colored" units.

   It must be pointed out that these data can be taken as only a representative, though significantly underestimating, indicator of the true participation. The numbers reflect only those men buried under the "standard issue" Civil War headstone and are found in cemeteries more than 100 years old that contain broken headstones, grown-over thickets, and probably unmarked graves. Therefore, the true number of Civil War veterans buried in Calvin cannot be accurately assessed from these data.

[13]Victor Lauriston, *Romantic Kent: The Story of a County, 1626 to 1952* (Chatham, Ont.: Shephard Printing Co., 1952), p. 456.

1863.[14] Of the entire force, approximately 100 were from the Calvin Township area.[15] In evaluating the role of the Calvin Negroes, Schoelzow comments:

> *The colored men of Calvin showed their appreciation of the*
> *effort made for their freedom by enlisting in great numbers in*
> *the Civil War. They organized a Post of the Grand Army of*
> *the Republic which had a large membership at one time.*[16]

The events of this period still live in the minds of the current resi-dents and in their public discussion. The Matthew Artis [Negro] Grand Army of the Republic Post No. 341 of Calvin still exists, and many of the respondents—white and Negro—that I contacted extolled the significant role the people of Calvin had assumed during the Civil War.

Post-Civil War adjustment and settlement

Negro Americans who served in the Civil War returned to some-what varied social orders. For a very few, positions of power were available in the postwar Reconstruction governments, some returned to an extra-legal system of bondage to compensate for past debts, many that originally were from the South were homeless, and a few others returned to northern areas such as Calvin Township.

Post-Civil War Negro migrants to Cass County did not represent a problem as they might have in previously all-white areas of the North. Negroes owned land in Cass County, they fought for the Union, and they returned home again to farm. In short, they *belonged* in Cass County. By the end of the Civil War, Negroes had been an everyday fact of local life for a generation. Many white men from Cass who fought in the war alongside their Negro neigh-

[14]Jno Roberson, *Michigan in the War*, rev. ed. (Lansing, Mich.: W. S. George and Co., State Printers and Binders, 1882), p. 392.

[15]Schoelzow, p. 73.

[16]*Ibid.*, p. 58.

bors had never lived in a social structure without Negroes. The end
of the Civil War meant a return to normalcy—not a departure from
it. Whites had no reason to fear Negroes, and Negroes no reason to
resent whites.

Shortly after the return to normalcy in Cass County, the Thir-
teenth, Fourteenth, and Fifteenth Amendments to the Constitution
were ratified by the states. In brief, these provided for the abolition
of slavery (1865), prohibition of abridgment of citizenship rights
(1868), and equal rights for whites and Negroes (1870). Whereas
the "immediate enfranchisement and full social participation guaranteed to the Negro by the Reconstruction Congress completely
upset former social relationships in the South,"[17] this did not occur
in Cass County. In Michigan these Amendments to the Constitution
were not ratified at gun point, or in defeat as part of the victor's
spoils. Rather, they were ratified as part of victory—as part of a
cultural reaffirmation. Negroes voted in Michigan only months after
ratification of the last of these amendments.[18] One of the respondents summarized the sentiment on this point when he remarked
that "Lincoln gave them the right to vote—period! This was the law.
Michigan took the Constitution for what it said." (WR–27.)

The Negro population of the county increased from 1,368 in 1860 to
1,810 in 1870 (an increase of 32 per cent). However, it must be
pointed out that while this increase indicated a continued migration
of Negroes into Cass County, the white population increased by
39 per cent during the same period. It may be reasonably concluded
that white immigration did not seem to be stifled by the presence of
Negroes. In Michigan, Cass County was surpassed only by Wayne
County (Detroit) in the number of Negroes in 1850 (Wayne—724
out of 42,726; Cass—389 out of 10,907). However, the proportion
Negro in Cass far exceeded Wayne County. In 1860, one of every
five Michigan Negroes resided in Cass County—in 1870, one in
seven.

Besides census materials, the most orderly and complete set of
records reflecting population origination and composition that I was

[17]John Dollard, *Caste and Class in a Southern Town* (New Haven: Yale University Press, 1937), p. 57.
[18]Roberson, p. 136.

able to utilize was the county records of marriage. Although marriages had been recorded since 1830, racial identification did not
consistently appear on the ledgers until 1868. After 1868 these records became valuable in that name, race, age, and birthplace were
uniformly entered. Although marriage data are of limited direct importance to the present discussion, their comprehensiveness allows
various forms of secondary analysis and interpretation.

Table 4 reports the birthplace of Negroes marrying in Cass County

*Table 4: Birthplace of Negro individuals marrying
in Cass County (percentage state of
origin by date of marriage)*[a]

State of origin	Date of marriage			
	1868–1870	1871–1874	1875–1879	1880–1890
Michigan	5%	13%	34%	63%
Indiana	19	32	24	13
Ohio	36	31	22	14
Other Midwest	0	1	1	0
Total Midwest	60%	77%	81%	90%
Kentucky	6	2	5	1
Tennessee	4	1	0	2
Virginia	11	12	5	2
North Carolina	13	7	4	2
South Carolina	4	1	2	1
Total South	38%	23%	16%	8%
Misc. East	1	0	0	1
Canada	0	0	3	0
Didn't know	1	0	0	0
Total Misc.	2%	0%	3%	1%
Total per cent	100%	100%	100%	100%
Total number	100	138	146	286

[a]Official records of Cass County, Michigan, 1868 to 1890.

for specified time intervals. In the earlier years, the proportion of individuals born in Michigan was quite low. Ohio, Indiana, and the border states were frequently cited as birthplaces.[19] In later years, the proportion born in Michigan steadily increased. Note also that between 1875 and 1879, 3 per cent were born in Canada (by subtraction of the respective ages of the individuals in the records, they were born in the 1850's).[20]

There is a dearth of data concerning the character of political and social life in the period prior to 1880, but some meager indications can be uncovered. As early as 1878, Negroes were elected to political office. In that year, a Negro was elected justice of the peace in Calvin Township. He served in this capacity for 24 years.[21] One of the respondents reported that in about 1880 the register of deeds for Cass County was a Negro. (WR–31.) Mathews, in his history of Cass County, asserts that in 1870 Calvin Township had approximately 400 voters, of whom 250 (62.5 per cent) were Negro.[22]

White and Negro children attended school together during this period. Several of the schools had classes taught by Negro teachers, and students in these schools were of both races.[23]

1880 to World War I

Shortly after the turn of the century (1903), Booker T. Washington visited Cass County to study the conditions in the Negro settlement.

[19]There is good reason to suggest that the high proportion of Ohio and Indiana births might be suspect because these states functioned as temporary stops in the flight from the South. Individuals reporting these data may not have known where they were born or may have been reticent to admit southern parentage because of the certain implication of slave status in the South.

[20]In reference to the discussion of origins in Chapter Three, it is significant to note that no migrants during this time came from the deep southern states.

[21]John C. Dancy, "The Negro People in Michigan," *Michigan History Magazine,* 24 (1940), 222.

[22]Mathews, p. 387.

[23]*Ibid.*

One of the older Negro respondents in this research remembers talking with him on this trip. (NR–34.) Washington remarked:

My attention was first attracted to this settlement some years ago when I was in South Bend, Indiana, the site of the Studebaker wagon factories. I noticed that the colored people of South Bend seemed to be an unusually prosperous and solid lot of people. . . . From this discussion of the condition of the colored people in South Bend, Mr. Studebaker called my attention to the large community of colored people in Calvin Township, Michigan, which is not very far from South Bend, since Cass County, in which Calvin is situated is the southern boundary of Michigan.[24]

From 1880 to World War I the Cass County Negro population suffered a fairly constant attrition as increasing urbanization was taking place in the United States. Cass County resembled other areas investigated by Baker, whose examination of agricultural northern areas indicated a declining proportion of Negro population between 1880 and 1900.[25] Booker T. Washington commented that the most general complaint in Cass County was that the young (Negro) men of Calvin "were too much inclined to leave the township and go to the large cities."[26]

Although faced with a declining number of residents at the turn of the century, the Negro community in Cass County seemed to prosper and appeared in no danger of collapse because neither mismanagement of the agricultural resources nor pressures applied by white settlers existed. The following passages, excerpted from interviews conducted by Booker T. Washington in 1903, underscore these impressions:

There is practically no difference in the material condition of the two races in Calvin.[27]

[24]Washington, *The Outlook*, 73, 296.
[25]Baker, p. 109.
[26]Washington, *The Outlook*, 73, 302.
[27]*Ibid.*, p. 304. (Quote from County Clerk.)

*I do not recall any instance where white residents of the
township have objected to colored people buying land there.
I do not think there is any depreciation in the price of land.*[28]

*Some of the best people in the county live in Calvin and
mingle with these people in a business way with no
distinction. I do not think that the fact of the colored settlers
being there is considered any detriment to the community,
although white people from communities which have no
colored settlers might be averse to buying land there.
Certainly land does not sell for any less there. The land in
Calvin is among the best in the county.*[29]

Washington then went on to reveal that the largest tax bill paid in
Calvin Township was paid by a Negro farmer,[30] and that many of
the Negroes owned their homes or rented them from Negro land-
holders. There were even a number of cases in which white settlers
rented property from Negroes.[31]

By 1910, the census reports the following indicators of a sizable
economic investment by Negroes in Cass County:

*1. The valuation of the Negro agricultural establishment was
over $650,000. This was almost one third of the value of all
Negro farms in Michigan and 4 per cent of Negro farms in the
five Midwestern-state area.*

*2. Negroes farmed 13,515 acres of land in Cass County. This
was 30 per cent of the figure for the state, and 5 per cent of the
East-North-Central states' acreage.*

*3. Finally, Cass County Negroes operated 171 farm units
in 1910. This is 27 per cent of the comparable figure for*

[28]*Ibid.* (Quote from Judge of County Probate Court.)

[29]*Ibid.* (Quote from County Clerk.)

[30]*Ibid.*, p. 299.

[31]*Ibid.*, p. 300.

Michigan, and 5 per cent of that for the East-North-Central states.[32]

In 1916, Corrothers' observations enhanced the meaning of the above data when he summarized the extent of Negro settlement at that time:

The descendants of these pioneer Negroes still possess the land in "The Chain Lake Settlement." Their community embraces all of "Calvin township," 36 square miles; and a portion of "Porter township," about two and a half square miles. Cassopolis, the thriving county-seat, eight miles from the Settlement, is the principal market and trading point for "Chain Lake" folk, many of whose farms consist of from 90 to 800 acres. Good roads, modern cottages, with roses blooming in the yards; great barns, windmills, schools, churches, country stores and telephones are common to their community.[33]

Although Negroes lived throughout Cass County between 1880 and World War I, they remained concentrated primarily in Calvin Township, as Corrothers' description implies. Because of the basic township system of government in Michigan, ecological concentration in Calvin gave Negroes representation and a political voice in the governmental process of the township. In addition, supervisors elected by the respective townships constituted the county governmental agency. The first Negro to serve on the County Board of Supervisors was elected from Calvin Township in 1899. Prior to this time, various other township offices of lesser status were filled by Negroes. In the election of 1901, Negroes were the successful candidates for the offices of supervisor, clerk, treasurer, as well as other public positions in Calvin, such as school inspector, justice of the peace, highway commissioner, and constables.[34] This pattern is maintained continuously from 1880 until World War I.

[32]U.S., Bureau of the Census, *Negro Population: 1790–1915* (Washington: U.S. Government Printing Office, 1918), pp. 642–673.
[33]Corrothers, pp. 18–19.
[34]*Cassopolis Vigilant*, April 4, 1901.

To the extent that partisan politics entered the township level, Calvin remained staunchly Republican. In 1889, out of 227 votes cast, 207 were Republican, 10 Democratic, and 10 Prohibition. The majority party in the county was Republican, and the participation from Calvin was appreciated.[35] In the elections of 1910, only the Republican ticket was nominated and therefore the Republican township officials were unanimously elected. The following editorial comments that Calvin was regarded—by the newspaper at least—as political profit:

No township in Cass County was worked so industriously by the wets as was Calvin, because Calvin was the banner dry township two years ago, and despite all the effort made there, Calvin still returns the largest dry majority in the county, making a gain of twelve over two years ago. Calvin demonstrated that she knew her own mind and resented outside interference in no uncertain words. Good for Calvin.[36]

The extent to which the Calvinite[37] was seen as a valuable asset in the political arena—and the degree to which he knew this—can be gathered from local newspaper articles. One, written by a white resident, basically explains why Calvinites should be "colored Republican gentlemen" instead of "Democratic darkies." The other, written by a Calvinite, reports that a Democratic speaker called the Calvinites in attendance "Niggers" and reported that he abused Abraham Lincoln and Frederick Douglass. The Calvinite then requested that Democrats stay out of Calvin.

One must remember that between 1880 and World War I, Negro Americans were being rapidly disenfranchised in many areas of the United States, especially in the South. As far as can be determined,

[35]*Ibid.*, April 4, 1889.

[36]*Ibid.*, April 7, 1910.

[37]"Calvinite," as used in the research, refers to the "old-time" Negro residents of Calvin Township. This is the name by which the Negroes are known in the area at the present time.

there is no question that Cass County Negroes continued to use the ballot as guaranteed under the United States Constitution. It would have been difficult to deprive Negroes of this basic right at a time when, with consent and acceptance of the white population, they were already wearing the uniforms of law enforcement officials,[38] the cloaks of jurors,[39] and the robes of judges.[40] A respondent stated the point simply: "The Negro was never denied the right to vote. Not because of being a Negro, but he was a human being and had the right to vote, period." (WR–27.)

The following observation from a Detroit newspaper of 1896 illustrates not only the uniqueness of the settlement and the political power involved, but also the profit that it represented to the Republican majority:

This township [Calvin] occupies a unique place in the
commonwealth of Michigan, and in fact, it is extremely
doubtful if its counterpart can be found in any state north of
the Ohio River. Here is a dusky little republic governed by
slaves and slave descendants of thirty-six square miles of
Michigan's choicest agricultural land. Since long before the
[Civil] War, a community has existed here in which the
Negroes outnumbered the white citizens two-to-one, have had
the reigns of local government in their own hands. Negroes
have filled the township offices, run the schools, handed
out letters and papers from post offices to their
white neighbors, and carried out the public improvements.
The little republic has on the whole been fairly well governed
too, and here at election time the most extraordinary GOP
majorities have been rolled up which have more than once
carried the day for county legislative and even congressional
candidates.[41]

[38]See, for example, *Cassopolis Vigilant*, April 4, 1901.
[39]*Ibid.*, September 3, 1891.
[40]*Ibid.*, April 4, 1901.
[41]*Journal* (Detroit), January 6, 1896.

Schools in Cass County continued to be integrated as in the past. My oldest Negro respondent, a former teacher, observed: "When I taught, a school would have a white teacher one year, colored the next. It made no difference. They mixed us up." (NR–34.) During her own high school days, she boarded with a white family in Cass-opolis and reported that she never detected any prejudice or encountered any discrimination when she taught in the county.

Local newspapers from the turn of the century constantly carried social news of Calvinites, but the word "Negro" was rarely found. The following social events in Calvin, taken at random from local newspapers, are perhaps sufficiently indicative of the character of social adjustment: an Emancipation Proclamation anniversary celebration (1889), a joint meeting of two literary societies in Calvin (1891), and a spelling bee followed by an ice cream social (1891).

The Judge of Probate Court in Cass County related the following to Booker T. Washington in 1903:

The material condition of the [Negro] people has greatly improved in the last twenty years. They have more wealth, better farms and homes—they live better. Their conditions have kept parallel with the whites. Considering their opportunities, they have advanced. Their moral condition has improved very much. There has been a great decrease in criminal conditions during the last twenty years. Calvin does not give us—the courts—as much trouble now as some of our white communities. There is increased membership in churches, and increased attendance at schools. There is more desire for education. There are six schools in Calvin in which white and black go together. The relations of the two races are mutually pleasant. . . . The colored residents have helped to contribute to the prosperity of the county, considering the opportunities they have had and the length of time they have had to earn money.[42]

[42]Washington, The Outlook, 73, 303–304.

World War I and the Great Depression

Throughout this period, Cass County retained an essentially Republican political character. In 1925 Calvin recorded 170 Republican votes and 3 Democratic votes on the state ticket.[43] Their township roster contained no listed Democrats.[44] In 1930, Democrats ran for only two county offices—they lost. With these exceptions, Republicans ran unopposed.[45] Calvin Township ran only Republican slates in both 1935 and 1939.

During this same period, such organizations as the Ku Klux Klan were reborn and flourished nationally. Although the movement was initiated in the 1860's, its influence steadily lessened after Reconstruction only to be rekindled following World War I. Thus, by the middle of the 1920's, it is reported that a peak nationwide membership of five million had been attained.[46]

It is somewhat difficult to measure the significance of the Klan movement on race relations in Cass County because of the relatively mild forms in which it appeared. Klan speeches were delivered before *interracial* audiences in the Cassopolis area in the 1920's that stressed American patriotism and appealed for a rule of law and social order.[47] Activities were then confined to speech-making and an occasional cross burning. In nearby Dowagiac, however, Klan parades were reportedly held. In addition to news coverage, several respondents reported these events from memory, remarked that no terrorist activities took place (NR–23) (NR–2), and that the "white-robed" participants "felt ridiculous in a short time." (WR–31.)

With the onslaught of the Great Depression, manifest Klan activities subsided in Cass County. Although there were some spurious emotional feelings about the presence of the Klan during the 1940's and 1950's, if any organized activities existed at that time in Cass

[43]*Cassopolis Vigilant*, April 9, 1925.

[44]*Ibid.*, March 19, 1925.

[45]*Ibid.*, September 30, 1930.

[46]C. Vann Woodward, *The Strange Career of Jim Crow* (New York: Oxford University Press, 1957), p. 102.

[47]*Cassopolis Vigilant*, September 6, 1923, gives an account of one of these speeches.

County, it was in men's minds rather than in their actions. I saw no signs that Klan activities were or had been the source of any sort of concern. Throughout the period, the character of interracial social relations was apparently dominated principally by a "live-and-let-live" spirit.

Following World War I, the number and proportion of Negroes in Cass County continued to decline. In 1920, 1,353 Negroes resided in the county (6.6 per cent of the population). By 1930, this number had slipped to 1,176 (5.6 per cent) for the county, and 14.4 per cent for the four-township research area. These declines can be attributed to a variety of factors. First was the continuing nationwide trend toward urbanization. Second, the county had a very restricted industrial base, and those individuals who wished to work in industrial jobs were forced to move to areas that provided a wider range of economic opportunities. Third, allure of the prosperity that abounded during the Roaring Twenties, and the knowledge that Negro areas could be found in the large urban centers, apparently proved a stronger pull than the restraining factor of better racial conditions in Cass County. Fourth, the Calvin settlement was contracting because of the attrition of the old settlers. They died, and their children, having left the county, did not replace them. Finally, the county was not significantly successful in attracting newcomers to replace those that had been lost. The resources that proved attractive in the years *following* the Great Depression mattered little *during* it. It is noteworthy that the percentage Negro in Calvin Township dropped to 50.9 in 1930. This was the lowest percentage recorded since before the Civil War. However, Negroes in other northern rural areas apparently suffered just as much attrition of resources. The value of land and buildings operated by Negroes in Calvin still constituted about 26 per cent of the total controlled by Negroes in Michigan and about 5 per cent of the total in the East-North-Central states.[48]

As economic prosperity returned following the Depression, the gradual attrition of the Negro population—proportionally and numerically—that had characterized the area for fifty years, ended. Although some of the data presented in Table 5 have already been

[48]U.S., Bureau of the Census, *Negroes in the United States: 1920–1932.*

Table 5: Negro population of Cass County,
1830 to 1960: number and percentage

Year of census	Number	Percentage of population
1830	1	0.1
1840	8	0.1
1850	389	3.6
1860	1,368	7.7
1870	1,690	8.0
1880	1,837	8.4
1890	1,609	7.7
1900	1,568	7.5
1910	1,444	7.0
1920	1,353	6.6
1930	1,176	5.6
1940	1,441	6.6
1950	2,309	8.2
1960	3,706	10.0

mentioned in the text, it is useful to study the long-range demographic trends as the examination of the historical period is concluded. Thus, this Table presents the number and proportion of Negroes in the county population at every census since 1830.

From these data it is immediately apparent that the Negro population of Cass County experienced sharp increases in size during the
twenty years prior to the Civil War. From 1860 to 1880 increases
were still typical but at a curtailed rate. From 1880 until 1930, each
census recorded fewer and fewer Negroes in the county. Incidentally, census data not reported in Table 5 demonstrate that each
census between 1870 and 1930 also reported fewer whites. Thus,
1930 was the low point for the number of whites, the number of
Negroes, proportion of Negroes, and total population size. Since that
date, the county has been experiencing a substantial increase in
both white and Negro population. Negroes have been moving into

Table 6: Negro population of Calvin Township and four-township area, 1930 to 1960: number and percentage

Year of census	Calvin Township		Four-township area	
	Number	Per cent	Number	Per cent
1930	370	50.9	679	14.4
1940	554	61.6	907	18.0
1950	617	61.9	1,155	20.6
1960	768	65.5	1,623	26.0

the county at a proportionately greater rate so that the percentage of the population classified as Negro has almost doubled from 5.6 per cent in 1930 to 10.0 per cent in 1960. Moreover, from 1930 to 1960 the number of Negroes in Cass County has more than tripled.

Relevant census data for townships were not collected between 1880 and 1920. Prior to 1880, the censuses of 1850, 1860, and 1870 report the Negro population in Calvin to be 25.3 per cent, 57.8 per cent, and 61.2 per cent respectively. Additionally, since 1930 complete census tabulations for township units are available. Table 6 reports the number of Negroes and their proportion of the total population since 1930 for Calvin Township and the four-township area that roughly constitutes the Cassopolis school district boundaries and the area of principle investigation of this research.

During the past thirty years, as demonstrated by Table 6, the size of the Negro population in Calvin Township and the four-township area has more than doubled. Presently, one out of every four persons in the research area is Negro. It is in this demographic perspective and with the knowledge of the historical antecedents and cultural tradition that a close examination of the contemporary social structure can begin.

The contemporary community

part three

five:

Economic

institutions

The origins of some of the most pervasive forces contributing to the generation and maintenance of patterns of racial discrimination in the United States are economic in character. Competition for scarce resources such as wealth, status, power, and prestige can certainly provide a sufficient motivation to attempt to control another's access in an effort to enhance one's own position. Arnold Rose finds that, in the North, economic competition between the white and Negro seems to be concentrated in two fundamental areas: employment and housing.[1]

Because of the traditional agricultural character of the Cass County region, these two institutional areas are by no means separate or distinct. Even though the agricultural establishment is playing a less important role than it once did, a growing importance of recreational pursuits still dictates that the questions of land acquisition, retention, and evaluation are among the more crucial issues in an analysis of local economic institutions.

[1]Arnold Rose, *The Negro in America* (Boston: Beacon Press, 1956), p. 313.

From the discussion of the historical evolution of the Negro settlement in Cass County, the following statements can be abstracted:

Prior to the Civil War, Negroes farmed approximately 1,500 acres of land located primarily in Calvin, Penn, and Porter Townships.

The agricultural census of 1910 noted that Negroes farmed approximately 13,000 acres of land still concentrated in the three townships mentioned above, but they gradually spread out to most areas of the county.

By the census of 1930, the number of acres farmed by Negroes had declined to 9,321. Nevertheless, this still constituted almost one third of the total land area farmed by Negroes in Michigan.

Securing and retention of land
by Negroes in Cass County

As part of the data collection, the most recent copy of the plat book (1957) for the four-township area was obtained and a "lot-by-lot" survey of land ownership was undertaken.[2] The results of this survey for Calvin Township are shown in Figure 5. The township is subdivided into sections—each area one mile square comprises 640 acres. Figure 5 reveals that Negroes currently own about one half of the land area of Calvin Township (10,000 acres). Negroes also control substantial acreage, but to a lesser degree, in several of the other townships nearby. The extent to which the contemporary patterns are similar to those of a half century ago can be noted by comparing the 1957 plat book with one circulated in 1915.[3] Not only have the

[2]Data relative to race do not, of course, appear on public records. This information was gained from my knowledge of the land owners and respondent reports.
[3]There have been no completely revised plat books between 1915 and 1957. Beyond making general observations regarding some over-all patterns, it is not possible to present precise data concerning the exact racial composition relative to the 1915 period.

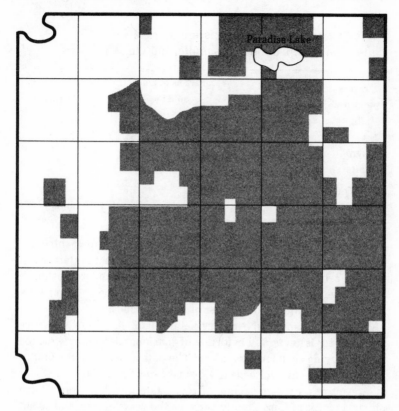

*Figure 5: Graphic representation of Negro land
ownership in Calvin Township*[a]

distribution patterns of Negro settlement remained approximately
the same, but in numerous instances the identical plot of land, retaining its same size, has been owned by the same white or Negro
families in both 1915 and 1957.

Currently, one third of the population of Calvin Township is white,
and one half of the land area is controlled by whites. Thus, it is
evident that whites have had substantial interests in Calvin Township throughout the recorded history of the area. Indeed, there is no
township in Cass County that is exclusively populated by one racial

[a]Shaded area indicates land ownership by Negroes.

*Table 7: Percentage land transfers by race for
Calvin Township, a random sample, 1960 to 1965*

Parcel purchased by	Parcels of land sold by		Total
	Negro	White	
Negro	64%	4%	68%
White	12	19	31
Total	76%	23%	99%
			(Number = 94)

category. Considering the relatively modest size of a township unit, what at first glance might appear to be a segregated pattern is, in part, an artifact of the modest geographical area under consideration. However, before accepting this assertion, the relevant data should be consulted on a number of related issues.

Are there instances of Negroes selling land to whites and vice versa? If so, is there any evidence of tension, friction, or violence accompanying such land transfers? The data concerning the first of these questions are quite clearly brought to bear in Table 7, which is a result of a random sample of real estate transfers drawn from official records of Cass County between the years of 1960 and 1965.[4]

The data in Table 7 confirm what previous analysis has already suggested—that the majority of land sales are intraracial. Only 16 per cent were interracial and 31 per cent involved the purchase of land by a white person.

In addition to checking public records of real estate transfers, several respondents were readily able to provide instances of interracial sales. Inquiries into the occurrence of tension in such cases brought an occasional semiaudible mutter that some people might not like "colored" moving in but that nothing would happen if they

[4]Although records of land transfer are "public information," their relative inaccessibility, added to the generally consistent image (when compared to firsthand knowledge and real estate sources), would make further probing of older records fairly unrewarding.

did. One respondent offered the following account of alleged interracial tension:

> There was a farm in the southeast part of Calvin that a Negro
> sold to a white man. There was a cross burned on the lawn.

He thought a moment and then added:

> But, of course, they were Catholic. [WR-11.]

Is it possible to document any cases of rapid alterations in the
racial composition of an area? In other words, are the ecological
processes of invasion and succession found to be in operation? Although most sections around Cassopolis exhibit a gradually increasing proportion of Negroes, Vandalia, the village in Penn Township,
has undergone dramatic shifts in racial composition over the last
twenty years. Prior to World War II, Vandalia's population was predominantly white with a few Negro families interspersed. However,
since World War II, the proportion of Negroes has been constantly
increasing so that now the village is estimated to be at least 70 per
cent Negro. (NR-22.)

Respondents report that whites have not moved away either as a
cause or a result of the changing composition, but rather, have died
out over the years. The village has not had great success in attracting younger couples, basically due to a lack of economic opportunity. However, many older Negro families have entered the community, and a substantial proportion of these people are living on a
marginal income, fixed retirement income, or both. Here, they have
found low living costs and have not suffered from racial discrimination. A moment's reflection reveals the strong attraction a village
like Vandalia would have on a retired Negro couple who wished to
remain independent of their children's families. In Vandalia they
are able to avoid both the rising costs of living associated with
metropolitan ghettos and the discrimination typical of the rural
South. In talking to many of the older people of Vandalia, anyone familiar with Chicago's South Side would be reminded of an
"old home week." Residents of Vandalia who are recent migrants

from Chicago still keep informed of events there and find that city a topic of mutual interest.

As a result of these forces—attrition of whites and in-migration of Negroes—the population size of Vandalia has held constant at 360 for a decade, but the racial composition has changed rapidly. In a sense then, Vandalia has undergone a "racial invasion," but a corresponding flight (succession) of the established white residents has not taken place. The remaining whites seem to be in no hurry to leave and do not appear to fear or resent living under a Negro mayor in a predominantly Negro village. This is the only situation I found in the area that could conceivably resemble an "ecological turn-over."

Many areas of the northern United States live under the belief that land values will depreciate if residential desegregation should take place. Is there evidence of depressed or inflated land valuation that might be related in any way to the racial composition of the population? Respondents stated that the price of farm land in Calvin Township averaged about $150 per acre and that other land in the county ranges between $100 and $200 per acre. These figures are, of course, subject to constant rise. Obviously, land bordering the lakes costs considerably more—between $30 and $100 per running foot—depending on the desirability of the lake for fishing, swimming, and scenic beauty. Several respondents maintained that Calvin land, although a little wet because of the low areas, contained some of the best farm land in the county. Its price reflects that this is true.

There seems to be neither a discernible trend of change in land values when Negroes become more numerous in an area, nor a general price depreciation in land already held by Negroes. While most respondents perceived no relationship between race and land values, several maintained that land values in the area had gone up because Negroes are willing to pay more to avoid enduring discrimination elsewhere (NR–22), or because Negro people from higher cost of living areas such as Chicago do not really know a fair price for land and thus tend to overpay. (NR–7.) One respondent maintained that the price of land decreased because "Negroes, especially new migrants, don't have pride in their homes like we do." (WR–24.)

Although real estate changes hands racially, it usually does so slowly, without fanfare, and without corresponding changes in its evaluation. Nevertheless, several Negro respondents expressed the belief that discrimination was encountered in attempts to acquire land or housing. White respondents were able, often unwittingly, to provide some illuminating commentary on the issue. Although these white respondents tended to deny discrimination on the basis of race, they did seem quite aware of the "sensitivities" of the neighbors.

Some people in some areas would rather not sell to colored in the same way that people in an older area might not like to sell to people with children. Race, religion, or politics or anything else like that doesn't enter into it directly. [WR—16.]

There are no policies around here about discrimination, but situations which would have repercussions would be avoided. For example, if one knows Joe Blow is dead-set against colored, one would not deliberatedly place a Negro near him. [WR–13.]

Sure, some people would like to sell but won't sell to colored. If colored insisted on seeing the property, they would be told that. This is not because they are colored or because of the people. The neighbors would object. You know that there is a class of colored around here who don't want to associate with other colored. Some are trash. (WR–14.)

It isn't that we don't like colored, it's just that nobody can stand living near these mouthy drifters. You can go down to Calvin Center, and they will tell you the same thing. You don't see the new ones moving into Calvin either, do you? [WR–17.]

I've always heard that colored like to stay around their own kind. I don't mind them being around, but if they feel that way, why can't we? [WR–29.]

It's not a matter of race, but sound property value. [WR–14.]

I really don't see why you are interested in asking about such boring crap. There may be discrimination around here, but it is

*not against any local people. The community would not stand
for it. [WR–24.]*

Upon closer probing it became clear that Diamond Lake (near Cassopolis—encircled by predominantly finer white-owned homes) was
the main area being protected. Even though practices of evasion may
not be the general rule, their existence is one of the first indications
that, although the area is visibly bi-racial, still, some tension between Negroes and whites may exist.

There seemed to be a fairly widespread notion that Negroes moving into the Diamond Lake area might present a somewhat "unpleasant situation." As WR–11 stated, "over at Diamond Lake some
are pretty choosey about their neighbors." One respondent reports
that several years ago a Negro attempted to buy a lake-front home
but was unable to do so after the neighbors "chipped in" and bought
the property. (WR–13.)[5] However, although Diamond Lake may be
predominantly white, at least one Negro family is reportedly living
there with no adverse results. It would appear, however, that Negroes generally seem to be excluded from the Diamond Lake area
because of the possibility of tension as well as inflated real estate
prices for property bordering the lake. Negro respondents tend to
emphasize the race issue more heavily, while white respondents
stress economic factors.

Possibly part of the reason why discrimination may well exist
around Diamond Lake is that whites from surrounding urban centers own a substantial number of summer homes on the lake. These
areas are not particularly known to be free of racial prejudice and
discrimination, and thus tend to reflect patterns more typical of the
urban North. Thus, integration of "the lake" area might impede the
input of "outside money" upon which the county is relatively
dependent.[6]

Among some Negro respondents there is a vague suspicion that

[5] I was not able to substantiate this incident.
[6] To show that *race* was not forgotten, the Cass County branch of the NAACP
petitioned the County Road Commission on December 1, 1959, to remove the
designation, "colored," following the "Paradise Lake" entry on the county road
map. This was done. (Paradise Lake is a Negro resort area.)

somehow Negroes have had land "maneuvered away from them."
Closer probing of this notion did not reveal anything more important than an occasional tax default case (and then only after an
extended time period of several years had elapsed with taxes in
arrears). Although knowledgeable respondents claim that there is
little or no difference in the tax defaults of Negro and white residents, it does appear that occasionally a retired Negro family in
Calvin or Penn Townships, no longer able to produce revenue from
idle land, finds it impossible to keep current on tax assessments.

Some of these very old people have very little but their land.
We try to look the other way as long as possible because they
are poor. Eventually, we have to do something about it. Often
a neighbor will buy some of the land to settle it up. [WR.]

I found no evidence to suggest that the power to seize defaulting
properties was influenced by racial discrimination.
  Perhaps most indicative of the general absence of major difficulty
that Negroes find in the procurement of real estate is evident in the
lack of success of a housing development recently established in the
area. A farm was purchased by an outside concern and promptly
subdivided into modest-sized tracts. The lots were advertised in regional urban centers because it was thought that they would have
appeal to Negroes there. However, little action has taken place and
little overt interest or enthusiasm has been generated.

I don't think that development would be attractive to a Negro.
Hell, when they can buy a place anywhere in this county,
why the devil should they hide out in a segregated
development. It doesn't make sense. [WR–20.]

Availability of credit for real estate

No discussion of the possibility of residential segregation is complete without an examination of the lending policies of a community's banking institutions. Withholding credit from Negroes who

wish to move into "white areas" is a common practice nationally. Thus, lending institutions, while usually denying practices of racial discrimination, often subscribe to the same notions of many real estate agents—that segregation must be maintained if an area is to hold its resale value. Credit and its availability are crucial variables in land use and occupancy patterns since few people—Negro or white—are financially capable of obtaining real estate without mortgage assistance. Lending policies that may be undertaken are illuminating for another reason. For, if a financial institution such as a bank is to operate successfully in a small community where everyone often knows the activities of everyone else, it must tend to uphold and reflect contemporary community standards.

Both of the two local banks are owned, operated, and staffed by whites. Knowledgeable respondents expressed the opinion that because appraisals were based on resale potential one might loan "a little" less to Negroes. Upon further examination, it became clear that there was no "rule of thumb" in determining how much less they would loan Negro applicants because, allegedly, the amount depended on the property rather than the person. Negro migrants are more likely to buy older housing in the villages, and banks tend to insist on higher down payments based on the age of the structure. Thus, respondents maintained that the criteria for granting loans to Negroes and whites were identical. One stated:

Negro customers are less delinquent in paying back loans than whites. Whether this is because we might be more harsh to begin with or that colored prize their credit more, I don't know—maybe both. [WR–24.]

Throughout conversations two concerns were detected: first, did the individual applicant's financial picture warrant the loan; second, was the applicant an old-time resident of the area. I suspect, however, that racial discrimination is prevented or at least minimized by the economic realities. In short, how could one discriminate in lending money to a Negro when "over 30 per cent of our business is colored." The answer is clear—they cannot. This is true not only because the "Negro community" is to be reckoned with economically, but also because the "white community" would not be willing to absorb or attempt to offset the losses certain to be incurred. Economic discrimination and deprivation may occur here and in areas of community economic life yet to be discussed, but the practices which give rise to such conditions are not inherent in the culturally approved behavior of the community. If discrimination were a structuring element of community life, it must be normatively supported and culturally legitimated. Often this can be done by simply defining who is "in" and who is "out" of the "community." Essentially, what is implied is that one cannot publicly and openly criticize a member of the in-group without calling into question the cohesion of that group to begin with.

Occupational access and comparative economic welfare

As I commented in Chapter Two, one half of the employed workers living in Cass County commute outside of the area to surrounding industrial and urban centers. Traditionally, the research area was primarily farming country. Recently the gradual sagging of agricultural prosperity has forced many residents to seek additional employment. However, the area has not been able to generate a sufficient economic base to absorb these additional workers. The resulting pattern has evolved from farming to commutation with "back forty" farming as a sideline.[7] Although the typical farm in Cass County is slightly over 100 acres, substantial portions of these lands lie idle. It is for these reasons that a discussion of economic discrimination must ultimately address itself to the question of wider employment opportunities.

Even a cursory glance at comparative economic opportunities outside the county will show significant degrees of discrimination in such cities as South Bend and Elkhart, Indiana, Kalamazoo and Benton Harbor, Michigan. Comparative economic welfare of local

[7]I would estimate from respondent information that Calvin Township has no more than 10 to 15 capitalized full time farms of which two to four are operated by Negroes.

whites and Negroes tends to reflect differentials that external job discrimination produces. However true this may be, the major concern here is with patterns generated by conditions *within* Cass County.

Questioning respondents concerning the existence of job discrimination in Cass County against Negroes produced variant responses. A few Negro respondents maintained that they had no knowledge, direct or otherwise, of any job discrimination in the Cassopolis area: "Never heard of anyone being refused employment if he had ability." (NR–21.) Some asserted knowledge of such incidents but tended to justify that the alleged actions were based on lack of seniority, education, or marketable skills: "Often times people can't find qualified Negro personnel. I'm thinking of taking two or three white people on the staff." (NR–5.)

However, most Negroes—especially migrants from the South or from northern urban centers—felt that job discrimination was widespread:

Let me put it this way. There are two banks, two drug stores,
three department stores, a bakery, and car dealers in Vandalia
and Cassopolis, and where are the colored? In the back of
the garages and cleaning up the shops. [NR–14.]

This portrayal is essentially accurate. Negroes are definitely underrepresented if not almost absent from the "visible positions" on the main street of Cassopolis.

On the other hand, white respondents either categorically denied the existence of any discrimination based on or associated with race —"so far as employment in this area is concerned, I don't think there is any difference between races" (WR–21)—or acknowledged that Negroes tended to be discriminated against but maintained that this discrimination could be objectively justified—"it's harder for the Negro to get jobs, but it's their ability. If ability is the same, there is no prejudice in Cass." (WR–29.)

To clarify some of the actual experiences of Negroes in the area, I requested that the Michigan Civil Rights Commission provide information concerning complaints or findings pertaining to unfair employment practices in the area. Although the Commission maintained that they did not process complaints by county and therefore could not provide any usable data, they did acknowledge the receipt of complaints concerning employment practices in the county and stated that they had authorized a public hearing against one employer. While they supplied no information that would divulge the identity of the employer, most respondents who were asked about this knew immediately which firm was referred to and stated that it "would not hire Negroes, period!" This situation has since been rectified.

The remaining light industrial firms in and around Cassopolis employ Negroes but mostly in menial, maintenance, or line positions. With the exception of establishments owned and operated by Negroes, respondents of either race were unable to cite an example of a Negro placed in a high-level supervisory position. Thus, the situation seems to repeat the pattern that was found in the retail establishments in Cassopolis—Negroes were hired, to be sure, but principally as stock boys or in other "behind the scenes" operations.

White respondents freely admitted the existence of this pattern but saw the cause not as discrimination but rather as indicative of a family owner-operator pattern—no additional help was needed. However, this does not satisfactorily explain why some find the necessity of employing *whites* who are not related to the employer in the positions that Negroes maintain are closed to them because of race. When questioned about this situation, several proprietors and managers of business establishments maintained that they would have no objections to the employment of Negroes nor would their customers, but that they were unable to locate qualified Negro applicants.

Because the perception of discrimination need not be grounded in fact, one can legitimately ask how much of the alleged discrimination is factual and how much is carried in and generated by the folk beliefs and legend. In an effort to weigh the validity of somewhat conflicting claims, census materials for Cass County were consulted. Table 8, reporting the relative occupational distributions of white

Table 8: Employed men in occupational groups for
Cass County, 1960: percentage distribution by race[a]

Occupational group of employed men	White	Negro
Professional and technical	5.5%	2.8%
Farmer and farm manager	8.4	2.2
Manager, official, proprietor	8.5	1.8
Clerical	5.0	2.7
Sales	4.4	2.8
Craftsmen	23.0	14.7
Operatives	27.0	33.5
Service	3.6	8.4
Farm laborers	3.7	7.4
Laborers (excluding farm)	4.8	14.8
Not reported	6.1	8.9
Total	100.0%	100.0%
Number	(8,363)	(774)

[a]Computed from Census of the Population: 1960, Vol. I, Pt. XXIV, Tables 84 and 88.

and Negro employed men, shows without any doubt that Negroes in Cass County do not fare well in comparison with their white neighbors. For example, more than 60 per cent of Negro men were either operatives, service workers, or laborers, compared to less than 40 per cent in the white category.

Based on these differences in occupational distribution, the data presented in Table 9 should come as no particular surprise: There is substantial inequality in income between white and Negro families. The median income of a Negro family is $3,600 while the median for the white family is $5,600. It is interesting to note that for the state of Michigan the comparable statistics are Negro—$4,400, and white—$6,400.[8] The respective figures for Cass County are substan-

[8]Census of the Population: 1960, Vol. I, Pt. XXIV, Table 65.

tially lower, but the absolute difference between the two groups remains the same: $2,000. Of course, one would be justified in pointing out that the lower the level, the more such an absolute difference means.

An even more relevant comparison for the present purposes is between the Cass County population and the rural nonfarm population in Michigan. These data show that, for whites, the percentage distribution of family income in Cass County is identical (within 1 per cent) to that for the state. However, the family income distribution for Negroes is considerably higher in Cass County than is generally found for Negroes throughout the state. As a result the median for rural nonfarm Negroes is $400 less in Michigan than in Cass County ($3,200 compared to $3,600). Income data controlling for occupation by race are not available for the county.

One additional measurement of the relative economic security of white and Negro residents of Cass County is the comparative level of unemployment that each group faces in the labor market. Table 10 reveals that the unemployment rate for Negroes is more than

Table 9: Family income for Cass County, 1959:
percentage distribution by race[a]

Income	White	Negro
Under $1,000	4.6%	12.6%
$1,000–$2,999	13.5	27.3
$3,000–$4,999	22.8	29.0
$5,000–$6,999	27.3	20.5
$7,000–$8,999	16.6	6.0
$9,000 and over	15.2	4.7
Number of families	8,460	844
Median income	$5,617	$3,620

[a]Computed from *Census of the Population: 1960*, Vol. I, Pt. XXIV, Tables 86 and 88.

Table 10: Percentage unemployed, controlling for race and sex, Cass County, 1960[a]

Sex	White	Negro
Male	*4.0*	*9.4*
Female	*5.6*	*13.6*

[a]Computed from *Census of the Population: 1960*, Vol. I, Pt. XXIV, Tables 83 and 87.

twice as high as that for whites. Almost one out of every ten Negro men is seeking a job but cannot obtain one.[9]

As significant as these figures demonstrating racial inequality may be, they do not prove that, even though both occupational level and family income of Cass County Negroes are considerably lower, they are *discriminated against because they are Negroes*. This is compounded since there is no assurance that each race comes to a job situation with equal skills, motivation, or education. Although it is impossible to measure accurately the effect of all of these variables because of the lack of cross-tabulated data, the census does provide us with information on the relative educational attainment of the white and Negro populations. As can be deduced from Table 11, whites' educational attainment (as measured by years of school completed for those 25 years of age or older) far surpasses the average levels attained by Negroes.[10]

In conclusion, by almost any criteria one might wish to employ, the data support the contention that there are pronounced economic disparities between whites and Negroes: Negroes are employed in a lower status occupational grouping, tend to make a significantly lower family income, and are more than twice as likely to be unem-

[9]Since employment rates are quite volatile, the absolute levels are not important; however, the differences are.

[10]One could, of course, carry the argument further by maintaining that Negroes face discrimination in the schools. However, because this question is beyond the scope here, it shall be examined in a later chapter. For the moment, it should suffice to indicate that no data uncovered in the field research suggests differential treatment in the local schools.

ployed. However, what can one definitely conclude about the *cause* of these disparities? In short, are economic disparities per se a reliable index of discrimination against Negroes *because* they are Negroes?[11]

Certainly, these data reveal that Cass County Negroes possess a significantly lower level of educational attainment: 56 per cent of the Negroes compared to 36 per cent of the whites have gone no further in formal education than eighth grade.[12] Although the data definitely document disparity and possibly appear to indicate racial discrimination, many more aspects of community life must be examined before it can be stated with certainty that racial discrimination is indeed present in the community.

Table 11: Years of school completed for persons 25 years and over for Cass County, 1960: percentage distribution by race[a]

Years of school completed	White	Negro
None	0.8%	2.5%
Part grade school	14.6	37.3
Eighth grade	23.3	24.5
Part high school	23.8	18.6
High school graduate	21.2	12.3
Part college	6.8	3.4
College graduate	3.9	1.3
Number of persons	17,874	2,030

[a]Computed from *Census of the Population: 1960*, Vol. I, Pt. XXIV, Tables 83 and 87.

[11]This the data do not show. A disparity exists but the *meaning* of this disparity remains unclear.

[12]The most desirable data for the present discussion would obviously be a cross tabulation of educational attainment, occupational position, and income by race. Unfortunately, the census data I was able to obtain were not presented in such degrees of adequacy or comprehensiveness.

Ownership of recreational
facilities and industry by Negroes

Chapter Two noted that a "Negro recreational area" is found near the village of Vandalia. Paradise Lake is a relatively small lake around which are clustered an assortment of summer homes, a few year-around homes, a small hotel, several motels, barbeque stands, and other recreational enterprises which are owned and operated by Negroes. Paradise Lake has been known as a predominantly Negro summer resort area for many years. However, there is a more developed area in Lake County, Michigan that provides Paradise Lake with rather stiff competition.[13] Nevertheless, the existence of Paradise Lake and its reputation in Chicago and Detroit tends to bring in numerous vacationers during the summer.[14]

Many of the Negro residents of Calvin Township reveal a substantial amount of disdain for the lake and will not visit the area or permit their children to frequent it. Despite the glowing reports in the various Negro news media about the lake and its attractions, it is not very glamourous or "gala." As one long-time Negro resident said: "Why should I go there when for ten dollars I can go to the Holiday Inn in South Bend?" (NR–30.)

The respondent's point is well taken. One of the greatest attractions that Paradise Lake can offer is an absence of embarrassment, harassment, or outright refusal typical of treatment of Negroes in most parts of the United States. I rather suspect that this has been a major factor in sustaining the Paradise Lake area over the years. We

[13]See Chapter One for a brief discussion of this area located in northwestern *lower* Michigan near Baldwin. The area, called Idlewile, is more developed, considerably larger, and tends to receive far more coverage in Chicago and Detroit newspapers, as well as in such publications as *Ebony* magazine, than does Paradise Lake.

[14]"American Traveler's Guide to Negro History," recently distributed by the American Oil Company, cites the Cassopolis area Underground Railroad marker as one of four attractions in Michigan. The September 1963 issue of *Ebony* magazine also calls attention to the same marker. These forms of publicity would also tend to increase Negro tourism in the area. However, even without such "advertisements," the pressures placed upon the traveling Negro family, especially before the Public Accommodations Act, makes areas such as Paradise Lake relatively well known.

thus find that the community profits from the character of more prevalent racial prejudice elsewhere.[15] Most other recreational facilities in the county are not owned by Negroes, but, of course, are open to them.

In addition to the attractions at Paradise Lake, several other Negro-related facilities are located in the county. One of these is Camp Baber:

> Over 200 ministers of the African Methodist Episcopal Church gathered at a retreat at Camp Baber on Stone Lake [in Cassopolis] June 30. The retreat will continue until July 3, officially opening the church's 1964 camping season. . . . Camp Baber, established in 1948, is the largest and most modern church camp owned and operated by any Negro denomination in the U.S.
>
> More than 100,000 people are expected to come to the camp during the season which closes August 28.[16]

Another is Camp Sun-Chi-Win:

> Camp Sun-Chi-Win on the shores of Long and Baldwin Lakes is one of the most unique established camps in the country. Owned by the Sunshine Mission in Chicago, it is supported by donations from Christian people everywhere. . . . The words segregation and integration are unknown to the seventy boys and sixteen counselors. The present group has ten Puerto Ricans, seven whites, and fifty-three Negroes. Counselor for the eleven through thirteen age group is ———, a young white policeman, whose beat is in one of the toughest sections of Chicago.[17]

Finally, the Lake Region Conference of the Seventh Day Adventists —a Negro conference—owns a 120-acre church and school complex

---

[15]This same circumstance is evident in later stages of the analysis. It should be pointed out at this time, however, that many respondents were quite perceptive about this issue.

[16]*Cassopolis Vigilant,* July 2, 1964.

[17]*Ibid.,* August 29, 1963.

in Calvin Township. In addition to providing church services and elementary education classes for local Negro children, the installation is rapidly developing campground facilities to meet the needs of several thousand of its members from Michigan, Illinois, Indiana, and Wisconsin who attend the yearly ten-day religious convocation on the premises. As an indication of the extensiveness of the operation, more than $36,000 was spent several years ago on campground improvements.[18]

The presence of these installations has some interesting and extremely important implications for the study of race relations in the community. The institutions are located where it is assumed that no difficulties would be encountered either in the purchase of facilities or in their day-to-day functioning. In addition, the large number of people that are drawn to the area tend to inadvertently advertise the research area as a stable bi-racial community. I have spoken to Negroes in such divergent places as Chicago, Detroit, Alabama, and Canada who were well acquainted with the area. They had either visited there themselves or knew friends who had. Perhaps the most important contribution of the installations is that they also change the proportion of Negroes in the area. Although Diamond Lake attracts nonresident whites during the summer, the number added to the population base does not compare to the number of people brought in by the Negro establishments.

One might suspect that perhaps some of the recreational attractions for Negroes could provide a constant irritant to the white community and could thus serve as a basis of friction and tension. I have no evidence to suggest that this is the case. When white respondents discussed the issue of Negro tourism, they perceived the situation in terms of economic benefit rather than social disadvantage. Two or three respondents, however, had some qualms about the possible detraction Negroes could present to whites who came from surrounding cities and might be more accustomed to segregation and

---

[18]Lake Region Conference Souvenir Edition of the *Cassopolis Vigilant*, July 4, 1963. Although $36,000 is a relatively modest amount of money, it should be noted that when it is spent for improvements for a church-school complex situated in the middle of a corn field, in a rural township, in a county that is poorer than average, the effect is significant and visible.

other discriminatory practices. However, it is difficult to know whether these white respondents were forthright in their concern or were actually using it as a "straw man" to verbalize their own prejudices under the guise of concern for someone else's sensitivities.

In addition to the recreational and church-related establishments, there are three or four small industries owned and operated by Negroes in the four-township area. These industries include a casket factory, an industrial machine manufacturing plant, and a metal fabricator. None employs more than 20 persons. These, along with five or six retail establishments—taverns, barber shops, filling station, and sheet metal shop—owned by Negroes, are represented in the Cassopolis Chamber of Commerce. Thus, seven or eight of the approximately 80 members of the Cassopolis Chamber of Commerce are Negro. Vandalia concerns are owned by whites, with a few exceptions such as a tavern, two filling stations, and a nursing home in which public care patients of both races are placed and maintained by the county.

Public facilities

It must be stressed that in most northern states the denial of access to public facilities on the basis of race is illegal and punishable by law. Michigan, perhaps a bit more progressive than many states, passed an "all-inclusive" public accommodations law in 1931.

However, it is axiomatic that official and folk beliefs or practices are not always synonymous, nor are legal dictums always accompanied by uniformly vigorous application. The tasks, therefore, are to examine the existence of discrimination, or lack of it, against Negroes in Cass County; second, to ascertain what legal standards are upheld; and finally to carefully look at what possible avoidance mechanisms—direct refusal, evasion, or embarrassment—are employed.

Numerous cases were related to me and uncovered in other ways concerning alleged incidents of discrimination that occurred mainly in the taverns of nearby Dowagiac. Only once was an establishment in Cassopolis or the surrounding townships mentioned as practicing discrimination. Closer questioning of this allegation, that involved the use of the Cassopolis recreational facility, revealed that the respondent had not directly experienced discrimination but, rather, had heard that someone else had. The "someone else" claimed no knowledge of the incident.

That people in the area would not object to being served next to a Negro in a facility of public accommodation removes the commonly stated motivation for a proprietor to take discriminatory action. Of course, with the substantial Negro settlement in the area, a sizable amount of revenue could be lost by refusing, avoiding, or embarrassing Negro clientele. Lack of public sympathy for discrimination seems to dictate the validity of professing and exhibiting a willingness to serve all customers without regard to race.

The possibility of losing trade becomes an interesting and important economic motivation for the lack of discrimination in an area possessing recreational facilities primarily attractive to and frequented by nonresident Negroes. Paradise Lake, as one of the few major Negro recreation centers in the Midwest, is not a self-contained installation. Rather, it produces business and, thus, revenue for the local establishments run by whites. Although the local citizenry would have no reason to apply "either them or us" pressures, any act of refusing or embarrassing Negroes could economically damage the proprietors.

The discussion of public facilities has focused mainly upon recreation facilities because they are the most applicable to the region and would be the most likely area where tension could be found. However, a few words must be offered regarding other institutions of public service. The press is often in the position of subtly or overtly introducing issues related to race into its pages in much the same manner that it is capable of "creating" a crime wave.[19] After more than two years of close reading of the local newspaper, I had not

[19]This can occur if the newspaper selectively reports incidents, names race only if a minority group member is involved, or otherwise dramatizes some news item far out of proportion to its true significance.

seen any inflammatory or derogatory statement regarding any racial or ethnic group.[20]

I was able to uncover no evidence and none was reported to me that suggests either overt or "sneaky" discrimination in the treatment of Negroes in stores, by doctors or other professionals, in funeral homes, and so on. Several comments may illuminate this point:

For many years Dr. ——— [a Negro] practiced in Calvin Center. He delivered babies for whites and Negroes alike— it never made any difference. [WR–17.]

A while back, some Negroes with Illinois license plates on their car went into a store and asked if they could try on some sportswear. When they were told of course they could, they just left. I certainly don't see why anybody would bother to test that around here. [WR–24.]

Discrimination in public places? Hell no! [NR–2.]

---

[20]One of the few times I saw the local paper, the *Cassopolis Vigilant*, use the word "Negro" was in the following eulogy to President John F. Kennedy: "There are evidences of hate, bitter, deep and irrational, from other extremes. When news came of the death of the President, some Southern newspapers received anonymous, jeering calls, saying 'So they shot that "Negro lover." Good for whoever did it.' There were others along the same vein."

six:

The political

process

Introduction

Many believe that racial friction and antagonism in America can be essentially conceptualized as a conflict involving access to and manipulation of economic and political power. To a substantial degree, power is naturally centralized in the political process of the community. A recognition that the term "minority group" refers not to a numerical variable but rather to the differential distribution of power serves to underscore not only the potential role of racial identification in the structuring of power relations, but also the importance and effective use of the franchise. Even though our national legal structure is now replete with legislation designed to insure equal access to the ballot box and equal protection of the law, it would be naïve to assume that Negro Americans are permitted to vote and participate in the political process without reference to the existence of mechanisms of evasion, repression, or violence.

The use of the franchise is of less crucial concern to a minority when that minority constitutes a very small proportion of the population or if its vote cannot be effectively mobilized. However, in the research area it is quite clear that Negroes, by sheer number alone, do possess the potentiality of a formidable political force. How this strength is used, and what efforts are made either to accommodate or incorporate Negroes into the political process of the community is the central issue of this chapter.

The formal structure: on paper

In preceding chapters it has been frequently pointed out that Negroes generally concentrate in the townships surrounding the village of Cassopolis and particularly in Calvin Township. In most states, township units have little or no direct influence on the structure of county politics. However, as T. Lynn Smith has observed in his study of rural sociology:

In New York, Michigan, and Wisconsin they [townships]
perform many of the essential governmental functions
elsewhere performed by the county. In the other Middle
States their roles are of considerably less importance.[1]

The township *is* the basic unit of local government in Cass County. Each township elects a supervisor who, in addition to managing the political business of the township, automatically occupies a seat on the County Board of Supervisors. County governmental functions and services requiring coordination between townships are within the proper scope of this board. Because neither Vandalia nor Cassopolis are incorporated areas, their interests are represented in the County Board deliberations by the townships in which they are located. Thus, government on the county level is formally controlled by 19 men: one from each of the 15 townships and four additional members from Dowagiac. At the time of the field research, the County Board of Supervisors had one Negro member who represented Calvin Township.

[1]T. Lynn Smith, *The Sociology of Rural Life* (New York: Harper and Bros., 1947), p. 447.

County politics are conducted on a partisan basis, that is, a Republican and a Democrat usually oppose each other on the ticket. This has been true when the Democratic Party felt it could muster enough strength to enter all the races—which, historically, was not always the case. Village politics are *formally* conducted on a nonpartisan basis. However, local residents have little if any difficulty in identifying who is Republican and who is not. The villages have presidents, clerks, treasurers, assessors, and trustees.

The informal structure: politics and power

In an effort to learn concrete and definitive information regarding the characteristics of community leadership patterns, respondents were questioned: "If you want to get something done around here, who has the power to help?" It became clear from respondent comments that community leadership tends to be structured on three levels which relate to one another in a hierarchal order—Level One being the "highest," i.e., most powerful level.

Level Three leaders

Only rarely were township officials or the County Board of Supervisors named as likely candidates for this level, but, generally, respondents could list at least five men not *formally* involved in the political structure. For the most part, "established" members of the community were mentioned. The figures named seemed to possess nothing in common other than that they were known to be stable, tenure members of the community. Level Three leaders, while not possessing power in their own right, manage to wield influence because of the knowledge of and ready access to "those people who count."

They do not and probably cannot take the resolution of matters directly into their own hands, but would rather "feed them up" to those who could. Basically, Level Three leaders could be described

as peddlers of respectability in that their concern with a problem
tends to enhance the probability of its being regarded as a significant and true issue. The majority of this political level is white—
with only three or four Negroes qualifying for "membership." As a
result these Negroes have assumed an extremely powerful media-
tion and filtering role between Negroes and whites in the community. These men are called "white Negroes" by many of the recent
Negro migrants and "Calvinites" or "old-timers" by whites.

Level Two leaders

These individuals are usually elected or appointed officials. They
have gone out into the community to cultivate power and consoli-
date their position. They too are established residents of the area
and are generally descendants of pioneer families. These men seem
to wield power on a much broader base than their narrowly defined roles in the formal structure would seem to warrant. In addition to their elective positions, some also serve as visible standard
bearers of the Republican Party, usually head community groups
concerned with community issues, and play central roles in the few
voluntary associations that are actively operating in the community.
In short, these men are activists in the true sense of the word—they
are visible, concerned, dynamic, and busy. With the exception of
one Negro, these men, numbering about 15, are white.

Level One leaders

However, above Levels Three and Two there is definite power in the
community which is neither open nor visible to many community
members. Some of the Negro migrants, possessing an inadequate
knowledge of power and who holds it, were only vaguely aware that
those in the formal structure and the true power-holders were not
necessarily one-and-the-same. Generally, newer migrants had diffi-

culty identifying where they would go to get things done. Often a diffuse "over there" answer would be given:

That Republican syndicate in town—one big family affair is
all it is. You never really know who they are because they are
too sneaky. They set everything up under the table.
Just a set-up job, that's all it is. [NR–18.]

In other words, there are important economic and political inter- ests that lie, in the words of this Negro respondent, "under the table." Perhaps the term "under the table" indicates conspiracy, which is a more severe implication than is warranted. It is fairly clear to those defined as "in the community" who these individuals are. Level One leaders number about ten. All are white and mem- bers of established families. They are also inclined to be the eco- nomically influential business leaders and particularly prosperous farmers. These individuals very rarely take an open part in the resolution of issues, but rather, they seem content to manipulate events and influence others to "do their bidding." While it is true that there is substantial affluence in Level One leadership, the more important factor is that the affluence is inherited. The new rich do not lead. They have face respect only because their money com- mands this.

In conclusion then, the three levels of community leadership rest on the laurels of "respectability" rather than directly on any inher- ent objective basis. Negroes are almost entirely absent from Level Two because they have not been successful in placing men in key county posts. Despite the existence of an occasional prosperous Negro farmer in Calvin Township, Level One is "lily-white." The implication is obvious: the average recent Negro migrant negotiates with a "white Negro" or "old-timer" at Level Three to gain status for his particular claim. However, for a plea to reach any level where issues are settled, the old-timer must in turn negotiate, cajole, flatter, or twist the white power of the community. The search for authority generates a structure of deference: The migrant bows to the Calvinite, the Calvinite submits to the white power structure.

Those individuals in the community who feel out of touch with the power process may often know the identity of Level Two and perhaps some Level One figures but basically they have no legitimate way to approach them because they and their problems have been defined out of political existence at Level Three. It is the third level, assuming the crucial "filtering" role, that decides who is a "troublemaker." It is by way of this mechanism that the long-time resident, often by this fact alone and regardless of race, has ready access to at least the lower echelons of the power structure. Assuming that the knowledgeable access to power *is* a form of power, the established resident has acquired it by tenure alone.

The recognition that the possession of power is a function of "a seniority system" tends to enrage newcomers who perceive, quite accurately, that their voice has such little volume that it is unable to penetrate into the inner circles. It is even more enraging because the power of Level Three does not come from "below" (electorates) but rather from "above" (higher echelons of informal leadership).[2]

It is within the context of the dual structures presented (i.e., formal versus informal) that race and race-related issues assume a degree of importance. Individuals on these three levels who were interviewed were quite aware that they were operating in a bi-racial framework and that race might, under certain circumstances, become a matter of concern. In order to evaluate how racial identity feeds into the political system, it is first necessary to examine briefly the development of the local political system.

Race and politics

Negroes first voted in Cass County in 1870. They voted for the party of Lincoln and have been doing so, almost without exception, ever since. Throughout the latter part of the nineteenth century and the first half of the twentieth, Negroes were actors rather than issues in the elections. This can be contrasted to the more typical situation in which the "place of the Negro" is a political football in a game that bars him from play.

[2]For a cogent and comprehensive analysis of these and similar issues, see Floyd Hunter, *Community Power Structure* (Chapel Hill: The University of North Carolina Press, 1953).

For Negroes in Cass County, voting was not, nor is it today, a contested issue. The United States Civil Rights Commission reports:

Voting is no problem in Michigan, even in the most densely
populated non-white areas. We have found no evidence of any
attempt to deny Negroes the vote. In fact, every effort is made
to register non-white voters and get them to the polls.[3]

Part of the reason for the almost enthusiastic granting of the franchise to Negroes is that they have traditionally voted "the right way." The importance of this factor should not be underestimated. In his analysis of American segregation, Woodward comments on the issue:

If the Negro's affinity for the conservative whites had its
practical motivations of self interest, so did the conservative
interest in the Negro. The tradition of noblesse oblige and the
flattery of paternalistic impulses do not adequately account
for the pains the conservative Redeemers took to conciliate
the Negroes and attract their support. . . . Conservatives were
obviously in need of friends.[4]

Local newspapers, throughout the past century, constantly documented the existence of Negroes as a political force, but did not perceive them to be a political problem. In the late 1800's local papers often carried detailed accounts of violence toward and repression of Negroes in the South. The stance assumed by the newspapers was one of "finger-wagging" while an attempt was made to gain prestige and political mileage for northern Republicans at the expense of the southern Democrats.

Although Negro Americans were staunchly Republican following the Civil War, by the time the Democratic administration of Franklin D. Roosevelt was underway most had switched their allegiance to

---

[3]*The Fifty States Report*, Submitted to the Commission on Civil Rights by the State Advisory Committees, 1961 (Washington: U.S. Government Printing Office, 1961), p. 287.
[4]Woodward, p. 38.

Table 12: Percentage voting Republican for the
presidential candidate by political unit:
Cass County, 1944 to 1960[a]

Political unit	Election year				
	1944	1948	1952	1956	1960
Calvin Township	84.0	61.8	63.2	67.9	57.1
LaGrange Township (Cassopolis)	65.6	63.5	67.0	68.7	61.7
Penn Township (Vandalia)	74.3	67.7	71.6	71.4	62.8
Cass County	68.7	62.2	64.9	64.6	56.8
State of Michigan	49.2	49.2	55.4	55.6	48.9

[a]Official records of Cass County and census data.

the Democratic Party and have generally remained there ever since.
This pattern, found nationally, stands in stark contrast to Negro voting behavior in Cass County.[5] As one distressed Negro respondent
put it:

Negroes around here owe their allegiance to Abe and
therefore are Republican. If Negroes are any other, they are
classified as outsiders and trouble-stirrers. Here the
Democrats don't want the Negro and the Republicans take the
Negro for granted. [NR–2.][6]

The last time Cass County supported the Democratic national
ticket, aside from the 1964 election, was in 1936. Calvin Township,
reportedly, has never had a Democratic supervisor. Often, Calvin
Democrats have not been able to get anyone to run on their ticket.
The depth of the traditional Republican commitment is evident in
Table 12 which reports voting behavior in various political units for
the preceding five presidential elections prior to 1964.

[5]There is absolutely no way of obtaining precise voting records by race for the
county because the data have never been recorded in that fashion. Therefore,
voting returns by townships, in addition to respondent reports, will be used to
infer the probable patterns of Negro voting behavior.
[6]If one would bother to switch party labels, it will be noted that substantially
the same charges were leveled in the 1964 national presidential elections.

Taking into consideration the relatively large number of Negroes, their political concentration, and their voting behavior, it is quite reasonable to propose that the existence of Negroes would present a formidable force in county politics. However, this has been only partly true. Possessing a sizable Negro population base and harnessing that potential power are two quite different things. The inconsistency has led some local Negroes to criticize the Negro population strongly for its supposed lack of interest in getting out the vote:

A potential one-third voting strength ratio held by Negroes in Cass County falls far below in its registration of qualified voters. The medium of information through the Negro press strongly advocates taking advantage of voting rights. Failure to register hinders our progress.[7]

Later in the same year, this column reported:

A fortnight ago the election returns substantiated the statement, "You don't have to worry about them, Negroes won't support a colored candidate." The most depressing angle is that the two colored candidates, if elected, would have provided six jobs. The one-party system in this area presented an excellent opportunity for the minority faction plus the vote of the Negro, who constitute one third of the county's population [census data including comparative age structures of the Negro and white population indicate about 10 per cent Negro in the county and 26 per cent Negro in the research area at this time], to become equal to or exceed the number of the present single party.

In the November election we may elect the sole partisan candidate and have two of the six positions. The next generation warrants the immediate change of our lackadaisical attitude.[8]

[7]Lee Weatherspoon, "Cass County News," *Pittsburgh Courier* (Detroit edition), February 16, 1956.
[8]*Ibid.*, April 21, 1956.

In addition to drastically overestimating the proportion of Negro residents—fairly common among *Negro* respondents—the context of local politics makes this newspaper comment an appeal to join ranks with the Democratic Party which, over the years, Calvinites have been quite loathe to do. The relatively greater importance assigned to party rather than to race was evident in a recent election in Calvin Township in which a Negro Democrat was soundly beaten by a white Republican. This outcome can be interpreted to mean that either the Republican Party is too important to leave or that race is not that significant an issue to Calvinites.

Before 1964, the Negro vote in Cass County and especially Calvin Township was *not* a race vote, nor was it really an issue vote either. Rather, it was a "party" vote—a vote of sentiment, of loyalty, and of tradition. To this extent, Negroes have not delivered a viable bloc vote because Calvinites did not switch their vote. This situation was fairly well recognized in the area:

On July 9th, the last day for registration, the records were
swollen by many new registrants. Many registered for the first
time. Some pale-faced comments were "don't worry, those n's
won't stick together anyways, so you don't have to worry
about them voting for a colored person."[9]

A comment by a white respondent, while considerably different in tone, basically reflects the same perception:

Negroes are smart enough to know that Democrats can't do
anything for them in this county. Their party has always
been the Republican Party. [WR–20.]

Although the Negro vote has been basically immobile, few politicians would care to ignore its existence completely. Negroes, especially the old-time Calvinites, were *occasionally* "courted" for their vote. For example, compare a comment made by Simeon Booker in *Black Man's America* and the comment of a white respondent.

[9]*Ibid.*, July 21, 1956.

Booker:

It's a common GOP practice to give Negro ministers money and expect them to preach on Lincoln freeing the slaves.[10]

Respondent, running for public office:

I gave $25 to the NAACP and have several Negroes down in Calvin working for me. [WR.]

Finally, here is the published comment of a local Negro:

Most of the candidates were inexperienced in campaigning in front of Negroes. Several commented on the virtues of Abe Lincoln.[11]

Thus, the role of the Negro population as a political force has not been enhanced by their basic lethargic immobility at the polls. Their partisan traditionalism has not made the vote work for them. In short, Calvinites were "safe" from a Republican standpoint and impenetrable from the Democratic point of view.

Political participation by Negroes: appointive and elective positions

The flurry of appointive positions following an election is one of the most time-honored (perhaps dishonored!) practices in American political life. Do Negroes receive appointive positions from the political machinery? The following list of Negroes occupying public and political positions will demonstrate beyond a doubt that they do:[12]

Regular service on jury duty regardless of the race of the defendant

Acting chief of police, Dowagiac (later made chief)

[10]Simeon Booker, *Black Man's America* (Englewood Cliffs, N.J.: Prentice-Hall, 1964), p. 104.

[11]Weatherspoon, *Pittsburgh Courier* (Detroit edition), November 1, 1958.

[12]This is only a representative listing from early 1964. The character and extensiveness of the list is subject to constant change.

Negro deputy sheriff in uniform (one of twelve)

Detective, sheriff's office (the only one)

Service on tax allocation boards

Members of school reorganization board

Assistant county librarian (since appointed librarian)

Several county highway department employees

Deputy county clerk (one of three)

Road commissioner (one of four)

County park trustee (one of four)

Bureau of Social Aid caseworker (one of three)

Assorted office girls in county governmental offices

Republican and Democratic Party convention delegates

Court reporter

In addition to the above list of positions and political control of Calvin Township, three of the six members of the Vandalia village council are Negro (NR–22); Dowagiac has a Negro alderman; the assessor and justice of the peace for Vandalia are Negro, as are two trustees.

The preceding analysis has only vaguely implied some of the characteristics of informal Negro leadership patterns. While it is true that the essence of the internal leadership of the "Negro community" is political, the problem of internal disunity and discrimination in "the community" is even more fascinating to examine. For this reason such issues will be discussed in Chapter Eight.

1964: The year of miscalculation

Because the data collection phase of the research spanned a period of several years, it is possible to report the slow building of tension before the 1964 presidential election and the resulting implications for the political structure of Cass County, including the changes directly or indirectly affecting Negroes. In general the conservative citizenry of the county made an enormous miscalculation relative to the attractiveness of the Goldwater ticket, and who they thought was politically safe.[13]

Evidently the tenets of the state Republican Party did not seem sufficiently conservative for some local residents. The first president of the Conservative Federation of Michigan was a Cass County resident.[14] According to the president, their main purpose was:

> ... to seek out qualified individuals of like minds and get them
> elected to public office. He added the purpose has been
> effective in Cass County where such men have been elected
> to the Board of Supervisors from both parties.[15]

The Conservative Federation of Michigan strongly endorsed the candidacy of Goldwater for president. Several of my respondents estimated that this organization had some 1,000 members in Michigan of whom 200 to 300 were residents of Cass County. There were approximately ten Negroes involved, including, allegedly, a Negro supervisor of Calvin Township and a Negro official from Dowagiac. In addition, several respondents maintained that the John Birch Society had strength in the area: "This is a hotbed of the John Birch Society" (NR–2); and "part of the opposition to my election came from the John Birch Society." (WR.)

The conservative perspective and attitudes held by some in the community can easily be seen in the following news item entitled "Tip Romney and Skirt Cass":

> Niles—A radio warning to the Romney [Republican Governor
> of Michigan] cavalcade approaching Cassopolis Thursday
> afternoon sent the governor's car skirting the center
> of town. . . .

[13]Part of the mistake was similar to that made on the national scene: talking only to one's friends and fellow Goldwater supporters, thereby fatally overestimating the political attractiveness of the conservative appeal.

[14]*The Niles* [Michigan] *Daily Star*, August 13, 1963.

[15]*Ibid.*

*A Goldwater group, irate about the alleged connection of
Romney volunteer groups with the ticket-splitting campaign,
awaited him on a street corner across from the Cass County
Courthouse in Cassopolis.*[16]

  For six months before the election I inquired of most respondents
how they would vote in the presidential election and how they
thought local Negroes would vote. Most white residents expressed
the opinion that Negroes in Cass County and especially those in
Calvin Township would support Goldwater:

*Negroes will vote for Barry Goldwater. Many whites are in
favor of George Wallace [segregationist Governor of
Alabama], and I suppose Negroes are too. [WR–11.]*

*We've got to lick this slavery known as international
communism, and who knows what slavery is better than the
colored. [WR–19.]*

*Yes, Negroes in my township will definitely vote for Goldy.
[WR–12.]*

*A colored man talked to me and said, "That Civil Rights bill
took rights from all of us and gave rights to no one and
Goldwater saw that." [WR–11.]*

*There was a Democratic booth at the [county] fair and it was
manned by an obnoxious sort of colored guy. That should
have made 1,000 Negro votes for the Republicans. One-time
colored Democrats around here are all going for Goldwater.
[WR–19.]*

*This will be one of the last places where Negroes would leave
Goldwater. [WR–27.]*

*Some have fallen for this New York [NAACP] propaganda
that Goldwater is against colored, but most haven't. It's not
true. [WR–19.]*

[16]South Bend Tribune, October 30, 1964, p. 34.

A few white respondents were not quite as certain of the political allegiance of Negroes in the election. One, in fact, accurately perceived some possible implications, if not the results, of the coming election:

Goldwater may take Calvin because of old-time Republican
allegiance. If they vote Democratic, it will show that the
people are feeling more than saying about civil rights.
[WR-24.]

They did feel: the election, 1964

When Cass County voters kick over the traces—they really
kick them over. The county went Democratic with a
vengeance, with but two exceptions, giving a majority of votes
to Governor George Romney and to [the] County Clerk. . . .

Three other Republicans in the county survived because they
were without opposition. Even veteran ———— [state
representative] failed to carry his own county of Cass for the
first time in his long political history. . . .

President Johnson led all Democrats on the county ticket,
polling 8,789 votes. Goldwater received 5,925 votes.[17]

Thus ended, at least temporarily, an era of solid Republican control of county politics. As Table 12 has suggested, during the past thirty years the Republican presidential ticket polled an average plurality of 63 per cent in the county. In 1964 this sagged to 40 per cent. However, Calvin Township shifted its allegiance even more drastically. From an average Republican plurality of 67 per cent, Goldwater bagged a mere 23 per cent of the vote. The comparable statistic for Michigan was 33.1 per cent. Not even Romney, the Republican candidate for Governor who seemed to be a pre-election favorite in Calvin, managed to carry the township. It is interesting to

[17]Cassopolis Vigilant, November 12, 1964.

note, however, that of the seven Republicans running on the *township* level, six, including the supervisor, were voted into office.[18]

In part, of course, Calvinites followed the national landslide for President Johnson. However, since they had resisted national Democratic landslides before, why did they join this one? Before the 1964 election, the state Republican chairman flew a distress flag over the county when he stated that diminishing GOP power in the area could be attributed to "complacency by the Republican leaders and voters, lack of a strong grass roots organization and a better organization effort by the Democrats."[19]

Although both respondent comments and the election results in Calvin Township would strongly indicate a complete lack of Negro support for the Goldwater ticket, exact data are not available. The smallest political unit in the research area is the township. Below this there are no meaningful precinct data, as there are no political areas composed solely of Negroes.

The lack of Negro support for Goldwater in Cass County should have been evident when the Republican candidate spoke at a nearby rally prior to the election. Although local newspapers estimated that several thousand people were present to hear his remarks, I observed less than ten Negroes in the entire crowd—several of whom were wearing "LBJ All the Way" buttons.

Negroes' dissatisfaction with the Republican standard-bearer can be traced to a combination of the following factors:

1. An increasing number of Negro residents in the research area and in Calvin Township were not born there and do not feel as bound to the constraints and "understandings" of the previous generations. Most Negro migrants to Cass County in recent years have come directly from the South or the rural South by way of the urban North—both traditional bastions of Democratic power. Whereas the

[18]The Freedom Now Party, a third party movement, had advertised the following in the *Michigan Chronicle,* a Negro-oriented paper published in Detroit, on July 25, 1964. "Attention: Negroes, Want to Hit Back at Goldwater and Republicans? Join the Freedom Now Party." One of their offerings was "literature on Romney Volunteers." The party had placed a candidate on the ticket in the race for the governor's chair. He received 16 votes of the 14,400 cast in the county and 1 out of 400 in Calvin Township.

[19]*Cassopolis Vigilant,* November 14, 1963.

old-time Negroes voted Republican because it was the respectable thing to do, the younger generation increasingly perceives this action as a manifestation of "Uncle Tom-ing it."

2. Because of the intense activities of the Conservative Federation of Michigan and other conservative organizations, the local Republican leadership appeared to be in a "tight" situation. Although denied by some representatives of these organizations, Goldwater's position on States' Rights and the Civil Rights Bill, to say nothing of courting the southern vote, did have embarrassing and definite racial overtones.[20] This situation forced several local Republican politicians to either denounce Goldwater or attempt to sooth away the damage by vague references to Lincoln, emancipation, or Johnson's alleged ambiguous position on racial issues.[21] The ruse did not work.

3. Profound changes are taking place, not only in the composition but also in the structure of the Negro community in Cass County. Years of disinterest in external civil rights controversy are being replaced by careful scrutiny of those race-related issues which might possibly have a local effect. Because such changes in awareness have potentially important implications for a range of other topics, they will be examined in greater detail in Chapter Eight.

The political alteration

Even after a year had passed since the Republican Waterloo in Cass County, the election was still an object of day-to-day speculation,

[20]In a mass printed letter dated October 28, 1964, bearing the heading of "Conservative Federation of Michigan" and a note that the letter was produced at the private expense of one person "and has not been authorized by the Federation or its officers," is found the following comment: "Who are the Romney backers? ———— of Flint, *a Negress,* of the Romney Volunteers of Flint; and ————, said also to be *a Negress* of Grand Rapids and identified as chairman of the Romney Volunteers in that city. . . ." [Italics mine.]

[21]A political advertisement sponsored by the Cass County Republican Committee in the October 29, 1964 issue of the *Cassopolis Vigilant* asked: "Since LBJ refused to protect Negroes against lynching and was called a 'racist' in 1963, is his 1964 Civil Rights stand a 'Johnny-come-lately' stunt to gain votes November 3rd?"

reflection, and lamentation. However, as a result of the political character of the Republican nominee for president and the subsequent role Negroes played in 1964, one could draw the conclusion that Negroes were not just the political actors of past elections but were becoming an issue too.

The stunned wake of election eve generated a number of stories that were inclined to blame the Democratic victory on the Negroes.

They [local Negro Democrats] couldn't find recognition in the Republican Party because they are not the caliber of Negroes. The Democrats can have them. [WR–21.]

The Republicans lost because they [Democrats] took every colored by the hand to the polls. [WR–27.]

I tell you, when it comes to voting, some of these Negroes can be sneaky. They talk Republican and then turn on us and vote for the Democrats. [WR–24.]

Before very great spurious animosity was generated, the Republican and Democratic Parties apparently buried their mud-slinging activities and undertook a competition for the allegiance of the Negro voter. This is a comparatively new element in county politics. Previously Democrats made little effort to attract Negroes because of organizational weakness and Republicans were too "fat" to worry about drumming up additional business. Both parties now seem to be attempting to outdo each other to win back or retain Negro votes.

Republican officials have made speeches in Calvin Township stressing the future role of Negroes in the Republican Party. Republicans have held party meetings in the township hall and churches, and have thoroughly denied that they are a "lily-white" party. On the other hand, Democrats have also conducted meetings in Calvin that have been attended by "big-name" old-time Negro Republicans from the area. At these gatherings the Democrats have explained the provisions of the most recent civil rights legislation, sent local Negroes to Washington receptions, and so on.

There is, though, an essential difference between the activities of the Republican and Democratic Parties. The Democratic Party appears to be much more willing to match actions to verbiage. For example, following the 1964 election the vice-chairman of the Cass County Democratic Committee was a Negro from Calvin Township. She replaced a white from a township with few Negroes. Also, of the delegates elected to attend the state party convention (post-1964 election), at least three were Negro. (WR–36.) Comparable steps were not taken by the Republican Party. Thus, in the Democratic Party, Negroes are assuming positions of *countywide* influence, whereas in the Republican Party they generally tend to gain power in areas with a concentrated or majority Negro population.

What the outcome of the political competition will ultimately be is only speculation but there is some basis for an educated guess. I would propose that the Democratic Party has made permanent inroads into the Negro community in Cass County. It was Goldwater's 1964 campaign, despite persistent denial, that interjected race as a political issue as never before. Thus, Negroes can no longer ignore the implications of their political affiliation.

Many local Negroes may return to their ancestral political party, but nevertheless, the election and its aftermath have altered the image of the Democratic Party from a group of "outside troublemakers who are never satisfied" to a legitimate political force that presents a bona fide opposition in the community that must be recognized, dealt with, and compromised with. Negroes are playing important roles in the development of the county Democratic machine and are not likely to forget their successes for some time to come.

Nor is either party likely to view the Negro vote with "fat-cat complacency." Negroes proved that they can be a potent and mobile force in county politics. One would suspect that vague references to Abe Lincoln are no longer going to be sufficient to command the loyalty of Negro voters to the Republican Party. Perhaps the more active functioning of *liberal* Republicans in the area could offset the image generated by the conservatives, which, presently, makes the image of the Republican organization Goldwater's party, not Lincoln's. At this point, however, these remarks are in as speculative a vein for Cass County as they are for the nation as a whole.

seven:

Interaction, friendship, and status

Introduction

Although each of the specific forms of community function examined in the two preceding chapters was quite different in substantive surface detail, both had an essential similarity: namely, contact between whites and Negroes could proceed on an impersonal and instrumental basis. Furthermore, although the relative lack of discriminatory actions could be related to patterns of cultural tradition, it must be recognized that they were also influenced and perhaps molded by economic advantage and political profits. In this and subsequent chapters, we shall venture into areas of interracial contact that are not necessarily or directly controlled by political or economic benefit. Whereas the preceding chapters have questioned the presence of discrimination *as an action,* now the possible existence of prejudice *as an attitude* will be examined.

In economic or political arrangements, the respective status of the participants as individuals need not come into play. However, the character of interactive relationships formed for social purposes may well have definite implications for the status and possible status change of the participants. If Negroes are perceived to be an essentially undesirable segment of the community, then they who interact with Negroes as status equals can come to share the same derogatory definitions. Thus, the character of social contact becomes a mirror where the platitudes of "fine race relations" begin to wash away and expose the bedrock of social distinctions. It is in this context that Peter Rose observes: "The more personal the nature of a potential situation for social interaction, the greater are the barriers to primary and intimate 'intergroup' participation."[1]

As a result of these "barriers," Williams reports that "even in the northern-most areas, informal social interaction between Negroes and whites was very infrequent."[2] The forms of social participation and informal social interaction that shall be examined here are: educational institutions, religious participation, voluntary organizations, friendship choice, intimate acquaintance, intermarriage, and finally, the nature of prestige and status in the community.

Education: a community function

Education of the young is one of the most crucial functions that a community assumes. Thus, the school is perhaps the most logical place to examine the character of community relations because it is charged with not only the transmission of knowledge and skills, but it also serves to impart values, beliefs, and motivations to the young. Johnson in his study, *Patterns of Negro Segregation*, maintains that "the school policy regarding racial separation is perhaps the most obvious index of the racial 'climate' of a region."[3]

The role of the school is crucial for other reasons beside tending to reflect and uphold contemporary community standards. For most children, attendance in school marks the acceleration of social awareness, of interacting with others in a peer group relationship,

[1] P. Rose, p. 59.

[2] Robin M. Williams, Jr., *Strangers Next Door: Ethnic Relations in American Communities* (Englewood Cliffs, N.J.: Prentice-Hall, 1964), p. 253.

[3] Charles S. Johnson, *Patterns of Negro Segregation* (New York: Harper and Bros., 1948), p. 12.

and indeed, of a formulation of social identity.[4] The school thus becomes an extremely important setting for the rudiments of interpersonal living. Perhaps this is much more true in a rural community such as the research area. The school system in Cassopolis serves as a place in which to receive an education and to carry on social interaction, as well as a central focus of many activities related to the community. In short, the school is a central institution in the minds of the people. It was in recognition of these facts that I chose the outlines of the Cassopolis school district as the major variable of area delimitation. This is a unit of ecological identity which covers the Cassopolis-Vandalia-Paradise Lake-Calvin Township areas and binds them together into a comprehensive whole.

The Cassopolis school system

It was noted in Chapter Four that Cassopolis and surrounding environs had bi-racial schools as early as the post-Civil War era. In the middle and late 1800's, Negro and white students went to the same schools and both were taught by Negro and white teachers. *No essential change has taken place.* For the duration of the field research, the proportion of Negro students in the Cassopolis school system was at least 25 per cent. Moreover, there is no school in the district that is completely Negro or completely white. Discrimination and segregation are prohibited by law in the Michigan public school systems,[5] and, as was observed with respect to public facilities, the law is upheld.

[4]In this context, it might be illustrative to relate an amusing story told by one of the Negro respondents. One day a little white neighbor girl came home from school and told about a squabble the teacher had broken up on the school yard. As a matter of curiosity, the parents asked the second grader the identity of the teacher. The child, searching her mind for some variable of adequate identification, finally blurted out, "Oh, you know, the lady with the long fingernails." The teacher, noted for her long fingernails, was the only Negro in that particular school.

[5]The Michigan Supreme Court, in *The People v. Board of Education of Detroit,* in 1869 ruled that resident children have an equal right to public education regardless of religion, race, or color. In addition, Article VIII, Section 2 of the Revised Constitution of the State of Michigan incorporates the historic *Brown v. Board of Education* ruling striking down the separate but equal doctrine.

There are five elementary schools and one junior-senior high school within the jurisdictional boundaries of the Cassopolis school district. The system provides education for approximately 1,600 students (1963–1964) located in an area of about 150 square miles encompassing and surrounding Cassopolis. The schools are controlled by a seven-member Board of Education. These posts are filled by popular election. Recently a well-qualified Negro woman ran for one of the posts but was defeated. Reportedly, the Board of Education has never had a Negro member. (WR–5.) However, Negroes do serve on various committees such as census enumeration for the schools and architectural selection committees.

Race and education: enlightenment in action

While questioning a Negro respondent regarding integration of the school system, I inquired about the racial composition of the teaching staff. His answer, accompanied by a blank look, was: "Why, they usually are integrated, aren't they?" (NR–11.) In the eyes of the respondent, the question was somewhat naive because the only schools with which he had any direct contact had always been bi-racial.

Because of the rural nature of the area, the concentrated settlement of Negroes in Calvin Township, and the character of historical tradition, one is not surprised to learn that some of the teachers are Negro while many of their students are white. However, the rural elementary schools (occasionally referred to as "orange-crate schools" by some respondents) are not the only schools in the system that have integrated teaching staffs. In 1964, for example, the Cassopolis school system employed 63 teachers holding "straight academic" appointments. Of these, seven were Negro. According to respondents, four were employed in the Cassopolis High School. One held the position of chairman of the mathematics department; another was president of the local teachers' society and was also the Cass County president of the Michigan Education Association.[6]

[6]*Cassopolis Vigilant*, February 20, 1964.

Many, if not most, respondents in the community tended to regard the Negro mathematics chairman as one of the finest teachers they had ever met and felt very fortunate to have acquired his services. In addition to the teaching rosters, supporting staffs in the school system are bi-racial. At the time of the field work, the school system employed five Negro bus drivers in addition to three custodians and two cooks.

Evidence of enlightenment regarding education and the functioning of the system is contained in the following remark:

*The Negro teachers that we get are top-notch. In many cases
we get them because better paying systems will not hire them.
In this way, we benefit by discrimination elsewhere. . . .
If new teachers consider themselves to be prejudiced, for
their own good, this is a good place to stay away from.*
[WR–5.]

There is no evidence of friction generated because of either the interracial character of the student body or the many classes headed by Negro teachers. It must be stressed that we are talking *only* about the Cassopolis school system. As one travels away from Cassopolis, one hears allegations of discrimination, and, in some cases, brutality directed at Negro students.

Comparative achievement and recognition

In a booklet distributed by the White Citizens' Council, Carleton Putnam, discussing the area of Canada referred to in Chapter Four, states:

*If we are to compare averages, there is probably no better
laboratory than the rural areas around Chatham, Ontario,
Canada. Chatham is a town in the northern end of the pre-Civil
War "underground railroad" where a community of the
descendants of escaped slaves has existed for 100 years. The*

*social and economic situation of Negroes and whites in the
rural area around Chatham is approximately equal. The
schools have always been integrated, yet the tests of Negroes
in these rural schools show them, after 100 years, to be as far
below the whites in the same schools as the Negroes in the
schools of the South are below the whites in the schools of
the South.*[7]

The interracial character of the Cassopolis school system allows
further reflection upon Putnam's "proposition" that Negroes either
will not or cannot be expected to achieve adequately, or as well as
whites, in the educational system. Although academic performance
in school can be related to one's socioeconomic background, and
Negroes in Cass County are not on a general economic par with
whites, these factors do not seem to provide any startling differences in class achievement between whites and Negroes in the
school system. Table 13 presents the mean grade point average of
the 1964 graduating seniors from Cassopolis High School.

The slight differences that are found in the cells (focusing upon
either race or sex) are not significant because of the modest case
bases and related socioeconomic conditions. However, the relative
equality of performance could be deceptive if one racial group had
a significantly higher drop-out rate than the other, thus functioning
to render graduating seniors unrepresentative of their respective
classes. During the 1963–1964 academic year, nine of the 26 drop-
outs (35 per cent) were Negro. Considering that at least 25 per cent
of the students are Negroes who come from a more modest economic background in general, this does not appear especially surprising. A further complication in the interpretation of these data
could be the existence of reverse discrimination; that is, awarding
equal grades to Negroes for lesser levels of academic achievement.
Nothing suggests, however, that such a mechanism is in operation.

Grades are not the only basis of recognizing or evaluating excellence of academic achievement. In December, 1963, the Cassopolis
Chapter of the National Honor Society held its annual induction.

[7]Carleton Putnam, *Race and Reason: A Yankee View* (Washington: Public
Affairs Press, 1961), p. 25.

*Table 13: Mean grade point average of graduating
seniors by race by sex, 1964*[a]

Sex	White	Negro
Male grade point average	2.53	2.50
Number of male seniors	28	8
Female grade point average	2.68	2.21
Number of female seniors	25	11

[a]Computed on a four-point system.

From the newspaper story and accompanying picture, it was determined (by a knowledge of family names) that out of 22 inductees,
five or six were Negroes. This is what one would expect from a
system in which approximately 25 per cent of the students are
Negro. During 1965 a Negro student served as president of the local
honor society chapter. A Negro girl was also a member of the student council and had been both treasurer and secretary of her class.
It might be mentioned also that this same girl was named the winner
of the county Daughters of the American Revolution (DAR) award
for good citizenship which "is based on dependability, service, leadership, and patriotism."[8]

Extracurricular activities

Athletics is the primary form of extracurricular activity, at least it
receives the most press coverage and generates the highest degree
of interest. All of the school teams are bi-racial and have been so in
the past. One respondent commented that the Cassopolis team—the
Rangers—are sometimes called the "Brown Rangers" in the surrounding areas in which they play. (WR–21.) Negroes also participate equally in dramatic productions, debate, and forensics. Students of both races attend social activities such as dances, but there

[8]*Cassopolis Vigilant*, March 18, 1965.

tends to be little interracial dating, although it is not unknown. In 1963 the homecoming queen was a Negro girl who was elected by a popular vote of the student body. (WR–17.) Summer Red Cross swimming classes, sponsored by the schools, are bi-racial. The life guard for these classes was a Negro. (WR–17.) The research uncovered no indications or reports of any serious difficulties arising from the interracial character of participation in any of these events or programs.[9]

Religion: a semi-social function

While religious activities are not usually conducted for the manifest function of enhancing one's social position, social participation and contact are certainly very important latent functions of a group's collective expression of its religious beliefs. Religious worship may be of central importance on Sunday morning, but one would be hard-pressed to explain the deeply religious significance of fashion shows, knitting circles, bingo games, mission societies, and coffee clubs that seem to sprout like branches from most churches. Thus, although religion may be instrumental in one's salvation, as a group activity it is certainly functional for social prestige, participation, and contact. These associational aspects of religious participation may be important motives in urban America, but they attain even more importance in the rural community. T. Lynn Smith, in his study of rural sociology, observes: "Religion ranks with education as a social force in rural America; in importance as a farmers' institution the rural church is rivaled only by the country school."[10]

[9]There is only one difficulty in the school system that seems to be race related. Every summer a number of students—primarily from Chicago—reportedly attempt to live with relatives in the county, thus allowing them to enter the school system in Cassopolis rather than attend the schools in the district where their parents live. As a result, the district will not accept nonresident students without local legal guardianship. This is not much of a difficulty, but it does serve to indicate that perhaps the school system has a certain attraction primarily to Negro students from outside the district.

[10]Smith, p. 418.

In the research area there are over a dozen churches of various Protestant denominations and one Roman Catholic parish. The predominating Protestant denominations are Baptist, United (community), Methodist, and African-Methodist-Episcopal (AME).[11] In addition, there is one Gospel Church, a Jehovah's Witnesses, a Seventh Day Adventist, and a Friends (Quaker) meetinghouse. As the distribution of the churches would imply, the area is entirely gentile and essentially Protestant in character, with approximately half of the Protestant denominations bordering on "restrained fundamentalism."

The most truly integrated church in the research area is the Roman Catholic parish in Cassopolis. The parish is composed of approximately 180 families of whom about 30 are Negro:

They are well-accepted, excellent Catholics, officers and members of all societies, and altar boys. About one third are converts from this area, about two thirds from Chicago. The parish has had Negro priests in to help with the work. One was here for about two months and received a very favorable reaction. (WR-3.)

The likelihood of finding a Negro priest in a small village church in rural Michigan is not considerable when it is realized that there are, reportedly, only a few Negro Catholic priests in the entire United States.

With the exception of the Catholic parish, the remaining churches in Cassopolis are predominantly white:

Most of the Cassopolis churches are pretty white. I don't think that they deny Negroes. It's just that the Negroes don't want to mix that much. If 25 of them decided to go to a white church some Sunday morning, they would just go and no one would say anything about it. [WR–27.]

[11]Several Negro respondents claim that the "A" in AME stood for "Allen" (the name of the founder of the AME churches) rather than for "African." The word "African" has, to say the least, no positive attraction for the respondents.

No respondent, white or Negro, felt that there was any policy against Negroes in the churches. The "white churches" have an occasional Negro family in their membership. However, there was the thinly veiled feeling that Negroes generally go to "their" churches and "we go to ours." Although there are no prohibitions of any sort, a Negro attending a white service might be made to feel "conspicuous" and would not be likely to feel at home. That respondents can say "white church" and "Negro church" without misunderstanding supports the assertion that a substantial degree of mutually recognized separation exists.

Arnold Rose, in his study of the Negro in the United States, observes:

> In the North the few Negro churches before the Civil War
> served much the same functions as they do today. Many of
> them were also "stations" in the "underground railroad," and
> centers of Negro Abolitionist activities.[12]

Several such churches, founded prior to the Civil War, are located in Calvin Township. Although they tend to provide opportunities for social contact between the established Negro families in the community, religion seems to be taken quite lightly. For example, contrary to more "normal" studies of Negro communities, the Negro ministers do not occupy leadership roles in the community. Not once did any respondent mention a minister as one who held power or could help him. Other evidence of the weakness of the Negro churches is that the ministers either "circuit ride" throughout several counties or work at other pursuits such as "back-forty" farming or in factories. Although Calvin Township Negroes are not highly prosperous, it seems plausible that they could support two or three ministers if sufficiently motivated to do so. In short, religious activities in the Calvin Township area generally assume the role of spurious Sunday-morning adjuncts to community life.

Partially because of their historical connections and significance, the Negro churches are said to distinguish in membership between

[12]A. Rose, p. 276.

old-time Negroes and newcomers. Chapter Eight points out that this situation has become a source of deep-seated bitterness among newer Negro migrants. One Negro respondent pointedly observed: "The [Negro] churches in Calvin are getting so nice they now integrate with Negroes." (NR–32.) The strong implication in this and similar statements was that the Calvinites do not quite think of themselves as Negro, and thus, they have been more than a little unwilling to accept migrant Negroes into their churches as status equals.

It is most likely that the initial founding and subsequent existence of "Negro churches," together with the geographical concentration of Negroes in and around Calvin Township, contributes to the comparative lack of widespread integration in the churches. No Negro respondent asserted that these patterns arose as a result of either prejudice or discriminatory action. In short, religious separatism does not seem to be an issue of active concern. Nevertheless, whether voluntary or involuntary, from tradition or policy, widespread integration of religious institutions *does not exist.* Although one often suspects that Negro ministers actually function as a restraint to integration to protect their establishments, no data substantiates this in the research area. This situation can be related to the notion that there is basically little to protect because the churches are not particularly a going concern. If enhancing membership and insuring continuity of the establishment were of a high priority, one would not expect the "choosiness" of membership toward the migrant Negro.

Voluntary organizations: "The people here use velvet to discriminate"[18]

The number, character, and reputation of the organizations one belongs to often serve to classify one on the basis of status or prestige. In the Cassopolis area, few respondents had much difficulty in identifying "the organizations" in the community. It is perfectly obvious

[18]NR–23.

to anyone who would care to look that the membership roles of
social organizations vary as a function of both prestige and race:

*There is only one real social club. The Dance Club has a
membership committee and a waiting list. There are no Negro
members because there have been no applications from
Negroes. I think if we had a Negro teacher with a stable
marriage [italics mine] apply, there is a good possibility that
he would be admitted. [WR–20.]*

The same story is repeated in several other professional, business,
and social clubs: "No, there are no Negroes, but none has ever applied." However, white respondents sternly deny that a Negro
would be refused admittance *just because he was a Negro*, and
Negro respondents sternly maintain that they would not apply for
membership because they feel that they are not wanted. Both positions appear to be essentially accurate.

The forces that tend to keep many clubs segregated are informal
pressures such as avoidance of rebuff or embarrassment and a general lack of communication. Negroes claim that they do not apply
because they would feel "out of place." The lack of applications, of
course, removes the possibility of an "unpleasant situation." Although such organizations would not categorically refuse to admit
a Negro, they might well be overly selective. Perhaps it would be
illustrative to propose the term "super-Negro" to signify the need
for the Negro to "compensate" for his racial identification by sur-
passing the whites on a series of cherished attributes. In this light
the "stable marriage" qualification of WR–20's comment becomes
illuminating. Would this variable occur to a white respondent if a
white family were involved?

There is, then, the implication that the "type of Negro" who would
apply knowing that there is little precedent for this action would be
"pushy" and therefore, by definition, the probable forthcoming refusal would not be on the basis of race, but "pushiness." This attitude demonstrates a salient feature of the social life of Negroes in
the county: they are accepted to the degree that the whites voluntarily wish to accept them and not one inch more. If they "push,"

acceptance quickly diminishes. This pattern exists in many voluntary associations and it is maintained by the heavy-handed influence of tradition. This tradition could be broken, but it would demand overt action which few in the community, including Negroes, would sanction. Some Negroes are aware of this situation and heated disputes are provoked that basically are concerned with the validity of aggressiveness versus accommodation as the most efficient stance.

In addition to the "white organizations," Negroes have formed their own Masonic lodges in Vandalia and Calvin Township, an American Legion post in Calvin, a Rod and Gun Club in Vandalia, social clubs, and various "circles" connected with the churches in Calvin Township. There is the feeling among respondents that whites would be admitted to these organizations, but not without some discomfort. The amount of discomfort would probably be about the same that a white organization would generate in a Negro applicant.

Some of these Negroes segregate themselves. You can't blame the white man for that. They segregate themselves. Some of them still carry malice against the white man because of what happens in other places. [NR–32.]

If a white tries to step into completely colored groups, they resent it. I don't know why, but they do. [WR–24.]

You as a white man would not be welcome at some of the gatherings. [NR–14.]

The most uniformly integrated forms of organized social activities are those associated with children. Boy Scout, Girl Scout, Cub, and Brownie troops are integrated throughout the area. To the extent that the activities of children involve the adults, they too are integrated.[14] Finally, the Knights of Columbus, a Catholic men's organization, is integrated, and so are various groups formed for civic improvement and charitable purposes.

[14]For example, Scout Masters and Den Mothers of either race head up integrated troops. This is particularly relevant when the concept of role emulation is mentioned.

Friendship choice and intimate acquaintance

In a report submitted to the Commission on Civil Rights is found the comment:

It has come as a shock even to us on the Advisory Committee to realize how very little social communication exists between white and non-white groups. It is a rare white family in Michigan that has ever visited on a basis of equality in a Negro home; it is as rare for a Negro family to visit on a basis of equality in a white home. Each race has thus developed a stereotype image of the other based largely on fear instead of fact.[15]

Based on evidence to follow, I would submit that the above comment is not entirely applicable to the character of interracial contact in Cass County. Rather, the patterns of interpersonal relations which Gans describes for ethnic groups in his study of Park Forest, Illinois, can be applied readily to the present discussion.[16] Thus, there is a distinction between daytime interaction, largely generated by economic functions and interchange, political relations, or incidental contacts in which little or no racial distinction is made, and evening acquaintances, which are based more on personal friendship between two or more people with like interests and tend to involve the same race. Common personal interests and friendships with members of the same race tend to provide the basis of interactive relationships which in turn enhance the sentiment attached to the relationships and promote further in-group contacts.[17] Thus, a circular tendency is generated. Although Negroes and whites meet in almost all facets of the normal day-to-day functioning of the community, most of these contacts possess a minimal degree of emo-

[15]*The Fifty States Report*, p. 288.
[16]Herbert J. Gans, "Park Forest: Birth of a Jewish Community," *Commentary*, II (April 1951), 330–339.
[17]The implied process is of course that which George C. Homans proposes in *The Human Group* (New York: Harcourt Brace & Co., 1950).

tional significance. As a result, nighttime contacts between Negroes and whites are less frequent. Nevertheless, there are bi-racial adult clubs, neighbors of both races often play cards together, and so on.

Perhaps the issue of friendship choice and intimate acquaintance becomes most crucial when adolescents are involved. Not only are such contacts likely to imply a comparative gain or loss of status, but also the "ultimate" issues of dating, intermarriage, and kinship ties are thrown into question. Children play together at school during the day, and share scouting and other recreational activities at night. However, when respondents were probed on the patterns of interracial friendship, the question of dating was invariably brought up. In this context, Simpson and Yinger remark:

With the approach of adolescence and the beginning of "dating" the line between proper and improper associates is likely to be drawn sharply and categorically by the adult society, whereas a somewhat more tolerant attitude is usually shown toward interracial or other intergroup activities of small children.[18]

Similarly, respondents commented on the separation and the "mechanisms" to foster and insure such separation:

Come fourteen or fifteen, the kids separate because they are entering a different social life. When they are young they play together; there is some dating, but as they grow older, they tend to lean away from each other. [NR–18.]

Oh sure, small children play together, but you don't see interracial dating. There is interracial dancing but very little. [WR–5.]

I think parents should talk to their children about the practicality of social situations. But, in the last analysis, it's their decision. [WR–20.]

[18]Simpson and Yinger, p. 179.

*My son was dating a colored girl. She was a very nice person,
but I told him that it might not look very good for the son of
[a public official] to be dating colored, but I suppose that
really wouldn't bother too many. [WR.]*

*The teens around here don't socialize too much—most of
them would rather be among their own. [NR–4.]*

*The line is drawn at the social dating to avoid intermarriage.
[WR–24.]*

Although these comments do reflect concern about the issue of interracial social dating, I would maintain that the relative lack of
emotionalism generated by the topic should be evident. In many
cases, white respondents seemed to regard interracial dating with a
shrug of the shoulder and a mild comment that they would rather
it did not happen, but "you know how kids are these days."
There is, nevertheless, a "line" that is usually drawn at the onset
of dating. The pressure to maintain the line is largely informal. It is
maintained through the motivating force of pragmatism and the
powerful mechanism of "respectability." However, little or nothing
happens when the line is broken.

Of course, the line is not often overlooked although it is not uncommon to see mixed double dates—one couple Negro, the other
white—nor is it uncommon to see a mixed couple having a coke and
hamburger. It is, however, unusual that an interracial couple would
come to a school dance, take part in the function, and leave the
dance together. This behavior might lead to raised eyebrows and
generate rumors of late activities on a lonely country road. The
social definitions of "respectable behavior" operate with some energy, but are not strong enough to define interracial dating as taboo.
Therefore, interracial dating, while not particularly common, does
occur in the community:

*At night, white and Negro sweethearts are common. Oh, of
course around here, you can't tell who is what anyways.
[NR–2.] [Respondent was referring to the comparative
lightness of color of most Calvinites.]*

*Some whites enjoy going to Paradise Lake because they can
do things there and be with people there that they wouldn't
do in their own town. [NR–9.]*

*There is an honesty about it [interracial dating] around here
which I like. There is no sneaking around. [NR–28.]*

*Oh sure, there is interracial dating—the power men know
about it and don't care. [NR–30.]*

Intermarriage

To many people, especially whites, any discussion of patterns of
interracial contact can be reduced to the *ultimate* issue: intermarriage. Although the level of this concern is the subject of much contemporary humor, the sociological implications of intermarriage
between two definable categories are quite important. Drake and
Cayton observe:

*Social segregation is maintained, in the final analysis, by
endogamy—the rule that Negroes must marry Negroes, and
whites must marry whites—and by its corollary that when an
intermarriage does "accidentally" occur, the child must be
automatically classed as a Negro no matter how white his
skin color.*[19]

Michigan, like other northern states, has no legislation barring interracial marriage. However, even with the absence of any formal
prohibitions, in most northern areas public opinion utilizes such
tools as ostracism and condemnation and can operate to define intermarriage as a normative infraction and thus make its occurrence
infrequent. The high degree of ecological segregation typically
found in northern areas also lessens the formation of cross-sex interracial friendships by holding most informal interracial contacts
at a minimal level of frequency, duration, and intensity.

Unfortunately, there is a paucity of meaningful data regarding the

[19]St. Clair Drake and Horace R. Cayton, *Black Metropolis: A Study of Negro
Life in a Northern City* (New York: Harper and Row, 1962), I, 127.

actual occurrence of Negro-white intermarriage in the United States. In 1960, the *Vital Statistics of the United States* indicated that there were not enough reported cases to compute accurate or reliable statistics. In 1961, the same source reported that in only about one half of the marriages contracted was there an indication of the race of the participants. Of this half, about one-half of 1 per cent of the marriages recorded involved a white and *non-white* party. Presumably, the rate for white-Negro would be considerably less than this already low figure. These data combined with research done by Barron[20] and Gordon[21] would suggest that considerably less than one-half of 1 per cent of marriages contracted involve a Negro and a white.[22]

Probing the topic of interracial marriages met with quite diverse reactions among the respondents in the present study. The following comments have been selected from *white* respondents that demonstrate the variety and shades of opinion, latent fears, and reservations betrayed by such discussions:

The real answer to the race problem in America is intermarriage, but it is progressing too goddamned slowly. [WR–20.]

Relationships up to intermarriage are okay, but that's where I draw the line. [WR–5.]

I hear that there is a strong desire on the part of some Negro men to marry white women or at least light Negroes. [WR–11.]

From *Negro* respondents came the following:

As far as mixed marriages are concerned, my criteria would be if the boy came from a respectable family, in other words, are they the type of people I would want in my home. [NR–12.]

[20]Milton L. Barron, *People Who Intermarry* (Syracuse, N.Y.: Syracuse University Press, 1948).

[21]Milton M. Gordon, *Assimilation in American Life* (New York: Oxford University Press, 1964).

[22]When an estimated 80 per cent of Negro Americans are actually only part Negro, any attempts to assume a uniformity in data compilation leads to nightmarish methodological problems. Additional complications arise from the inconsistent application of inconsistent legal prohibitions as well as other equally confusing considerations.

*I would not let her date white boys because I don't think the
world is ready for it. They are just borrowing trouble. [NR–31.]*

*As far as dating and marriage are concerned, some of these
white girls have such hot pants for a Negro boy. They really
go after it. [NR–35.]*

Most respondents assumed a "negatively neutral" stance, that is,
little violent reaction one way or another, but with pronounced un-
easiness at the thought of racial intermarriage.[23] Respondents tended
to agree that intermarriage did take place in the area but not very
often. A sizable minority were able to cite definite instances. Once
again, most comments, especially those from Negro respondents,
tended to be of a laissez faire variety. For example:

*[A local Negro] married a white woman. One night he shot her,
but she sure as hell deserved it. Still, he got two to ten years
for it. [WR–10.]*

*There are quite a few mixed marriages in our church.
It doesn't raise a lot of question. [NR–5.]*

*There is considerable interracial dating and marriage. The
higher elements do this, not lower. It is not for intercourse but
[because they] have learned to respect each other through
association. [NR–30.]*

*I don't think there are any pressures. This is a place where a
couple can lose themselves. [NR–28.]*

*There are quite a few intermarrieds out at Paradise Lake. No
one pays much attention to them, and there is no
discrimination. [NR–14.]*

Whereas the respondents were correct in maintaining the existence
of interracial marriages and the comparative lack of attention they
create, there seems to be a general overestimation of the frequency
of occurrence. Table 14 reports the percentage distribution of mar-

[23]I heard no comments referring to stereotyped biological disadvantages (i.e.,
inferior racial strains or "mongrelization" of racial purity, "race-mixing," etc.).

*Table 14: Percentage of marriages by race in
Cass County: 1930 to 1963*[a]

Year interval	Percentage of marriages by race			Total number
	Both white	**Both Negro**	**Inter-racial**	
1960–1963	88.4	10.9	0.7	1,342
1950–1959	90.4	9.2	0.4	2,273
1940–1949	92.0	7.8	0.2	2,005
1930–1939	91.8	8.0	0.2	910

[a]Official records of Cass County.

riages by the racial composition of the partners: both white, both
Negro, and interracial.

Although the data in Table 14 would certainly suggest that the rate
of intermarriage in Cass County is higher than various estimates of
national trends, several important notes of caution must be introduced:

First, there is always the question of subjectivity in the recording
source. Because of varying legal and social definitions of "Negro,"
comparative statistics have only a limited validity or utility.

Second, Cass County borders the state of Indiana which was very
tardy in removing its legal barriers to interracial marriage. They
finally did so with legislative action in the spring of 1965. Thus, the
statistics for Cass County may well be inflated by couples from
Indiana who marry in Michigan. Although the case base is small,
eight out of 21 intermarriages that occurred since 1950 were between two nonresidents of Michigan.

Third, a complication which is the reverse of the second caution is
that Cass County residents who intend to intermarry leave the area
before doing so. Although these data are quite difficult to acquire,
several respondents reported that they had knowledge of this occurring. When it did, the Negro partner was able to pass for white and
consequently did so.

Fourth, it was already remarked and it will be stressed in the subsequent chapters that many Negro residents in the research area, especially descendants of Calvinites, are light enough to pass for white, and some do. However, in a small community such as the area under examination, this is a rare phenomenon because almost everyone has a comprehensive knowledge of who belongs to what family.

As a result of both the initial data concerning intermarriage and the subsequent complications, I would suggest that the rates of Negro-white marriages may be higher than is typical nationally, but significantly less than one would be led to expect by previous analysis concerning the number of local Negroes, the character of race relations, and the existence of and attitudes toward interracial dating.[24]

The question of how many mixed couples actually live in the community cannot be met with any exact data, partially because of the general lack of controversy such action generates. Respondents do not seem concerned enough about the issue to carry the tabulations with them. To the extent that Negro and white respondents were willing to offer an assessment, their estimates suggest that perhaps 10 to 15 couples in the Calvin Township area are interracial.

Because of a basic and prevalent racist philosophy, most mixed marriages in the United States become, in effect, "Negro marriages." It is a mark of caste-type endogamy that results in a couple and their children automatically assuming the lower status of the Negro partner.[25] In some cases, however, an interracial couple and their children seem to meet with more vitriolic prejudice because they have flaunted the taboo and therefore must pay for their alleged transgressions.

In Cass County the children of interracial marriages, and those Negroes who inherited fair complexions, are not regarded as "really Negro" by the community. Although the preceding analysis was

[24]This discussion has some obvious implications for those who assume "wholesale" intermarriage will occur at the first sign of the "erosion" of segregated institutions.

[25]As is the trend nationally, the majority of interracial marriages in Cass County (77 per cent) involve a Negro male and a white female.

accurate in describing the conditions faced by "the Negro" in Cass County, it must be stressed that local residents draw finer distinctions. Thus, there are whites, there are Negroes—and there are Calvinites. Calvinites tend to straddle the fence of racial identification. To be succinct, Calvinites look upon themselves, and are often regarded by a majority of the community, as one respondent put it, as "light, bright, and damned-near white."

Social status roles in the community

The question of friendship and interaction patterns in a community can be related to the maintenance of status and to the distribution of high status roles. Because status is a scarce commodity, its possession must be based upon—or justified by—an interweaving of those roles or traits which are deemed desirable. It is upon these decisions, then, that a substantial degree of explanation of friendship patterns rests. Social interaction of a personal and meaningful variety cannot but serve to influence the relative status positions of the participants.

In many studies of the distribution of status, the question of racial identification seems to be ignored. I would submit that this is not because race is irrelevant, but rather that the magnitude of social implications assigned to race makes all other variables pale by comparison. As a result, most investigations of social status and prestige would find it quite impossible to derive an adequate method of treating race as just one of many criteria of status. However, because of the nature of the present study, race cannot be ignored.

One of the more unusual aspects of the question of status distribution in community relations is the lack of attention given to the "standardized variables" of income, occupation, and education. Rarely did a respondent make a spontaneous reference to any one of these variables that could be used as a criterion of respectability, prestige, power, or status. The most salient variable, as judged by spontaneous report and directive questioning, seemed to be: Is the person from an old, established family in the community?

The "established" variable is not another way of saying affluent. Rather, it refers to "being known" as a long-time resident of the area. In a sense, however, the old-timer-newcomer distinction does not necessarily assume importance in itself, but rather because of the inference that it allows the respondent to make. The "length of residence" criterion becomes associated in the mind of the respondent with *reverence for the status quo.* Upholding tradition seems to be the prerequisite for community respectability. Affiliation with the Republican Party, at least traditionally, was an indicator of the emphasis that behavior should be based on tradition. Property ownership is valued, but not because of its economic implications— rather, because it has ramifications for the stability of one's attachment to the community.

The composite image of the low status of the newcomer is essentially explained by a constellation of variables opposed to those cited above. The newcomer has a propensity to question cherished aspects of tradition, is a member or follower of the Democratic Party —traditionally at least; and lacks real holdings in the community, thus suggesting lesser attachment.

The ranking system outlined above transcends the issue of racial identity. Among Negroes, the image of high status is characteristically projected by the Calvinite, and low status by the migrant Negro. In this sense, then, nothing approaching a caste system, which would ultimately rest on the implicit assumption that all whites are "better" than any Negro, can be found in Cass County. Not only do patterns of association and status tend to contradict any notion of caste, but, what is perhaps more important, so do social rules of endogamy. While it is true that racial intermarriage is discouraged, marriage across the "new-old" lines is not endorsed either. Chapter Eight contains reports of "social freezing" because of a marriage between an old-timer and a newcomer of the same race.

In conclusion, it would be accurate to state that social status in the community derives from a land tenure system which is embedded in the tradition of the community. Status is basically influenced by the dead hand of the past. Social mobility, except as a function of tenure, is difficult to achieve. The old-timer is granted a position of authority without any real economic basis, and therefore the new-comer cannot "buy his way up." With the exception of "sitting it out," the only other method of upward mobility seems to be strong, loud, and lasting support of the status quo.

eight:
Social
relationships:
cohesion and
disunity

Because of the particular set of historical circumstances surrounding the original Negro migration to Cass County and the subsequent incorporation of Negroes into the social rubric of the community, Calvinites have been separated from the mainstreams of Negro life in the United States. By the same token, the white residents, having grown up in a stable bi-racial community structure, are relatively free of many of the general stereotyped attitude patterns. E. Franklin Frazier, in his comprehensive study of the Negro American, sums up several of the crucial subcultural differences that are so typical of the research area:

Although the free mulatto families have had a history different from the mass of the Negro population, they have, nevertheless, gradually become identified more or less with the Negro group and furnished many of its leaders. In this respect they may be distinguished from those families of white, Negro, and Indian ancestry, living in isolated communities in various parts of the country, that have

*remained outside the main currents of Negro life. Whereas the
free mulatto families and their descendants have generally
formed an upper class in the Negro group, the families that
have formed these isolated communities of mixed-bloods have
often regarded themselves as an altogether different race
[italics mine].*[1]

Thus, Calvinites, because of isolation and a unique combination of
cultural forces, have become marginal men. Although neither they
nor whites accept that they are "really" Negro, they are visibly not
white. As one Negro respondent succinctly put it:

*My daughter does not realize that there are white and Negro.
I am trying to tell her that she is part of these demonstrations
on TV. She watches the demonstrations on TV, and she might
as well be watching a fairy tale as far as she is concerned.
[NR–31.]*

The groundwork of intraracial friction

In the early 1930's, a new set of interpersonal relations was introduced into the social fabric of the area by the southern-born and
northern urban-bred Negroes who migrated to Cass County. It will
be remembered from Table 5 that 1930 marked a low ebb in the size
of the Negro settlement. This was followed by a substantial and
continuing increase in the Negro population. The majority of this
increment is attributable not to natural increase but rather to increasing migration from the southern states and such urban centers
as Chicago and Detroit.

  The influx of newcomers, predominantly Negro, introduced a new
element in the social equations. Namely, what *is* a Negro? The white
community has already attempted to answer this question by com-
partmentalizing the social world into two categories: local white and
old-time Calvinite versus "other." The "other" included a complex

[1]E. Franklin Frazier, *The Negro Family in the United States* (Chicago: The University of Chicago Press, 1939), p. 215.

interweaving of the "evils" of urban America, Democrats, Negro slums—in short, outsiders. Such a "we-they" dichotomy may have flourished in the absence of any outsiders or newcomers to challenge the system by calling forth firm definitions. However, a redefinition was inevitable because the localistic "we-they" dichotomy had, of course, transversed numerous crucial sociological variables —most notably race.

The influx of Negro migrants with the attendant need to place them in some meaningful category forced the following "either-or" type of decision to be made: *Either* the newcomers with variant *cultural* attributes were outsiders to be "kept in their place" as separate from the main stream of social relations between the whites and Calvinites, *or* they were Negroes, just as the Calvinites were—although many whites had really forgotten this—with the *same* racial attributes. Sociologically, the decision depended upon the salience of racial versus cultural identity.

The eventual decision was a crucial one for all concerned. If newcomers, suspected for that reason alone, were looked upon as "really the same as Calvinites," the following results would emerge:

First, the structure of interracial social relations would have to be altered based on a "we finally woke up to the Negro problem" rationale.

Second, the image of many of the local heroes would become tarnished and therefore some redefining and remolding of the meaning of historical events might be necessary. Thus, ancestors whose actions were thought to be motivated by a deep and abiding concern for the rights of their fellow man might suddenly be perceived as having been "duped."

Third, Calvinites, who were regarded as "exhibit A" of the possibility of a stable on-going interracial cooperative effort, would have to step down from the elevated "Calvinite status" and assume a lower position called "Negro." The new status would, by definition, carry the overtones of "outsider."

Fourth, as the perception of the new threat became self-generative and circularly reinforcing, certain other events besides a perception of social differences would result. For example, would one want to live next to a "different type of person," send one's children to a school with "those people" to be taught by "one of them," or more precisely, would one want "his daughter to marry one of them"?

In summary, drawing the "we-they" line to exclude Calvinites from "our kind of people" would have profound implications for the meaning of race, the conception of historical purpose and cultural uniqueness, the status of the Calvinites, and finally, for the complex interweaving of Negroes and whites in the residential, economic, political, and social patterns in the community. In short, the perceptual import of the "community" would be altered by a redefinition of the Calvinites' "place."

The resulting upheaval should not be underestimated. A social change of this magnitude would require a careful examination of the relative desirability of the various alternatives. To categorize the newcomers as different from any of the various elements then in the community would imply the following results. The variables concerned parallel those previously discussed:

First, the character of social relations would be reaffirmed even though they deviated from the majority of the United States. This would imply that the local citizenry was awake and that it was outsiders who were sleeping and were unaware of the true dimensions of the situation.

Second, a general reaffirmation of the character of the historical process would be in order. Not only would it be necessary to bolster up even higher the character and motivations of one's ancestors, but again, their apparently contradictory behavior—when compared to the general trends of the time—would have to be explained by reference to the shortsightedness of others.

Third, the obvious racial identification which Calvinites and migrant Negroes did in fact share would have to be overlooked. Instead, actual or imaginary cultural differences would have to be stressed in order for a "line" to be drawn—not on the visible symbol of categorical membership (race)—but rather on some more elusive variable such as "understanding the local situation." In addition, Calvinites would have to work openly and actively to see that the social definition of the newcomer "stuck." This would require for-

saking what racial identification they had and joining in the deroga-
tion of the "shifty newcomers."

Fourth, to enlist the support of the Calvinites—and this was crucial
—any existing manifestations of prejudice or discrimination along
strictly racial lines would have to be struck down—or at least well
covered up. In other words, construction of the social "fence" some-
where *within one*—not *between* racial categories—required that
Calvinites never look back over their shoulders to their racial origins *and* that whites never build another fence between Calvinites
and themselves (or refuse to tear down any vestiges of fence that
might be there).

It should be recognized that these two alternatives are essentially
polar opposites and that to postulate a general perception of these
implications would be to attribute to a population an overwhelming
sociological "sixth sense." It is also possible, indeed, undoubtedly
probable, that neither of these abstract and opposite alternatives
would be wholeheartedly embraced, but that some precarious accommodation between the two realities might evolve. I say precarious because, among other things, the behavior of Calvinites was
crucial. They had the choice of jumping in to defend the status quo
—or more precisely, to extend it—or reaffirm the meaningfulness
of *racial* identification, or do nothing. But "doing nothing" in an
emotional situation is not likely to be perceived as affective neu-
trality, but rather a subversive sign that one or the other stance
was taken.

Pragmatically, it could be proposed that although both of the above
alternatives imply change, the second would be more likely to occur
simply because it is more comforting to assume that those people
who see a situation differently are wrong. To the extent that Calvinites were aware of the larger patterns of race relations, they would
seem to be extremely reticent to forsake a basically privileged position by identifying with Negroes; and the increased commitment to
an interracial social order that might be called for would perhaps
speed up the progress in this direction, but the direction was already
assumed. It is within this context of alternative paths of social
change (combined with a comprehensive knowledge of the historical precedents) that I propose that much of the nature of the con-

temporary social structure can be understood. Not only do patterns of interracial social relations become meaningful when seen in context, but so do the character and functioning of economic and political institutions, the sources of community cohesion and disunity, and, the nature of the accommodations necessary in the face of continuing externally generated social change.

The meaning of "Negro"

How whites interpret racial identity becomes crucial when it is recognized that their conception of Negroes will serve to structure a sense of group identity—or lack of it—among Negroes and, ultimately, will control the central question of what it means to be a Negro in the community.

Most of the respondents were quite unwilling to make blanket or stereotypical statements expressing their attitudes toward Negroes without benefit of the "old-new" qualifiers. However, those few who did seemed worried about such questions as (1) racial difficulties invading the community, (2) the possibility of conspiratorial contacts between Calvinites and newcomers that would define race as the salient structuring variable in community relations, and finally, (3) the possibility of Negroes retaining animosity toward whites.

One: The possibility of racial conditions external to the area influencing conditions in the community.

The Communist Manifesto said that races would be used to make trouble. This is coming true in the city. You know, it's almost as though Marx lived in Chicago. [WR–11.]

I have known Negroes all my life and they were always good people and liked Cass as a home. Unless the Negro has stability, the Chicago situation can get contagious. [WR–27.]

Increasingly colored here are getting like any place else—they have a chip on their shoulder and are always demanding things. [WR–29.]

If I was a Negro in Chicago, I would be so goddamned mad I'd be carrying signs too. But at this time we don't want that here. We don't want to risk everything we have. [WR–20.]

**Two: The possibility of an alliance between Calvinites
and newer migrant Negroes from Chicago.**

*In this town [Dowagiac] there is a feeling that when trouble
comes and gives a reason for the old and new to hang together,
they will do it. [WR–14.]*

*Today the old and new Negro are becoming more unified.
In the last few years they have been contacted by political and
racial interests. In this last campaign, they were more unified.
They are a political factor; no one knows how far this is going
to go. [WR–27.]*

*The old and new Negroes pretend they don't even know each
other, but they do. They say that they don't associate, but
they do. You know, the colored are a cagey race. [WR–12.]*

*The racial situation has been very definitely altered. Those
people have changed. They are drifting back to the thought
and action of their own race more than reliance on the white
people. [WR–26.]*

**Three: Assertions that Negroes tend to exhibit hostility
toward whites.**

*I live in Calvin Township and they Jim Crow me. I guess you
could say that I'm white-balled. [WR–24.]*

*I do feel that they have a deep-seated latent hostility against
the white. [WR–20.]*

With the exception of the above comments concerning "Negroes"
per se, the vast majority of attitudes expressed by white respondents stressed internal differentiations within the "Negro community." That Calvinites enjoy a privileged position as "white Negroes"
is quite obvious in the following comments:

Issues involving the privileged position of Calvinites

One: The stability, desirability, and "adjustment" of Calvinites.

*We get along with colored. The older colored are very good
and never give anyone trouble. The young out of Chicago are a
different matter. [WR–14.]*

*The colored situation is different here because colored in
Cass County have been here for generations. With these type
of colored you wouldn't expect to have problems. [WR–30.]*

*Calvinites are an entirely different class of people from
Negroes. [WR–29.]*

*The old-timers have made a place for themselves and are
respected. [WR–31.]*

*Negroes in Calvin feel that they must advance more in skill
before they can ask for equality. They don't participate in
demonstrations and fights. [WR–17.]*

*So far the old-timers [Calvinites] have managed to keep the
new ones in their place. [WR–29.]*

Two: The distaste with which whites view Negro migrants.

*There is no real tension, but rather disapproval of the conduct
of these rowdy newcomers. [WR–13.]*

*The name for these big black newcomers is niggerhead. The
new ones are ignorant and undesirable. These people are the
prolific ones. They should have their children taken away.
It's funny, the old ones are so different! [WR–29.]*

*Sure there are knifings in Dowagiac, but what the hell could
you expect from these disorderly transients. [WR–21.]*

*The newcomers are so different. They are not like the
old-timers. They are a little touchy. You say something and
they get mad so fast. [WR–31.]*

**Three: The firmly held belief that Calvinites share
the whites' distaste for migrant Negroes.**

*Of course there is segregation in Cass County, but not between
the Negro and white. It's between the Negro and Negro.
[WR–29.]*

*The fights that occur in the bars are started by Negroes from
the big cities. The local Negroes frown on these people.
[WR–17.]*

The churches in Calvin won't even accept these new ones.
[WR–29.]

There is a hard conflict between the Negroes. It's a question
of law and order versus the mouthy and crude. [WR–21.]

When . . . [a Calvinite] ran for office, he got the whites to
support him so he wouldn't have to go to that goddamned
NAACP bunch of commies. [WR–11.]

If you want to see racial prejudice, don't look at the white,
look at the Calvinite. He knows what he's doing. [WR–29.]

It is apparent, in the preceding observations from white respondents, that race is not a dead issue. However, most whites are more than a little reticent to condemn on a racial basis because of the fear of an alliance between the new and old. The possibility of an alliance, demonstrations, and "boat rocking" worry them. Ultimately, it should be clear that the whites feel a fair amount of paternalism for Calvinites, which will continue as long as the old-timers realize what might be lost if they start to "act like Negroes."

Calvinites look at race

In the only recent published description of the Calvin area, Dorson, who is primarily interested in the content of Negro folklore in Michigan, observes:

These were strange people, the descendants of Calvin's Negro
pioneers—caught between cultures, thin of body, yellow in
color, reedy of voice, sapped of energy. Some could easily
pass for white and several showed discomfiture at my
questions about their past. The township supervisor, a pudgy
little man who worked in the county rest home, supposedly a
jocular fellow, shifted uneasily during our brief interview, said
his folks came from Ohio and dismissed me with "we're a
forward-looking, progressive people here; we don't look

back." Others, less conscious of their position, spoke candidly and even brutally about their own and their neighbors' genealogies, tearing apart the polite veil of Ohio origins to reveal direct connections with slavery.[2]

Dorson's description of the fair color of the average Calvinite is accurate. In Chapter Three several authors commented on the light skin tone of the average fugitive who escaped North via the Underground Railroad. Additional supporting data for the Cass County Negro population can be derived from 1910 census data. Using these data, Table 15 reports the percentage of Negroes considered "mulatto" as opposed to "black" in the five East-North-Central states and Cass County.[3] Although the data cannot be regarded as precisely accurate, as color is more a matter of subjective judgment than an objective measurement, they are indicative of my previous assertions and of Dorson's estimations of complexion.

Table 15: Percentage of Negroes considered "mulatto" as opposed to "black" in Cass County and the five East-North-Central states[a]

Geographical area	Number of Negroes	Percentage mulatto
Cass County	1,444	76.9
Michigan	17,115	47.0
Wisconsin	2,900	39.4
Illinois	109,049	35.6
Ohio	111,452	35.2
Indiana	60,320	24.1

[a] *Negro Population: 1790-1915*, Table III, pp. 798-839. Data generated from the 1910 census.

[2] Dorson, p. 3.

[3] Only one other county in these Midwestern states with 500 or more Negroes had a higher percentage of Negroes than Cass County. This is Hamilton County, Indiana, with 82.2 per cent Negro population considered to be "mulatto."

Calvinites by no means ignore the implications and meaning of race and color. Rather, they would just as soon be left out of conversations concerning these issues. Several respondents expressed a degree of animosity when I inquired if they met with discrimination or prejudice because of their race. After some initial puzzlement, I discovered quite clearly what my mistake was when I discussed the matter with a recent Negro migrant:

Of course, the Calvinites don't like to talk about Negroes.
Many of them claim that they were all free men of Irish,
Scottish, and Egyptian blood. [NR–2.]

This impression seemed to be borne out by several comments made to me by Calvinites:

I really wouldn't know about this race business because, you
know, I'm not really a Negro. [NR–7.]

When I was a girl, I was never taken for colored, I was taken
for Indian. I never have lived among colored people, so I really
wouldn't know what causes the problems with them. I'm
really neither white or Negro. [NR–34.]

Because Calvinites seem quite loathe to talk about themselves in racial terms, some of their attitudes regarding race became more manifest when talking about newcomer Negroes:

The trouble is that everyone gets blamed for what one damned
fool out of Chicago does. [NR–21.]

There is no discrimination here because in Chicago the
Negroes never know how to live decently. Here we people
have money and there is no crime or that stuff. [NR–4.]

These city Negroes have no sense of personal worth. Paradise
Lake is a conglomeration of everything—money, rackets,
Chicago people, prostitution, and high living. [NR–5.]

There was no trouble [around Dowagiac] until Kaiser-Frazer moved in and brought in a new class of people. This was about ten years ago. [NR–23.]

These new Negroes have a lot to do for themselves. Too much dropping out of schools, too low morals, they need more pride in their property and keep it up. I say this all the time. [NR–21.]

Some of the churches around Calvin won't accept the Vandalia people, but, of course, they are from Chicago. [NR–7.]

The Negro in the South and Chicago has trouble because he moves around without jobs or security and causes trouble. Here we are different. [NR–11.]

Newcomers: race and reaction

At this point, the reaction of migrant Negroes to the pressures applied by whites and Calvinites could well be predicted. The migrants perceived quite clearly the implicit alliance between the two and deeply resented it. Resentment and hurt seemed to be most sharply directed not at whites who created the situation, but rather toward Calvinites who allowed and encouraged its continuity. The new Negroes act almost as though they expected the whites to harbor prejudice and practice discrimination because many of these Negroes have known no other treatment from whites. What baffles, discourages, and actually outrages migrant Negroes is that Calvinites have also turned their backs on them, thus encouraging and perpetuating the snub of whites.

Reports of rejection by Calvinites

In Calvin Township, the mulattoes mix with white but they won't let the newcomer in. [NR–32.]

The "*I was born here, you weren't*" attitude of the Calvin
people makes us outsiders in our own community. [NR–31.]

The Calvinites marry their own cousins to avoid marrying
others. I think this close intermarriage has worked on their
minds. [NR–32.]

They resent the outsider coming in because they have been
here since the Emancipation and don't want any other Negroes
around. [NR–14.]

I can't understand them. They don't like me as a Negro, and
they don't like whites. I don't know who they like. The old
ones handed down the idea of not associating with darker
Negroes. Now their children act the same way. [NR–32.]

They are old, secure, have their families. They are on a
pedestal. They don't want to disturb their position. Why, the
old-timers even had a demonstration against the NAACP.
[NR–2.]

If a newcomer marries a Calvin girl, he runs into resentment
because he is from some place else. [NR–16.]

  Reports or feelings of rejection are not new. The following comment appeared in a local newspaper in 1892:

We are informed that some of the [Negro] school teachers in
this township [Calvin] are making some little trouble in their
schools trying to establish the color line, and they also make
sport of teachers who are not as light colored as they are.
We should never ask any people to remove the color line until
we first remove it from our schools and churches.[4]

Accusing Calvinites of playing Uncle Tom and deriding Negro identity

They [old-timers] think the darker complected are inferior to
them. They are so prejudiced against color that they will

[4]Cassopolis Vigilant, December 22, 1892.

marry each other to avoid darkness. They think they have more white blood in them and want to keep it. [NR–14.]

The old-timers are brainwashed. They think they are better because they got that light hide on them. [NR–2.]

They refer to Chicago Negroes as "damned niggers" or "darkies." [NR–14.]

I used to go down to Calvin but was run out of there because I was too dark. [NR–30.]

I tried to teach that Calvin crew to be proud of Negro blood and it didn't work. [NR–2.]

He [referring to a Calvinite] is a Doctor Tom. A Doctor Tom is a professional Uncle Tom. He won't stick up for colored. He stays with the white and sides against us. If you are studying that underground railroad bunch of Abe Lincoln Negroes in Calvin, you should really call it Dr. Tom's Cabins. [NR–30.]

The Calvin Negroes were taught that they were better than other Negroes. Lot of them could pass for white. The trouble with them is that they are shooting for Abe Lincoln freedom. [NR–2.]

   When comparing the hostility expressed toward Calvinites, whites, although indicted, receive a comparatively mild sentence:

The white never really made me feel a part of this community. [NR–18.]

There is trouble between the races when the people don't understand each other. If they got to know us better, it would be better. It's that way in all races. [NR–9.]

There is more hypocrisy here than anywhere else in the U.S. Everyone was friendly to me until I joined the NAACP. Now, they look right through me. [NR–30.]

Oh sure, you can get along with the white around here, but you have to be pretty sneaky. [NR–14.]

To the white man, the lower class Negro is the best because they know how to grin better than we do. [NR–2.]

Whites and Negroes just don't like each other. The tradition is instilled; it is learned. [NR–9.]

It's a hoodwink situation that makes you feel like not part of the community. I couldn't really say we have good relations, the whites and us. [NR–18.]

A mutual low opinion of newcomers is implicit in the alliance between whites and Calvinites. Although there seems to be some small evidence that newcomers, by sheer force of the environmental demands, have learned to accept a negative self-definition, most statements concerning the self seem to stress pride in their racial identification:

The newcomers are better educated. We resent the attitude of Uncle Tom. The newcomer sees this and tells the old-timer to stand up like a man. The old-timer goes to the white and tells him that we told them to defy the white. [NR–22.]

The old Negro here had no problem because their qualifications didn't allow them to challenge. Now, new ones are better qualified and question new areas. [NR–27.]

Negro children should be proud of their race. We should point out the outstanding men of the race so they can be proud. [NR–10].

The higher IQ in Negroes are among the dark-skinned Negroes. [NR–28.]

You can always tell where a newcomer lives. They have "johns" inside and make improvements. [NR–14.]

The structure of Negro leadership

The crucial question of power is at the heart of intraracial friction and animosity among Negroes in Cass County. Calvinites and new-

comers are jockeying for power—Calvinites to maintain what they
have and newcomers to grab some of what they do not have. There
is only one difficulty. The power that Calvinites possess stems not
from themselves but rather from their mutually accommodative relationship with whites. Calvinites have the power of respectability
and therefore the power to isolate the newcomers if they so choose.
Newcomers do not have to petition whites because they are already
ignored by these quarters. The power newcomers possess is the control and manipulation of a grass roots protest against the conditions
of life. It is in this sense that new Negroes are the "natural leaders"
whereas Calvinites are the "installed leaders."

Calvinite leaders find themselves in an increasingly difficult position. They have, traditionally, always been the undisputed leaders.
They did not, therefore, have to take any actions or arrange any
issues to secure their position of leadership. However, a substantial
amount of energy was devoted to prevent the boat from rocking.
This was an acceptable role for the Calvinites because they basically did not identify with the plight of the dispossessed or the
migrants.

However, the migrants did not come with leadership patterns that
they could readily use. Those patterns that functioned for them in
the city were in disrepute in Cass County. Political power could not
be called upon because the Democratic Party was weak and unable
to help, and the Republican Party was too fat to be interested in their
welfare. Civil rights organizations were also helpless, for the large
part, because of the solid white-Calvinite bloc vote against them.

The migrants' only recourse, in the absence of home-grown leadership, was to accept the leadership of the Calvinites who were somewhat antagonistic to newcomers. Such acceptance demanded that
the new Negroes "petition" to get into the Calvinite churches, forsake interests in "race betterment," refrain from disturbing the status quo, ignore civil rights, cease from protesting, and, finally, go to
the Calvinites—who are among "Level Three filters"—for redress of
grievances. This, of course, proceeded to strengthen the Calvinites'
position as "brokers of respectability" for it gave them another
trump card: the ability to keep newcomers in their place. So that
whites might not suspect under-the-table dealing, Calvinites, by

word and deed, increased social distance between newcomers and themselves. By so doing, Calvinites made it unnecessary for whites to deal directly with newcomers. Thus the breach between whites and newcomers widened. These forces tended to make Calvinites the respectable pivot men who successfully dealt with "the lower elements" but really could not "understand what made them tick."

Because of the disorganized political condition of migrant Negroes and the incorporation of Calvinites into the political process of the community, it is not particularly productive to discuss the "Negro leadership class" as a separate or subcommunity entity. In this sense, "Negro leadership" is nonexistent.[5]

To maintain the image—fictional at least—of being a different race than Negro, Calvinites have found it necessary or at least advantageous to avoid religiously any identification with civil rights groups or Negro self-help organizations. This was basically easy to do because the Calvinites actually had very little to complain about. Their position was secure as long as they remained a working part of the social structure, which they had every intention of doing because it was to their own self-interest.

Traditionally the NAACP, the only civil rights organization working in Cass County, has been an "off and on" arrangement—actually more off than on. It is perhaps remarkable that in a county with over 3,600 Negroes the history of an NAACP chapter is one of alternating collapse and rebirth. White respondents tend to feel that community interest in the NAACP is quite low, especially among the Calvinites.

You know, the old-timers around here don't believe in the NAACP. They have no need of it. [WR–18.]

The Calvinites feel that the NAACP is a commie front organization, which of course it is. [WR–29.]

[5]Chapter Six commented that informal leadership consisted of three hierarchal levels. Level Three ("the filters") contains three or four Negroes. These are all Calvinites who possess "respectability." Only one Negro in the research area can be considered to be a Level Two leader (position in the formal structure with broad-based power). Once again, he is a Calvinite. No Negroes are found in Level One leadership slots ("hidden influentials").

None of the Calvin Township Negroes belong to the NAACP.
I really don't know about the Negroes in Cassopolis. The
Calvin area has no NAACP members. They are not in
sympathy with the racial demonstrations. [WR–17.]

Calvinite respondents generally substantiate the impression that they were not particularly interested in the NAACP activities in Cass County, and claim very little knowledge about either its whereabouts or activities:

Yes, there is an NAACP here, but I don't know where it is.
I don't have no trouble at all. [NR–17.]

The colored don't support the NAACP because they want to
feel like part of the community and don't want to do it as a
member of a racial group. [NR–13.]

Despite Calvinites' denial of knowledge of the NAACP, they know quite well where it is, who is running it, and what it is doing. Although the county chapter is quite weak in representation from Calvin Township, township residents do seem to support the general aims of the organization even though their support is covert:

The local chapter has about five or six active members from
Calvin Township. But there are forty or fifty that are
members-at-large.[6] They are there but we don't know who
they are, and they are not about to tell us. [NR.]

The following article which appeared in the *Pittsburgh Courier* in 1955 explicitly states much of the situation:

NAACP members "fret and stew" at the lackadaisical attitude
of their leaders. Problems of employment and civic interest
would be solved if discussed with the appropriate people
(white) who hold the keys to enable qualified persons to get

[6]These are members who have sent their membership dues to the national headquarters but are not identified with or affiliated with local chapter activities.

*jobs in schools and industry. It would be easy if a few would
drop their covering of aloofness.*[7]

The complaint of newcomer Negroes, as they view the lines of
power and communication in the area, is even more succinctly
stated in the following passage from the "Cass County N.A.A.C.P.
Newsletter," which is dated November, 1959:

*As in every evolution, creation and criterion, there must be a
starting point, so let it be in Cass County—this N.A.A.C.P.
Newsletter is a beginning. With the beginning of the
N.A.A.C.P. Newsletter there is a beginning of a New Negro
(yes, this is past time for a beginning). Taking the 11th verse
from the 14th chapter of I Corinthians which reads "When I
was a child I spake as a child, I understood as a child, I thought
as a child: but when I became a man, I put away my childish
things,"—the New Negro in Cass County is born. Ever since
the days of the Underground Railroad, the Negro of Cass
County has been complacent.*

*As president of the Cass County Branch of the N.A.A.C.P.,
I bury Abraham Lincolnism and christen the New Negro, for
we are men now. Why must there be a beginning of a new
Negro in Cass County to fight for his inalienable rights?
Why? Because the end is inevitable.*

Despite this statement of principles, the local NAACP chapter has
remained organizationally weak because those with sufficient resources to bring about social change show little interest in disturbing the status quo. To bolster up the organization, a form of "Negro
identity" has become the rallying point. Although this has little
appeal, it functions to rule out the NAACP as a legitimate protest
group for the complaints which Calvinites and others might have.
The basic lack of protest issues, but at the same time the organizational need to keep the structure alive and in the spotlight, has
occasionally made the group look irresponsible in its charges even

[7]Weatherspoon, *Pittsburgh Courier* (Detroit edition), July 23, 1955.

though its officers are not negligent themselves. Thus, a lack of support, a paucity of issues to complain about, and a tarnished image have all contributed to the weakness of the only civil rights organization in the area.

Most lower class Negro migrants were born and bred in a social structure—the urban ghetto—where a sense of racial identity was inculcated. They migrated to Cass County to find that here were Negroes who owned land and enjoyed other earmarks of success. But they denied their identity as Negroes, and yet wanted to assume Negro leadership. The contradiction is obvious. Lower class Negroes (and migrant Negroes in general) turned to the NAACP as a source of racial guidance because they found that Calvinites, as the professed leaders, have been coopted by the white power structure. The Calvinites' behavior is influenced by white interests from above rather than Negro interests from below. In effect, this reflects a "Negro revolt" in Cass County—a revolt not directed at whites or their power structure but at the old line "Negro leadership."[8]

In general, one could propose that the mobility system is, in itself, a coopting process—the most able of the lower class, those who could provide effective leadership, are systematically siphoned off through the adoption of middle class value patterns. As the acculturation process continues, the areas of common interest between Negroes and whites of middle class status increase. Not the least of these interests derives from the notion that both groups feel threatened by lower class Negroes in the ghetto.[9] Middle class Negroes,

[8]Although the NAACP is currently enjoying increasing verbal support, especially among newcomers, this interest does not seem to generate action. As of 1965 Cass County no longer had a branch of the NAACP because the Dowagiac branch nominally oversees the few members in the research area. The paid membership of the NAACP ranged between 35 and 40—a modest number. However, the potential for growth is present. The obvious question emerges: What about the influence of external civil rights controversy and tension? In a real sense, the answer is partially in view. The expulsion of the Republicans from political office, a sympathy march for Selma, a memorial service for Reverend Reeb—all point to a gradual increasing awareness of race in Calvinites, in newcomer Negroes, and in white residents.

[9]It has been recognized that great disparities have traditionally existed between the socioeconomic status of whites and Negroes. However, important as these data may be, the averaging process tends to conceal what may be an even more

157 Social relationships: cohesion and disunity

wringing sufficient profit from the system to generate a vested interest in the maintenance of the status quo, become—perhaps with mixed emotions—partners with middle class whites. Even though these Negroes request a more equitable share of community life, they are inherently interested in the basic continuity of the system rather than its upheaval. Acceptance of middle class Negroes as middle class Americans rather than as Negroes is possible only if areas of common interest are enhanced by playing the part *and* simultaneously extending the differences between the middle and lower classes.

significant trend, namely, the increasing inequality of income distribution *among* Negroes. Essentially, the "Negro community" as a class-related concept may be losing its utility. To employ a statistical analogy, as the variance within categories rivals that found between them, the basic conceptual framework may well be in need of alteration.

Summary and implications

nine:

Summary:

the status quo

and social

change

It is the mark of a dispossessed people to feel that there is nothing to protect in the status quo. However, for everyone else, social change is met with at least ambivalence and often resistance. In Cass County, tenure residents—Negro and white—who possess social and political power have worked together to protect their interests. These to a large extent have been identical—attempting to maintain the status quo. Both tend to view the new impinging external elements as a possible threat to the system.

Here is an area that, not unconsciously, has had at least partial success in preventing the inroads of bitter racial antagonisms that are so typical of the majority of the United States. Although it might not be wise to draw too strongly upon the analogy, the Cassopolis region has an air of self-containment. Yet, the existence of this insularity in the face of external influence has had other implications. The message of the Vidich and Bensman study, *Small Town in Mass Society*, has a striking degree of applicability for Cass County—neither area can repel social change.[1]

[1]Arthur J. Vidich and Joseph Bensman, *Small Town in Mass Society: Class, Power, and Religion in a Rural Community* (Princeton, N.J.: Princeton University Press, 1958).

Areas of change

Political restructuring

For many years, the county had a reputation as the conservative stronghold of southwestern Michigan. The first and most profoundly visible political change in the community was demonstrated by the Democratic landslide of 1964. Not only did the reins of political power change hands but so did the political forecast for the future. In a region known for conservative traditionalism, Goldwater, as a self-professed conservative, lost as no Republican presidential candidate had in the history of the area. Although the county as a whole backed the Democratic ticket, voting patterns (see Table 12, p. 100.) suggested that 1964 signaled a divorce between Cass County Negroes and the Republican Party. In some ways, this split formalized a separation which has been slowly but pervasively taking place over the years.

However, some local Republicans could have pulled the election out of the fire had it not been for the profound fear that Goldwater's political views instilled in many Negroes. For example, I was present at a discussion between several local Negroes who were talking seriously about the employment possibilities in Canada should Goldwater win the election. They perceived his possible victory as creating conditions which could be personally dangerous. A Negro respondent commented:

There has been no violence in Cass County yet. However, if
Goldwater is elected, we will have violence within two years.
He frightens us. There will be bloodshed in Cass County.
[NR–23.]

Many Negro respondents saw Goldwater not as the Republican standard-bearer, but rather as a candidate who sought to organize both fear and hatred as a political force in his behalf. Thus, they saw racism as a definite issue in the election. This same type of fear, as a result of political maneuvering, was held against the Democratic

Party in the late 1880's and, at least in part, formed and fashioned the Negroes' original allegiance to the Republican Party. It was not Goldwater's conservatism that turned the election against him, but rather the idea of the Senator as a leader of a white man's party. The depth and magnitude of these feelings should not be underestimated. These Negroes were solid and staunch Republicans who chided the administrations of Franklin D. Roosevelt for their "bold-faced give-away programs." [NR–7.]

One sees, in the 1964 election, a political alteration: race was made a political issue, which did great harm to the local Republican leadership. Before 1964, race was race (of little interest) and politics were politics (of great interest). As a result of the 1964 campaign these two elements became interdependent and their marriage brought subsidiary issues into the forefront of the political community. Lincoln's party had been dethroned in Cass County.

A changing economic base

For some years, predominantly rural areas in much of the country have been experiencing an attrition of both agricultural acreage and residents classified as farm personnel. The proportion of the population engaged in agriculture in Cass County has been steadily decreasing in recent years and can be expected to continue to decline. Some of this attrition can be attributed to a general lessening prosperity of agricultural pursuits. However, it will be noted that Cass County is situated between two Standard Metropolitan Statistical Areas (Kalamazoo, Michigan, and South Bend, Indiana). As a result, it has been slowly changing character from a rural area to an urban fringe: lands bordering the various state highways in the area are increasingly being used for ranch houses—several attempts to subdivide the land have been made; and a very high proportion of the residents work outside the county. Thus, according to a report prepared by the Cass County Conservation Needs Committee, lands currently being used as cropland and permanent pasture are expected to decrease in the immediate future. This acreage will be replaced by reforestation, urbanization, and recreational use. Subdivisions are expected to remove 400 to 500 acres annually from agricultural usage from now until 1975.[2]

With a growing population base in Cass County and especially in the surrounding counties, the profusion of lakes, the wooded lands, and the lower land values have an obvious implication as an increasingly important recreational establishment. Real estate agents are quite aware of this possibility when they send their listings to Chicago brokers or advertise directly in Chicago newspapers. County officials are also cognizant of the advantageous prospects. It would be impossible to ignore the heavy stress that is being placed on recreational development for the future.

It does not seem likely that industrial expansion will become a new future trend. While some respondents reported to me that Cassopolis is willing to offer some lands to new industry, I saw very little if any evidence to suggest that aggressive concern or attention was being given to the problem of attracting industry. This becomes difficult to square with economic reality when it is remembered that not only is a substantial proportion of the work force required to seek industrial employment elsewhere, but also that unemployment rates are already not low.

Because industrial employment is not increasing, the waning agricultural establishment might well be expected to displace more manpower than the rise of tourism could offset. With these thoughts in mind, the economic base of the area does not seem likely to grow by any substantial amount in the years ahead, just as it has not particularly grown in years past.

I propose that the lack of foresight in planning for industry is not a result of ignorance of the prosperity industry would bring, but rather, a resistance to the changes new industry might introduce in the community. Discussions with respondents on the possibility of bringing in additional industrial concerns emphasized basic and pervasive ambivalence. Of course greater economic prosperity would certainly be welcomed, but only if no substantial price had to be paid. Thus, many wondered about the "undesirables" that might be attracted to the area. At first, I assumed that the term "undesirables"

[2]*Looking Ahead,* Cass County Conservation Needs Committee (Cassopolis, Mich., April 10, 1962).

was a euphemistic way of saying "Negro." It appeared, however, upon additional investigation, that southern whites were the group feared.[3] Negroes especially tend to fear that southern white in-migration might lead to unpleasant interpersonal situations. In general, discrimination was not perceived to be a possible result of this in-migration because of the controls of community legitimation. Whites also seemed to fear this possible in-migration for two reasons. First, *any* in-migration would present "socialization" problems with the incursion of outside values, interests, etc. Second, and far more important was the very pervasive feeling in the area that lower class whites could endanger the status quo by straining or rupturing delicate interpersonal balances.[4] This would happen if and when southern whites "mistreated our colored residents" thus encouraging Negroes to identify more strongly with their race, and enhancing the possibility of an "old-new" alliance or coalition. As has been seen, many actions and perceptions of the white community are predicated on and structured by the fear of this eventuality. The evidence feeding this fear is increasingly abundant—the reasons are essentially political (first, in the partisan sense and second, in the "tradition-maintenance" sense). First, it is reasonable to assume that if a partisan coalition were to take place between Calvinites and newcomers, the marriage would be under the aegis and with the blessing of the Democratic rather than Republican Party. The reasons for this are both national and localistic. The second sense, that of tradition maintenance, is far more serious. Calvinites have been viewed as an integral part of the community because they imbedded themselves in the local subcultural tradition. They were, of course, the prime beneficiaries of this tradition. If they now coalesce with

[3]Parts of northern Indiana have experienced somewhat rapid increases in the number of southern white migrants. The negative definitions that these migrants generate is compounded by the fact that many white migrants in southwestern Michigan are just that—migrants. Fruit crops create a heavy demand for seasonal labor.

[4]Lower class whites have not been focused upon in this research because there are exceedingly few in the area. As was pointed out, traditional income, occupation, and education variables of socioeconomic status carry comparatively little import when confronted by the issue of community tenure. In-migrants have been predominantly Negro, hence lower class.

the fate of the newcomers, who are defined as the villains par excellence of social change, the whole edifice could be shaken.

Demographic change

For the most part, the migrant is considered a prime source of cultural diffusion as he carries "external" culture and influence. The Negro resort activities around Paradise Lake, the various church-affiliated camps, and a modest but increasing reputation as a stable bi-racial area all tend to function as inadvertent advertisements for Negro in-migration. Although probably an overstatement, NR–7 reports that "this area is known all over the country as a predominantly colored area." NR–32 stated:

Every time one Negro comes out here, there is a possibility of three or four families coming. They hear about us from their friends and relatives.

Since 1930, the proportion of Negroes in the resident population has been rising. The average percentage increase in the Negro population for each of the last three decades has been 46 per cent in the four-township research area and 34 per cent in the county. The comparable figures for the white population increase are 13 per cent and 20 per cent respectively. The total percentage increase of Negro population in the research area during the 30 year period is 139 per cent.

Reflecting on this situation, respondent NR–7 commented:

There has always been a harmony between the races here. Though, if Negroes keep coming in, can the few that are here sweeten up the whole new mess?

The words of this Calvinite pinpoint a very crucial question in the minds of many Negroes: What are the possible implications of the increasing proportion of Negro residents from outside the area?

It is especially within the demographic structure of the community that a deep and profound source of conflict between the old and the new groups lies. Unavoidably then, migration, too, has assumed a racial implication because of the changing proportion of Negroes. Although whites tend to view this situation with some concern, Calvinites express outright alarm and, at times, hostility. The underlying dissension which it manifests is not at all unusual and can be viewed as part of a more general phenomenon. Almost every generation of Negro Americans has identified and labeled the "new" versus the "old" Negro. The conflict of means and objectives between W. E. B. DuBois and Booker T. Washington seem to emphasize best the contemporary frictions in the local situation.

Cass County: bi-racial or integrated?

It appears that Cass County presents a unique demographic profile for a northern rural area. Furthermore, its history and cultural traditions are certainly deviant, and, to some extent, so is the degree of mutual cooperation in economic and political matters. However, residential separation does exist and upon closer investigation, social distinctions are evident. What then, in summary, can be said about the degree of "stable integration" in Cass County?

Certainly, "stability" exists in the Cassopolis region in the sense that there has always been and is at the present time a complete absence of interracial social violence or overt rancor. However, how may we interpret the absence of social violence, conflict, or even friction? Vander Zanden observes:

It is not unusual for people to conclude that the absence of conflict in a relationship is an indication that the relationship is highly integrated, stable, and secure.[5]

It is fallacious to use the presence or absence of violence as the only measure of racial disturbance because violence is only one mechanism of social control or form of conflict among many possible ones.

[5]James W. Vander Zanden, *American Minority Relations: The Sociology of Race and Ethnic Groups* (New York: Ronald Press, 1963), pp. 183–184.

Clearly then, more is implied by the term "stability" than a lack of violence and overt conflict. An additional measure of stability would be the extent to which the ecological processes of succession and invasion play a part in the physical complexion of the community. In this regard, it is crucial to note that land changes hands intra- and inter-racially, but it does so slowly and with few racial implications. Whites purchase land in Calvin Township and Negroes purchase land in adjoining townships. It is, therefore, impossible to find a "tip-point" in the area—no evidence suggests that a certain concentration of Negroes will trigger white out-migration. There should be no doubt at this point then that Negroes (regardless of the old-new distinctions) and whites have created a stable bi-racial social structure.

Going further, in the present study the term "integration" means that Negroes are not only accorded full and equal treatment in community facilities, but also that they are accepted as being *part of the community*—its economy, its political structure, its social life. In short, integration is taken to mean that they "belong here." In these areas of community living, however, the experiences faced by Negroes in the Cassopolis region are not consistent in character. Although a substantial amount of integration is found in economic, political, and educational functions, one still finds separation in the patterns of residential distribution as well as in social relations.

Although the present research has stressed heavily the crucial role historical antecedents and cultural tradition play, this is insufficient for a total comprehension of the patterns of interracial relationships. In an effort to evaluate the underlying factors of racial interaction in this community more adequately, it is instructive to pose two questions:

1. *Is it possible to conceptualize whites and Negroes as maintaining two systems of interaction? If so, at what points do they separate, at what points do they appear to converge, and why?*

2. *What effects, if any, might the rural character of the area have on patterns of social interaction and community integration?*

Systems of interaction

In regard to the first question, it is not productive to conceptualize the "white" and "Negro" into distinct social systems or "communities" unless one pays a proper degree of attention to the "old-new" dichotomy so prevalent in community relations. Patterns of perception and social distinction prevent any casting of a "Negro community" without reference to *which* "Negro community." Indeed, it is both accurate and productive to conceive of Calvinites, newcomers, and whites as having systems of interaction which mesh to a degree in some areas of community life, but appear separated in others. These areas are economic-political and residential-social respectively.[6]

It has been established that there is a substantial degree of race-related residential separation in the research area. However, for Calvinites this is a result of historical process rather than of contemporary segregation. That is, prior to the Civil War and thereafter, the most certain sign of safety to Negroes was not the Quaker broadbrim, but rather another Negro peaceably established in a region. Agricultural prowess became evident in the process of farming successively larger plots of land adjacent to original holdings. This "natural growth," combined with slow rates of change over time, has perpetuated the pattern. However, even though the residential pattern can be related to historical forces of acquisition and retention of land, several contemporary results are clear.

The research area can be divided into neighborhoods that have become associated with meaningful social distinctions. To an extent, the township has become the unit of area symbolization. It is then no accident that the term "Calvinite," which is a respondent term, not an artifact of the analysis, assumes a high degree of meaning. It is also instructive, I think, to be aware that the label "Calvinite," as a term of geographic reference, conveniently avoids having to discuss these people in racial terms. Perhaps this is one of the

---

[6]For a comprehensive treatment of this approach, see Talcott Parsons, "The Principle Structures of Community," in his book, *Structure and Process in Modern Society* (Glencoe: The Free Press, 1960).

strongest indications of the racial marginality of the settlement.
Whites living in Calvin Township are *not* called Calvinites. Furthermore, no other township name in the county can be associated with
any meaningful social distinctions.

Newcomers in the research area generally concentrate for non-
historical reasons in Vandalia, Paradise Lake, and the southern
portion of Cassopolis. Whites populate the remaining portion of
the four-township area. Residential distribution then becomes an
analytic device that allows one to explain, at least partially, patterns of social interaction.[7]

If one accepts the term "community" as denoting a geographically
based social system, there are essentially communities *structured
initially on a residential basis.* However, even though ecologically
based social systems have arisen in the research area, the possibility of social integration is not automatically precluded. Calvinites
have developed an identity of their own but the maintenance
of this identity does not prevent full participation in community
life. Only in the most "in-groupish" of social functions is the
"line" found. Certainly, this line is no more impenetrable than that
often found between socioeconomic classes, ethnic groups, religious
groups, and so on. If by "integration" we mean that a category of
people is defined as an integral part of the community, then Calvinites are partially integrated while newcomers definitely are not.

Shifting to consider the economic-political functions of the community, one finds patterns of a different character. People participat-
ing in these functions tend to interact less on the basis of attributes
of individuality and more as occupants of functional status categories. This distinction is necessary because community life is a
combination of "personal" and "status" relationships. The implication of this distinction can be seen in the Mayo and Bobbitt study
of bi-racial identity of rural locality groups.[8] They report that, although separate white and Negro neighborhoods could be deline-

[7]It will be remembered that the four-township area is closely related to the
boundaries of the Cassopolis school district and that Cassopolis, and to a lesser
degree Vandalia, serve as economic and service centers for the four-township
area.

[8]Selz Mayo and Robert Bobbitt, "Biracial Identity of Rural Locality Groups in
Wake County, North Carolina," *Rural Sociology*, 15 (1950), 365–366.

ated in their study, a "community of mutual interests" tends to integrate and override the separate residential areas.

I suggested earlier that Calvinites represent—at least traditionally —a "profit" to the white community in terms of mutual defense of the past, Republican allegiance solid enough to insure "safe" elections, and revenues, either gained through economic self-sufficiency or jobs outside of the area that are not dependent upon the community's origination. On these levels of contact, there is almost total integration between the Calvinite and white communities.

The newcomers, however, are considerably less established. Politically they tend to be "dangerous" when they put pressure on the status quo that they feel has isolated them. Economically the newcomers would be "costly" if they demanded equal treatment in the competition for jobs—which are often nonexistent to begin with. Calvinites, as holders of a marginal but privileged status, must look to the white community for cues. The cue is clearly to socially isolate the newcomers. What develops, in addition to pressures of "appropriateness" between whites and Negroes, is that contact between Calvinites and newcomers, while both nominally Negro, becomes ridden with social distinctions. Resisting "intermarriage," barring newcomers from certain churches, describing Paradise Lake as "undesirable," maintaining a slight separation of clubs and social activities (e.g., the Grand Army of the Republic versus the NAACP)—all are taken as indicative of relatively distinct systems of interpersonal relationships among the two categories of Negroes.

There are, then, distinct systems of social relationships. However, there have not been the years of complete isolation or self-containment that might be expected to produce a severe internal structuring of a community solely along lines of racial identification. As a result, while somewhat residentially and socially separate, old-time Calvinites have not been so removed that meaningful "we-they" distinctions could be generated or maintained. The inability to use the noun "Negro" without a qualifying adjective is taken as indicative of the awareness of this internal differentiation. Thus, Calvinites and whites perceive internal gradations in the other so that "The Negro" presents no threat to "a community of mutual interests." Figure 6 allows an inspection of variations in both de-

*Figure 6: Degrees of integration into areas
of community life*

Subgroup	Degree of integration			
	Total	Substantial	Partial	Minimal
Tenure white	Economic Political Residential Social			
Calvinite Negro	Economic Political	Residential Social		
Newcomer Negro			Economic Political	Residential Social
Potential Southern migrant white				Economic Political Residential Social

grees of and areas of integration for the subgroups presently or
potentially found in the community.

Effects of rural character on
patterns of interaction

Various sociological works on mechanisms of social conformity
and control have stressed the point that definitions of "place" are
more adequately handled on a personal level of interaction (racial
etiquette) in the rural area than in an urban environment where contacts are generally more impersonal. An essential point is that the
rural area tends to be less functionally differentiated.

Whereas economic and political contacts in an urban environment are more likely to be based on competition and perhaps conflict, the diffuseness, the comparative lack of differentiation, and the egalitarianism of rural life combine to produce cooperation at best and accommodation at worst between racial collectivities. This, of course, assumes that past traditions are such that contemporary interaction can take place without a "backlog" of mutual fear, hostility, and resentment.

Thus, I would propose that the generation and maintenance of the unique situation in Cass County is, first of all, a result of a historical and cultural process. This subcultural tradition must be considered a living force in the community. Internal patterns, that initially may appear inconsistent, become more meaningful and relevant if discussed in the framework of separate "communities" which develop social systems that entail varying degrees of separation and intermeshing. Finally, in terms of economic and political arrangements, where impersonal competition would be likely to damage integration, the quality of rural life tends to enhance the validity of cooperative rather than competitive effort.

The future

Because the Negro population in the Cassopolis region is undergoing a compositional shift to the newcomers' advantage, accommodation will gradually be replaced by challenge to the "system." Clearly, no candidate for office or political party will gain power if the legitimate demands of Negro residents are not heeded. It is unlikely that other institutional areas in the community will exhibit any significant alteration. The higher levels of economic prosperity in surrounding counties will tend to remove local pressure to provide increased opportunities. Furthermore, all public facilities—especially the school system—already accord Negroes full and equal treatment.

The remaining question—that of social relations—is not likely to undergo significant alteration. Negroes do not seem willing to push

the system further and whites have already formed many friendship ties with Negroes. This appears a mutually satisfactory state of
affairs and may be expected to be maintained, especially between
whites and Calvinites.

However, the community has a long history of ignoring or resisting
social change. If alterations in the community are viewed as a
threat to the community as a whole, stability will prevail. However, if the whites or Negroes find grounds to blame the other, it
will provide the basis of a rupture of the stability that has characterized the area for over a century. WR–19 comments:

*We have no reason to worry—we have gotten along with
Negroes as equals for one hundred years and we fully expect
to get along for the next hundred years. We will be able to
avoid the Chicago-type problems. Both the Negro and white
are a stable people.*

Some implications

Now that the historical derivation and cultural evolution of a particular community have been examined, what part of the preceding
information and analysis might allow one to generalize about the
broader and more widespread sociological significance? Basically,
of course, we have been studying a community as a methodological
device to enable us to learn some of the day-to-day interpersonal
relationships which may or may not be socially structured along
lines of racial identity. Thus, I would propose that the present research has been what Hughes called a "conducted tour toward, but
not dangerously near, the extremes. (See p. 7.)

I realize that American sociology is currently oriented to the problems of an urban, mass, or industrial society. This is as it should be
and I embrace this orientation. We are an urban society and are
becoming more so. The large-scale and continuing migration of the
rural southern Negro to the urban North has set the stage for the
"race problem," which, in the end, is a problem that will be settled

in Chicago, New York, Detroit, and the other centers of the metropolitan Northeast, Midwest, and probably Pacific Coast.

With these thoughts in mind, I believe that an area such as Cass
County, while admittedly a particularistic study, holds some obvious implications. Perhaps, for my purposes, the single most influential piece of research is Morton Grodzins' slim monograph, *The
Metropolitan Area as a Racial Problem*. Here, Grodzins outlines co-
gently the dimensions of the problem and a series of possible
solutions.

It is quite obvious that "the city" is basically a political or adminis-
trative unit which often bears little relationship to the outlines of
what could be called the "functional community." Because most
large cities are "land-locked" by suburban communities with different political control, growth has increasingly meant not flight from
the inner core to outlying parts of the city, but a flight from the political city altogether. Basically, in accordance with Burgess' concen-
tric zone theory, the inner city becomes obsolete and deteriorated in
comparison with newer, modern housing in the fringe communities.[9]

Negroes who come to the metropolitan area are generally denied
access to the newer or more desirable housing either because of
their race or because they are poor and unskilled. However, the
deteriorated housing of the central city is available to them, and,
by moving into this area Negroes do not create the slum, they inherit
it. Therefore, the central cities with "open occupancy" are gradually
becoming "black," while the suburbs surrounding them are "white."

Thus established, the ghetto is self perpetuating. The continued in-
migration from the rural South puts more and more extreme pressures on the inner city to provide housing. Overcrowding is inevitable. It is unavoidable that the ghetto, as miserable as it may be, builds
its own internal interests to match the external interests in maintaining Negro segregation. External interests, such as keeping the
suburbs "lily-white" and gaining tidy profits by exploitation in the
ghetto, combine with political, economic, and social profits derived

[9]Ernest W. Burgess, "The Growth of the City," in Robert E. Park, Ernest W.
Burgess, and R. D. McKenzie, *The City* (Chicago: The University of Chicago
Press, 1925).

by some within the ghetto. Thus, Kenneth Clark observes that "stagnant ghettos are a monument to the dominance of forces which tend to perpetuate the status quo and to resist constructive social change."[10] Williams observes the result:

Each race develops its own closed system of interaction, and frequently feelings of hostility develop toward the outgroup. Thus, residential segregation goes along with a high incidence of interracial conflict—contrary to what many people have argued.[11]

Thus the racial problem is an urban one. Indeed, I find it justifiable to maintain that it is the problem facing the stability of the American society. What then is being done, what steps are being taken, where might a solution be? Grodzins suggests that there are at least five solutions to some of these trends. I would propose that they can be reduced to two simple but related issues: "urban reversal" and "Negro out-migration."

"Urban reversal"

Grodzins outlines under "urban reversal" the three steps he feels are necessary. First, the creation of a free real estate market. It is essential to allow Negroes and whites to select housing divorced from the question of race. Second, the return of whites to the central city. Finally, controlled migration, or more bluntly, "benign quotas," is necessary to insure a realistic racial composition.

"Negro out-migration"

Chapter One commented that Negro Americans are almost totally absent from most areas of the northern United States. Even a cur-

[10]Kenneth B. Clark, *Dark Ghetto: Dilemmas of Social Power* (New York: Harper and Row, 1965), p. 199.

[11]Williams, *Strangers Next Door*, p. 132.

sory glance at census materials, such as those presented in Chapter One, will substantiate this statement. Furthermore, Chapter One asserted that prevalent assumptions found in sociological literature concerning the genesis of prejudice and discrimination do not seem to apply to the "rural" North because that area has had neither a long tradition of racial animosity nor has it been faced with large-scale migration of a racial minority.

Grodzins proposes two possible solutions when he talks about out-migration of urban Negroes: suburbanization and migration to smaller cities. As he clearly states, suburbanization of Negroes raises the question of the desirability of encouraging "Negro" suburbs. Even though the housing would be in better physical condition, an all-Negro suburb is basically a "gilded ghetto." The question of substandard housing might be settled in this way, but the central issue of racial segregation and the resulting separate institutions, political structures, and schools remain. Unfortunately, this situation only reestablishes the "separate but equal" relation between Negroes and whites, and does not provide a structure for successful integration.

Myrdal's study, *An American Dilemma,* tells us that it is the rural North and smaller cities of that area that "constitute the most important of all community groups to which Negroes yet have to gain entrance."[12] Why then has so little sociological thought been expended on the implications of Myrdal's comments? It is somewhat doubtful that heavy Negro migration to smaller cities and villages could take place without significant resistance unless either market or legislative forces are able to offer some controls or brakes on the forces of economic and political conflict. Without controls, does it seem likely that "communities of mutual interest" could be forged out of the present chaos?

In short, one of the more general issues that must be faced is the possibility of exporting the type of relations found between whites and Calvinites to other areas. The probability that any such export could be successful seems dim. This is especially true considering that it is obviously not possible to duplicate the most deviant feature of the Cassopolis region—its cultural traditions. In addition, one

[12]Myrdal, p. 386.

cannot but help observe that nearly a century of mutually agreeable race relations did not really prepare the white community for the in-migration of Negroes following 1930. Rather, nonexistent and basically fraudulent half-way houses of racial identification had been constructed to avoid the inconsistency of saying "Negroes we know are not *really* Negroes." Thus, newcomers were deprived of "borrowing" status which the Calvinites had generated. In these semantic games lies the essential point: When under fire, local Negroes were defined as the exception, facilitating the entrance of the stereotyped rule.

To be sure, the Cassopolis region has presented a case history of the possibility of stable race relations. However, I propose that it would be deceptive to assert that the relative tranquillity is solely because whites and Negroes "know" each other. Socially, enough separation exists to strenuously question this assumption. *However,* at least the established Negroes and whites *do* know each other in a different way. Each knows that the other presents no threat to his own interests.

Thus, it seems highly tenuous that an artificial injection of Negroes into stable pre-existing communities will meet with much success—even in the rural North. This seems to be so because the migrant becomes defined as a threat to the status quo, a threat to meaningful relationships, and a threat to vested interests of various sorts, be they social, economic, or political. What would happen if it were possible to remove such threats and more important, the perception of possible threats? Some meager data are already coming in on this question from the integration of totally new and completely planned communities. The possibility of creating stable patterns of race relations in planned communities is both pragmatically possible and theoretically fascinating.

We know that a substantial urban growth will be forthcoming in the decades ahead. Presumably, this growth could well be "added on" to existing metropolitan complexes which are already often over taxed, over burdened, top heavy, and decaying, or, it could be channeled into the creation of new complexes. The most likely outcome is, of course, some combination of the two. Nevertheless, if that amount of time, energy, money, and talent is to be expended, it becomes imperative to launch an immediate investigation into the possibility of designing such arrangements in which intergroup relations would provide exciting diversity, not leaden danger.

One should not minimize the difficulties. The problem has had almost a half century to grow, mature, and compound itself in the urban North. Of course, monumental alterations will have to be made if we as a society have any sincere intention of incorporating Negroes into the mainstream of American life. I propose that there is enough evidence in this study and others to show that bi-racial stability and, possibly, integration *can* be achieved.

"Five years later"
—replication
and reflection

part five

Introduction to part five

The preceding chapters discussed the structural patterns and social processes of what I perceived, and still perceive, to be a unique, basically stable, bi-racial community. The field work for the original study was conducted over a two-and-one-half-year period, terminating in 1965. Many events have occurred in the community during these last years—much has altered the nature of race relations in the United States in general. The second edition constitutes a restudy of this community, relating the findings based on two additional periods of field research—one each in 1970 and 1971. Additionally, we shall examine a series of methodological issues which such a restudy literally propels to one's attention.

As a general overview, then, Chapter Ten will discuss the nature of community reactions to the first edition, the methodological difficulties which these reactions generated, and the consequent alterations in field techniques. As a result of the first edition, several years of further reflection, and two additional periods of residence in the community, I am convinced that the interactional relationship between investigator and respondent or informant makes it mandatory to present an exacting elaboration and analysis of methodological procedures. Many of these issues were suggested in the first edition and subsequently brought into a sharper focus. Some of them relate to the "problems" the respondent might inject (such as resistance, untruthfulness, over-cooperativeness); most are concerned with the often subtle ways the investigator perceives, categorizes, and presents the data. Many of these problems become complex when one examines the rationale for —indeed the necessity of—reanalysis of the community by the original investigator, replication by other scholars, or preferably both.

It is exceedingly fortunate for a more comprehensive analysis that a number of other studies have recently focused attention on this community. Due in large part to communication barriers across academic specialties, lags in production and publication of materials, and the endemic frustrations in interdisciplinary research, most of these studies were completed independently of each other. An annotated bibliography of these projects follows Chapter Twelve.

Because the contours of a community analysis are closely related to a particular period in time, Chapters Eleven and Twelve will review the emerging trends outlined in the earlier chapters and assess the degree to which events predicted or projected in 1965 did or did not come to pass. The reader should note *very carefully* that the analysis presented in the first nine chapters has not been altered in *any way* except for the correcting of misprints. It is indeed tempting to contemplate the possibility of "second guessing" one's own work because some changes that have taken place during these intervening years were predicted (such as the racial composition of the population in 1970); but other events have occurred that could not have been foreseen (such as a *symbolically* substantial influx of Black Muslims).

Perhaps the temptation to second guess, though fleeting, underscores a characteristic of much social research. Not all projections in a study function as proposed. One can, should, and must learn in retrospect from incorrect predictions or projections so that

these empirical reversals may lead to a greater and more productive understanding of the social processes involved. Chapters
Eleven and Twelve, then, report many changes during the last
years, some related to external conditions, some internally
induced.

Sociologists, I would propose, have always seemed a bit too
content to describe *social structures* in precise but static detail,
while mumbling something about *social process* in the last chapter.
We simply must develop a sensitivity to the types of structural
conditions which will, in probabilistic models, produce change.
What I am proposing, then, is that two or more "snapshot" analyses of a community begin to provide more realistically a sense of
process, a sense of adaptability, and a sense of viability. This is
especially so given the volatility of American race relations.

ten:

Methodological considerations

Community reactions to Black Neighbors

One of the crucial issues which must be faced in community studies is the nature of the relationship between the investigator and respondent, interviewee, or informant. Clearly, the gathering of information in the context of face-to-face interaction involves more than simple question-and-answer sequences. The investigator and the respondent are each playing a role—"managing an identity," if you wish. Each is continually making assessments of the other's behavior, deportment, and motives, and is thus structuring and altering his own behavior accordingly. A clear example of such interactive processes can be seen in the instance of a "break-off"—that is, a respondent, having originally agreed to participate in an interview, decides at some point during the contact that he or she no longer wishes to continue. The changed attitude *could* have been generated by a growing suspicion of the investigator's purposes, a resistance to questions deemed "inappropriate" (such as probes on income), a growing fatigue with overly long sessions, and so on. These types of situations are well known and thus can at least be compensated for by stressing the legitimacy of one's purposes and assuring the anonymity of the individual's responses. This chapter takes as its concern issues which, in the main, are far more subtle.

Because Part Five reports the results of a restudy by the same investigator with some of the same respondents (who may or may not have been aware of the results of the earlier analysis), the first major question concerns the degree of respondent or community awareness of or sensitivity to the earlier materials. Second, the nature of the reaction, if any, to that work must be evaluated.

During the two recent periods of field research (1970 and 1971), the level of reported public awareness *seemed* to hover slightly above zero. Earlier respondents, public officials, and new contacts either reported a complete lack of awareness or vaguely and distantly knew about my earlier published research, but had not read it. Initially this reaction seemed semi-plausible, mainly because of the normal marketing procedures for an academically oriented monograph. Only routine academic advertising efforts occurred and these were concentrated in professional journals that would not have had a direct effect or appeal in the research area. However, at least two local residents approached the publisher proposing to purchase quantities of the book for resale in local taverns, barbershops, drugstores, and the like. These inquiries went unanswered. Essentially, then, the book was directed to those with professional rather than regional interests. On the other hand, the local weekly newspaper *did* receive a copy and complimentary copies were sent to several of the more interested respondents. Given that the effects of possible feedback from the first edition could sensitize segments of the community, I was led to investigate the issue more closely, especially in view of the fact that an earlier work by folklorist Richard Dorson[1] stimulated an intensely negative reaction.

[1]Richard M. Dorson, *Negro Folk Tales in Michigan* (Cambridge: Harvard University Press, 1956).

A search of the circulation records in the four libraries directly accessible to the research area uncovered the fact that the book had been drawn out, on local library cards, over 60 times in the previous three years. Librarians suggested that this was an underestimation because it did not include bookmobile draws and regional libraries in some of the schools, nor did it record unfilled requests due to constant circulation and a lack of multiple copies. The effect of library activity on community awareness is not precisely measurable so some estimating is necessary. There is obviously no guarantee that a book, once having been drawn, was read by the borrower. Conversely, the number of readers per draw for a monograph in rural libraries is difficult to estimate. In addition to these considerations, it is difficult to gauge *community* awareness versus *individual* awareness or interest. For example, in at least one library, the book had been stolen and the librarian reported that "I didn't even know about the book or that it was missing." No library displayed the book to attract local awareness or interest.[2]

Additional probing revealed that the book was stocked by the bookstore of the local Southwestern Michigan College,[3] where about 60 copies were sold. It was required reading in at least one course and suggested reading in several others. Moreover, at least one public lecture-discussion in a local church had been based on the findings in the book.

On the basis of the above information, it was clearly unsound to conclude that the community could be restudied with no reference to the fact that at least some of the individuals whom I contacted had read the book and formed reactions, whether or not they chose to admit it. The following are a sample of stated reactions:

[2]One library listed it with new acquisitions and cataloged it under "sociology." (The staff at this library recognized the local relevance of its contents.) At a second library (where the book was a direct gift from two well-known local residents), it was listed under "race relations." In a third library it was placed under "Michigan history" (prior to its demise via theft). The fourth library cataloged it under "General Social Science."

[3]Southwestern Michigan College is a junior college which opened in the research area in the late 1960's.

I read the book myself and thought it was interesting. [WI][4]

There has been no reaction from anyone. [NI]

I think it would be unprofessional to mention it except in listing the title along with other new listings. [a librarian]

There was a lecture on the book by this psychology professor. They [local residents] didn't like the dreary picture it gave. [WI]

The kids are dangerous. If it's in print they take it as gospel. [WI]

Your book took so long to publish that by the time it came out it wasn't so good anymore. [NI]

Your book was the first thing they showed me [a local instructor] when I took the job. They thought it well to expose kids to things in their home county. The student reaction is simply "that's how it is, all right." They showed no excitement. I have had no Calvin blacks but the South Bend blacks didn't think the book was militant enough. [WI]

They [students] find it interesting and somewhat surprising that blacks were not more integrated into the economic mainstream. White students feel this for the most part, but also some blacks. [WI]

[4]The reader will note that, contrary to the practice in the first edition, "informants" are identified by race but not by number. The smaller number of individuals involved, a degree of overlap between original "respondents" and contemporary "informants," and the amount of material obtained from individuals in "visible roles" provided the validity for this alteration. Also, the reader will note the continued use of the term "Negro" in place of the term "black," which is often used in contemporary works. I have retained the term "Negro" for two reasons: first, I wished to retain continuity with the first edition; and second, the term "black" has a definite ideological connotation in the community. Thus, its appearance here would be an artifact of social changes in the academic community and portions of the larger society which the research area does not recognize.

Two final comments underscore the need to be sensitive to the effects of earlier exposure:

Lots of people won't admit to reading the book because
lots would rather not admit that Negroes even exist
around here. [WI]

People around here say that they don't read anything. They
think they will lose prestige. Only the more obscure
people read the book. [WI]

As suggested earlier, *Black Neighbors* is not the only recent work on this area. Thus, it is equally important to assess reactions to other studies involving local residents. The following analysis will examine such reactions and illustrate the types of situations which can arise during replication.

The nature and function of replication

It is axiomatic that the need to restudy, recheck, reexamine and doubt is an integral part of the scientific process. The concept of reliability suggests that if one is correct in one's formulations, other investigators using the same tools, talents, and techniques should be able to arrive at identical or similar conclusions. Thus, employing the concept of reliability insures that the research report will not be a spurious artifact of the idiosyncratic perceptions of one investigator. Imbedded in these comments is the clear suggestion that a full disclosure of procedures, methods, etc., is mandatory. It is only through full disclosure, sound field methods, and sensitivity to the perspectives of the respondent that a science of community sociology will grow. Growth in this sense means *cumulation* of results so that one study may build upon or enrich another rather than start again at the beginning.[5] On this level,

[5]See, for example, Willis Hawley and Frederick M. Wirt (eds.), *The Search for Community Power* (Englewood Cliffs, N.J.: Prentice-Hall, 1968); and Arthur J. Vidich, Joseph Bensman, and Maurice R. Stein, *Reflections on Community Studies* (New York: John Wiley and Sons, 1964).

replication and cumulation are mutually supportive goals. And yet, even the best of scientific intentions can fade when one realizes the tremendous difficulties involved in the replication of research.

Most community studies do *not* take the macroscopic nature of community structure as the unit of analysis, but rather use the community as a *locale* for conducting studies of more limited scope. Thus, we are presented with the community as the *unit* of analysis but such interests as race, social class, family stability, or criminal behavior as the *scope* of the analysis. As a result, community studies have become a rich source of data for the generation of knowledge in various substantive areas of the discipline. The empirical result is that one's image of Cass County, or Jonesville, or Springdale might well change as the limited interests of investigators A, B, and C change. These produce honest and legitimate differences but they nevertheless strain both reliability and replicability.

Prior to the 1965 field work, little attention had been devoted to this unique community, and most of that dealt with interpretations of historical events. Claspy, a local resident and writer, observes:

In considering the broad problem of the races, it appears remarkable that the interesting situation here in South-western Michigan has never been studied by research agencies.[6]

This virtual vacuum of scholarly activity was fortunate in one sense—it freed my initial study of some of the sensitizing problems involved in replication. The same cannot be said of the second edition. Many of the "reaction"-type issues that are of importance now were unimportant then. The single major exception to this was the work by Richard Dorson. (See references on pp. 18 and 145-146.) Numerous respondents reported both in 1965 and recently that they did not particularly enjoy being portrayed as

[6]Everett Claspy, *The Negro in Southwestern Michigan* (Dowagiac, Michigan: By the author, 1967), p. 108.

"reedy of voice" or "sapped of energy"; nor did they expect direct, identifiable references to individual respondents. One of my recent informants commented:

The reaction to Dorson was extremely bitter. In addition
to paying too much attention to the new arrivals, he poked
fun at the old-timers. [NI]

Claspy, for example, devotes two full pages of his work to expressing these local reactions to Dorson's study and suggesting data which could lead to alternative conclusions.[7] However, as another recent informant reports:

The day Claspy's book came out was the most exciting
night in the history of Calvin. Many of the people of Calvin
didn't appreciate seeing their names in print. [WI]

I suspect that, given that Calvinites are subject to the same vanities as the rest of us, many did in fact enjoy temporary notoriety, but the result of the dispute is not important here. What *is* important is that neither my research, Claspy's, other newer studies, nor the even earlier investigations by Dorson went unnoted. It will be seen that such levels of awareness forced an alteration in my recent field procedures.

When negative reactions to these research reports did occur, the most general basis of objection centered on printed comments that allowed interested readers to identify individuals by name. Implied characterizations of people "by class"—for example, "old-timers"—seemed to be received in a more neutral manner. Here, the investigator is clearly "walking a narrow path." It is completely unnecessary to name individuals and proper obfuscation can normally be employed. However, it *is* necessary to report enough background information to enable the reader to place the investigator's observations and analyses in a meaningful context.

[7]*Ibid.*, pp. 12-13.

At the most basic level, this decision centers on whether or not to identify the community by its actual name. Thernstrom, for example, heavily faults W. Lloyd Warner for using pseudonyms to mask both Newburyport, Massachusetts, and Morris, Illinois:

Like many another sociological field worker, Warner made evaluation and criticism of his work more difficult by obscuring the identity of the community studied with a pseudonym. The usual justification for this step is that it protects the identity of local informants. Whatever the merits of this argument, it seems clear that a latent function of this device is to lend an aura of typicality to the community in question: "Yankee City" is manifestly a place of more universal significance than Newburyport, Mass., "Jonesville" is more truly American than Morris, Ill.[8]

Thernstrom clearly raises an important issue—namely the applicability of findings to other communities. Warner himself claims the following about Jonesville:

Jonesville has been our laboratory for studying Americans. The social structure governing American capitalism lies within the actions of its people, for the lives of 10,000 citizens of Jonesville express the basic values of 180,000,000 Americans. The life of the community reflects and symbolizes the significant principles on which the American social system rests. Borrowing from the Gospel of John, we can say that Jonesville is in all Americans and all Americans are in Jonesville, for he that dwelleth in America dwelleth in Jonesville, and Jonesville in him.[9]

In addition to the claim of "typicality," one might be tempted to ask if pseudonyms serve any useful protective function. Following

[8]Stephan Thernstrom, " 'Yankee City' Revisited: The Perils of Historical Naiveté," *American Sociological Review*, 30 (April 1965), 235-236.

[9]W. Lloyd Warner, *Democracy in Jonesville: A Study in Quality and Inequality* (New York: Harper & Row, 1964), p. ix.

the passage cited above, Warner reveals the distance between "Jonesville" and Chicago, the population in 1950 and 1960, the status of "Jonesville" as a county seat, and the fact that a canal bisects the town. I defy any reader with a road map of Illinois not to discover via triangulation the true name of the community.[10] Similarly, the location of the Negro community in Cass County could not be hidden for more than five minutes from any intelligent and careful reader. Any attempt to conceal its location would have ruled out much of the analyses concerning the historical role of the Underground Railroad, the contemporary demographic uniqueness of the community, and the origins of both tourism and external influences.

The same rationale does not apply to the use of individual names. The right of the respondent to remain anonymous cannot be sacrificed merely because identification would facilitate replication. Such is the price that community research has accepted and will of necessity continue to accept. Research efforts which embarrass or embitter respondents can completely stifle any further attempts. For example, Dorson's work was published in 1956; negative reactions remained intense fifteen years later.

The above commentary is not meant to imply that research efforts can be done on a "hit and run" basis or that they can be done at no "costs to the data." The very act of examining a community brings new awareness, and possibly casts respondents in the role of "playing experts." All research efforts involving investigators and respondents in an interactive relationship "generate friction" and "consume" data. In short, one cannot really measure social phenomena without altering their character, if only minutely. Is the image received reflective of the community per se or is it refractive of either one's own preconceived notions or community reactions to earlier published investigations? In a classic comment with sobering implications, Dobriner asks:

---

[10]Accordingly, a number of sociological textbooks and secondary sources make it a common practice to insert the true names of communities following the pseudonymous ones. See, for example, Thomas E. Lasswell, *Class and Stratum* (Boston: Houghton Mifflin Co., 1965).

*One cannot help wondering whether, in the comparatively
slick and sophisticated suburbias of the college educated, the
awareness of class differences might in some part be due
to the social science courses these suburbanites took during
their undergraduate days. May it not be the voice of
sociology feeding back on itself through the voice of a
corrupted respondent?*[11]

The interaction of investigator and respondent

In addition to published materials which might be seen in the
community, one's own data collection procedures generate awareness and reactions. The fact that this should be so when one is
dealing directly with respondents is quite obvious. However, it is
not immediately clear that more subtle forms of data collection
may disturb or structure the data. They can and do. Several examples drawn from my field work will illustrate this point. In
each of the following instances, eyebrows were raised, questions
were asked, whispers were heard, or quizzical stares were seen.
In each case the data were collected at a cost—at the very least,
at the cost of awareness.

—One enters an office where public documents are housed and
requests access to the records concerning marriages. The most
recent book of such records is placed on the counter with the
probable expectation that one or two entries will be examined.
Instead, one stands for several hours tabulating data and then requests records from earlier periods—stretching back prior to the
Civil War. Inquiries must be made—for example, why does it appear that racial data had been erased during the period of Klan
activity in the 1920's?; what does "Mul" mean (Mulatto)?; how is
the race of the applicant judged and has the method changed?
—One is interested in the flow of traffic into and out of various

[11]William Dobriner, *Class in Suburbia* (Englewood Cliffs, N.J.: Prentice-Hall,
1963), p. 37.

recreational sites in the area. Accordingly, a tabulation is made based on identifiable license plate characteristics. Illinois uses city license decals which can be read at a glance, for example Chicago or Evanston. Indiana uses a digital system on state license plates to designate the registrant's home county, for example "20" for Lake County (Gary), "71" for St. Joseph County (South Bend), etc. Michigan codes the first three letters to identify home county. Thus, GPC to GPV were assigned to residents of Cass County. It is, however, difficult to stand at the roadside with a clipboard and remain unnoticed, or even to park on a state highway for any substantial length of time. The vigilant local constabulary soon inquires about one's presence and purpose.

—One walks into a local library to examine the extent of the collection of books in race relations. One is pleasantly greeted by name by a librarian who remembers discussions six years earlier and wonders what the purpose of the restudy is.

—One undertakes a comprehensive tabulation of downtown retail establishments to observe if Negroes are employed in visible positions and to note the racial composition of the customer traffic. Even with no evidence of paper and pencil, it is not normal to walk into a store, linger a while, and then leave without having shown any particular interest in the merchandise or in responding to the "You're new here, aren't you?" query.

—One visits the local newspaper office with full knowledge that it possesses the only intact set of back files and has allowed "local authors" to examine these documents covering numerous decades. One is asked what is of particular interest and an adequate reply is made. The office suddenly becomes exceedingly busy and remains so during subsequent data gathering attempts between 1963 and 1971. One is left with the question of the degree to which "intruding" questions stimulated work productivity.

—One visits a public official who is in possession of data that could legally be released and could make a significant contribution to the research. Yet the official feels that community residents might not appreciate these disclosures. The conversation turns into a maze of bureaucratic complications eventuating in "We will

give you a call when we find the information." The information
is never found.

—One examines records of land transfers. Such records are generally not kept in a form that sociologists or other individuals
untrained in real estate law can interpret. For example, what does
the notation "QCD" mean? An inquiry must be made. It, "of
course," means "Quit Claim Deed." But what does *that* mean?
(For an example of how a QCD is used in many states, consider
the instance of a married couple jointly owning real estate and
concluding a divorce settlement. Neither "owns" the property
solely, but one is granted possession. The person not receiving
this property might be asked to sign a QCD, thus "quitting" his
or her "claim" to former partial interest in the property. Or, in
the case of a jointly owned parcel of farmland, one of the two
owners could use a QCD to transfer his partial ownership to
the other.) Although one has secured the data with the assistance
of courteous and helpful personnel, one's visibility has clearly
risen.

—One is taken to a "civil rights" meeting by an individual with
whom previous contact has been made. A discussion ensues
among a number of participants in the meeting and a difference
of opinion arises. Gradually the stances become more polarized,
and suddenly one is cast into the limelight after having been
labeled an "expert" in race relations by a local resident.

—One spends a morning in a Negro church cemetery to chart
family names and kinship ties, and to note recorded Civil War
casualties. The minister happens to drive by and is intensely interested in knowing what would explain such seemingly bizarre
behavior.

—One finds a particularly knowledgeable informant and is gen-
erously and sincerely introduced to other contacts and identified
as "that Dr. Hesslink who wrote a book on us."

Each of the preceding incidents has a similar theme. In each
case, the data were useful to substantiate or enrich some part of
the analysis; in almost every case one could acquire the information through known, legitimate, and presumably low-visibility

channels. Yet, in these instances, the relatively "unobtrusive" methods resulted in awareness of the study and reaction to being studied, and, in a few cases, to denial of access to the data. The point is clear: there are very few if any data collection procedures that do not eventuate in interactive relationships with members of the community. In the case of the restudy, one simply could not drive into a town of 2,000 people in rural Michigan, reachable only by state highways, in a vehicle bearing California license plates, and commence data collection, without raising questions and probable suspicion. This is especially so for a population that has an increasing perception of its own visibility and that has been thrust into the status of a curiosity in race relations by several recent studies. Some populations, for example ghetto blacks, increasingly resent "data extraction" activities.[12]

The preceding issues deal with the steps that the *investigator* takes or might take and what the attendant costs might be. An intricately related issue is the behavior initiated by the *respondent* in this interactive relationship. Contrary to my initial hesitations, based on the methodological literature stressing ways of overcoming respondent resistance, I found my contacts generally quite helpful. They are also perceptive people who are able to "read" from one's face and demeanor what might or might not be of interest. On a crude level, the process of "out-guessing" the investigator may take place as a result of expectant gestures or leading probes. An investigator is able to get many respondents to agree or disagree with a wide variety of statements. For example, respondents in both 1965 and 1970 observed, somewhat facetiously, that racial frictions are low in Cass County because people ignore the subject. It is in this vein that Claspy comments:

---

[12]A recent research seminar which I directed was devoted to the problems of migration and adjustment of reservation Indians to metropolitan Southern California. Attempts at data collection were frustrated at every turn. In one memorable incident, we were informed that a nearby university regularly sent groups of students into urban Indian communities to acquire "practice" in interviewing so that they "could make mistakes where it didn't count" (preparatory to going into the predominantly black communities of south-central Los Angeles [Watts] and Compton).

"Some people may claim that one reason why race relations are so good in the county is that the problem is rarely discussed."[13]

Yet, both my initial study and the restudy were concerned with precisely these issues. In Chapter Two, I reported that non-directive interviewing regarding contemporary race relations was not extremely productive and that I had to assume the lead in focusing discussions. This, again, is clearly done at a "cost"—a cost which cannot be eliminated and consequently must be monitored constantly. The main danger is the subtle pressure to induce respondents to "manufacture" usable data. In a community study, such deliberate or unwitting "help" could seriously injure the analysis. This is particularly so because of the heavy reliance which is placed upon people's *perception* of reality, *versions* of history, and *estimations* of others' behavior. Sociologists have long been interested in social constructions of reality as well as in "reality" itself. Concepts such as "relative deprivation" suggest that often we are more interested in how respondents order their reality than in "reality" itself. The legitimation for this concern is found in the fact that individuals act on the basis of their knowledge of a situation and not on the universe of knowledge which a third party might possess. Sociologists have repeatedly suggested that what is perceived or expected to be true may well come to pass as a consequence of these expectations. The *version* of reality that respondents carry regarding the placement and historical origin of themselves and various sociologically significant groups in the community represents a "retroactive reconstruction of reality" or reality interwoven with mythology. Lowry observes:

But life in Micro City is built on a set of myths, and there is a gap between the myths and reality in the social and economic affairs of the town. Underlying them are historical myths—those beliefs that have a specific origin in the history of the community. . . .

The old-timers, those who have twenty-five years or more residence, consistently use an idealized and almost deified

[13]Claspy, p. 72.

conception of what the founding family did or might
have wanted for the community as a yardstick against which
to judge present social change.[14]

Thernstrom, however, does not seem to weigh "local history"
with the same set of scales which has been suggested here when
he observes:

Though he cited a few secondary historical accounts that
were tangentially relevant to his analysis, Warner derived
the main outlines of his romantic interpretation of "the
industrial history of Yankee City" from his informants in
the community in the 1930's. . . .

The distortions that pervade the Yankee City volumes sug-
gest that the student of modern society is not free to take
his history or leave it alone. Interpretations of the
present require a host of assumptions about the past. The
real choice is between explicit history, based on a careful ex-
amination of the sources, and implicit history, rooted in
ideological preconceptions and uncritical acceptance
of local mythology.[15]

Little would have been accomplished in the present study by insisting, for example, that Negro respondents seek out "the truth"
regarding the origins of their ancestors. The social life of the
community does not take cognizance of forgotten shreds of his-
toriography. Moreover, since local histories tend to agree with the
dominant local ethos of the time, often no sources of "objective
historical truth" can be found. Many of the concerns of the sociologist—group, position, historical events, and social status—must
be viewed through the eyes of the resident and not through the
eyes of the investigator.

Many of the preceding remarks suggest some of the obvious as

[14]Ritchie P. Lowry, "Who's Running This Town?" *Trans-action,* 3 (November-
December 1965), p. 31.
[15]Thernstrom, p. 242.

well as some of the more elusive potential pitfalls in field research, and out of each one can distill the very important and
basic issue of objectivity. To strive for objectivity is perhaps one
of the finest aims of sociology; to assume that we have reached
it would be a colossal fallacy. While value-free sociology may be
a goal, it is clearly not a fait accompli. While very few sociologists use the guise of dispassionate academic analysis as a vehicle
for their own hobbyhorses, none can escape the influence of cultural conditioning. As it is said that one man's passion is another's
poison, so too it might be said that one man's objective analysis
is another's value judgment. The claim that sociology has reached
the exalted state of insisting that "Thou shalt not commit a value
judgment" is not only inaccurate but also self-defeating. The
man who is convinced of his pristine purity is not likely to be engaged in the continued searching and questioning and doubt which
form the backbone of science.

It is certainly true that any investigator, whether or not he
chooses to admit it, will have initial reactions to a community.
Sociologists are not "brainless eyes." These reactions should be
examined and reported because it is probable that early investigations are being structured by, or at least tested against, these
preconceived images. Images are not just matters of prejudgment
—they flow necessarily from the background and training and
previous experiences of the investigator. Let us assume that the
reader has never visited Vandalia. Consider the following descriptions from two recent publications. Although both agree on the
faltering retail establishments, do they project the same "feel,"
the same "flavor," the same imagery, or the same emotive quality?

The small rural village of Vandalia in Cass County is
typical of the changes in black Southwestern Michigan.
Once a prosperous town serving the agricultural community
surrounding it, Vandalia today resembles a ghost town.
The once thriving stores have been abandoned, and are
vacant.[16]

[16]David M. Katzman, "Early Settlers in Michigan," *Michigan Challenge* (June
1968), p. 31.

Calvin Center has always been all colored, but Vandalia offers an interesting contrast in that it has remained integrated since long before the turn of the century. As in the case of the more recently integrated Covert in Van Buren County, the white and colored live on the same streets, and the visitor will look in vain for a segregated section, or even for a slum section. People who want to live in shacks, which are not uncommon, are apt to be located in the more rural parts of the townships. . . . The town long had a good business district but, like so many places under 500 in size, it has suffered in the automobile age and few stores are now open as its population now does its shopping in Cassopolis.[17]

These independently written statements evoke somewhat different images. We cannot fault either of them because we are all prisms, receiving similar sense data but refracting them in variant ways.[18] I, too, am a prism. I saw, heard, discussed, and interpreted such data. As related on page 15, I employed a focused interview technique rather than attempting to involve myself in the fabric of community life as one might do in *participant* observation. I chose to retain a degree of separation or aloofness because of my belief that more information could be gathered if I were able to avoid being identified with any one segment of the community. I chose the freedom to come and go at will—to gather data and reflect upon them while not under local scrutiny. Nevertheless, even though binding emotional attachments were not sought out, I did form personal opinions and evaluations about the community and "where it stood" in comparison to other interracial areas.

In the initial study, these opinions and evaluations centered on the hope that this community might be able to withstand growing interracial frictions generated elsewhere and perhaps lying dormant in the community itself. Underneath, I suspect that I feared

[17]Claspy, pp. 26-27.

[18]A more general description of the area (and one that includes Vandalia) can be found on pp. 17-18 in Chapter Two.

that I had stumbled upon a community in which people and groups would slide into patterns of behavior that would make interracial friction more likely and more threatening to the delicate fabric woven out of localistic understandings and "arrangements." In the restudy, I no longer fear this happening—it has happened. As a human devoid of scientific guidelines, I feel sorrow over some of the frictions and animosities presently surfacing. I do not see them as a lesson or as a new basis for social cohesion. As a sociologist, I can *understand* much of what has happened and why. Understanding the data is the sociological goal; feeling the data is a personal experience which is not easily conveyed.

In each of the analyses of Cass County, some issues are treated more intensively than others. This is a natural result of individual decisions stemming from the sifting and selection of data. For example, the first edition reports those aspects of the data that I perceived to be relevant to my stated purposes. Ultimately, no more than a fraction of respondent comments was employed in the finished work. Similarly, not every shred of the many scattered bits and pieces of data was employed. Such selectivity introduces subjectivity into the analysis—subjectivity that is unavoidable if one's analysis is to be more than a running stream of consciousness punctuated by purposeless data. The issue at hand is clearly not one of "fudging data." What *is* suggested is that the reader has a strong dependency on the sensitivity, the background, and the intellectual orientation of the writer. Unfortunately, the difficulty is compounded because such considerations are rarely discussed at any length in community studies. The reader *must realize* his dependency and be, accordingly, skeptical. Fortunately, one control mechanism is publication of materials that allows and, in fact, invites professional criticism and, if feasible, replication.

One possesses a self and a set of personal attributes. One of these attributes is clearly racial identity. I am "white" and I am in the process of examining a bi-racial community. It is a dead-end argument to suggest that a white *can not* or *may not* examine a bi-racial community because non-whites are present. If this were the case, then by the same reasoning, a non-white would be presented with the same sets of constraints. Clearly, a "mixed"-race interviewer would also be bound. Such arguments suggest that scientific investigation is impossible. What is called for is sensitivity to the possible impact that one might have—not ideologically based claims regarding who may study whom and under what conditions.

It must be stressed that "cultural conditioning," or concern with certain intellectual issues, cannot be used as a cover for the more obvious types of value commitments. One of these commitments, which is elusive but serious, is a possible preexisting, growing, or lessening attachment to the individuals and communities that constitute the data. For example, it is not at all unusual to hear anthropologists refer to their previous research area as "my village." A related difficulty can be generated by the growing investment an investigator has in his study. There is no journal of failed studies. Though there should be—mistakes and failures are often more illuminating in the long run than safe, contrived studies on "dime store" hypotheses.

Finally, a number of authors have struggled with the problem of segregation of audiences. There is no safety in the assumption that one's respondents will never be one's critics. They often *will* see and read about themselves. To the extent that they had an investment in their "side" of the story, they may well be dissatisfied by a more "objective" profile. The threat of contamination from the pressure of respondent reaction becomes particularly serious when one chooses sides in an issue, when one receives financial assistance from the individuals involved in the study, or when one is concerned with distribution in the local market rather than in the broader based "academic community."

The nature of restudy and "adaptive methodology"

The goal of replication, taken in its most rigorous form, would suggest that a restudy employ the same methods as those used previously, so that reported "changes" in the community would not be mere artifacts of an altered methodology. This is the ideal. In reality, because of the interactive nature of data collection, the unavoidable subjectivity, and evolving interests, perspectives, and perceptions, one can never go back unchanged. These factors make a restudy a relatively hazardous undertaking. Just as it is proposed that the structure of a community is a changing entity, it should be proposed too that applicable methodologies may well change. If, as it has been suggested, the answer one gets depends at least in part on the question one asks, any significant alteration in methodology must be reported and then examined for its possible confounding implications. This is one of the crucial reasons why the analysis contained in the first edition remains unchanged, namely to avoid the possibility of a retroactive reconstruction of reality—in short, projecting today's assumptions on yesterday's data.

The initial period of field work ultimately involved seventy-one respondents. They were subjected to a "low-key" type of interaction in which they were permitted to describe racial conditions, both historical and contemporary, in their own words. Although richly rewarding in the nature and amount of data collected, this form of research is "inefficient" and "expensive." Generally one cannot approach a research-granting agency for support to establish residence in a community for a number of years to see what, if anything, one might find out. Moreover, for such observational and seemingly casual methods to function at all requires an enormous amount of respondent cooperation in a relatively tension-free environment.

The necessary field work for the second edition took place in an atmosphere in which neither of the above conditions prevailed. First, my time was limited and second, respondents no longer were willing to muse for hours on end (up to sixteen hours in the initial study). Specifically, the initial field research involved nearly three years of residency near the community. The restudies were conducted in a month during the summer of 1970 and five weeks during the summer of 1971. As in 1965, the decision to terminate face-to-face contact was *not* made on the basis of a predetermined schedule but rather by determining the point at which little new information was being received. The 28 individuals contacted in the restudy did not function as diffuse observers of the changing scenery. In the main, they were persons with whom I had previous, and in some cases continuing, contact or who were in direct possession of information which I desired. The change from the use of the term "respondents" to that of "informants" indicates this alteration. An additional 15 individuals were contacted by letter.

The *most immediate* rationale for altered methodology was that the propensity to gossip was very low during the *restudy*. In Erving Goffman's terms, the amount of "backstage behavior" had diminished significantly. In 1965 most people were eager to discuss race-related issues with an off-the-cuff frankness. In 1970 and 1971 many individuals were talking *for the record*. In the first edition I had stated "Talk is a plentiful commodity and the ability to listen to spontaneous conversation saved much effort in the initial stages of data collection."[19] Talk had evidently become more "expensive" by 1970. Why this was so is partly conjecture at this point. I will simply cite those conditions with a likely relationship, and in the following two chapters I will undertake a more detailed analysis of those not discussed here.

1) There was the awareness of my earlier work as well as the work of others. Comments were more guarded. The "fish bowl" phenomenon had set in. That is, a number of contacts realized they were being subjected to repeated analyses that would be published. Some were flattered and some were fatigued.

2) The period between the first and second studies was a time marked by unprecedented national, race-related violence as well as by a significant increase in such activities in nearby population centers such as South Bend, Kalamazoo, Benton Harbor, etc.

3) Internal, race-related social and population changes had been taking place. The "balance of power" discussed in Chapter Nine continued functioning in a state of uneasy flux.

4) Patterns of migration to Cass County had assumed an unfore-

[19]p. 25.

seen and unexpected *symbolic* turn with the purchase of land by Black Muslim interests.

5) Respondents in the initial study supplied helpful "leads" and valuable information based on their "feel" for the area. Due to the "fish bowl" phenomenon, these types of referrals were more difficult to obtain in the restudy. Fortunately, they were not as necessary in 1970 because I had had at least yearly contact with the community and therefore knew where to go for needed crucial information. Thus, the continued collection of factual materials supplemented by field assistance from informants enabled me to get a firmer grasp on the situation in a relatively modest period of time. Finding efficient sources of information can easily consume more energy than does the analysis of the data that emerge.[20]

The labeling and identification of these conditions is not meant to imply that all problems have been (or can be) brought under control. The greatest difficulty was found in attempts to acquire data which, although legally open to examination, were obscured or otherwise made inaccessible by local individuals. Although county records are not found in the greatest profusion (for example, race is no longer listed on marriage data), these data *do* exist and county personnel have been consistently helpful to me. Evidently a student doing thesis research at a nearby university did not find this to be so when he wrote:

Since the County keeps no back records, the general feeling being that any record keeping is a sign of "creeping socialism," much of the work is based on local histories, newspapers, interviews with prominent figures, the few professional works done on the subject and, most importantly, the United States Census figures. An example of the dearth of records available can be seen in the fact that the County Clerk keeps records only of births, deaths and marriages. All the property records and individual census

---

[20]A perfect example of this is Claspy, who, in addition to having authored one of the cited works on the area, maintained "clip files" of regional daily newspapers which proved to be valuable for information relating to events in the years between the first and second editions.

records are either given away (usually to the Salvation
Army) or judiciously destroyed every so often. Because of
this, research in many areas is difficult at best.[21]

This general frustration is not unusual in research in small communities. Lowry underscores some of these difficulties:

From the outset they met enormous difficulties. Much of the
needed information was simply not available. However, in
some cases where data had been collected in an intelligible
and useful form for use by state or other larger regional
groups, both the student and the professors were refused the
information locally. Even contacts by the mayor, the
manager of the Chamber of Commerce, and a number of
other officials could not break the resistance. As one ex-
ample, the local employment office steadfastly refused to
divulge any statistical information whatsoever. Availability
of such information for research purposes is not only
standard practice in all urban communities, but such data
must be collected locally in Micro City and sent to the head-
quarters in the state capital for later publication.[22]

In the case of Cass County, no newspaper maintains any sort of comprehensive index or clip files which could be personally examined. The only access to desired information is by the examination of each and every paper for the time period in question. This normally could be done at the county library but, unfortunately, papers are kept there for only a short period of time and then destroyed because of space limitations. Additionally, the local newspaper was somewhat selective about giving permission to peruse series of back issues. A local author of one of the recent works on the county commented:

[21]Robert J. Kundtz, "A Short History of Cass County, Michigan, and the Development of Racial Tension Through Demographic Shift" (unpublished senior honors thesis, Dept. of History, University of Notre Dame, 1970), p. 1.
[22]Lowry, p. 33.

Because they have been subjected to deplorable mutilation, copies of the Vigilant, *from its inception, were not available for general use. Thanks to [managerial] trust, I had immediate access to them.*[23]

Excellent writing, coupled with a well maintained file of back issues, has made research by this author much easier.[24]

Unfortunately, I was not a local resident so I could not draw upon this asset to generate trust or rapport in order to gain such access. It should be made clear that the issue is not one of unethical denial or distortion of information, but rather one that involves the types of "credentials" that various investigators are able to present. Known and respected local residents are able to impose in a way that "outsiders" are not.

Gathering what should have been very accessible legal information proved to be equally difficult. Contacts with the regional office of the Michigan Civil Rights Commission in Benton Harbor, which assumes jurisdiction over Cass County, seemed frustratingly inefficient in 1965 and absolutely irritating in 1970. When, during an interview on August 20, 1970, I requested data concerning incidents of alleged or actual racial discrimination, the local director (a Negro) made the following comments:

I truthfully don't know where to tell you to go to get information on discrimination in Cass County.

Any complaints made to us are confidential all the way through unless one of the parties wishes to make it public.

Yes, they would file complaints with us but we would not have records on how many. Maybe the Detroit office might know.

[23]Lois Webster Welch, *A Diamond Sparkles: The Facets of Diamond Lake* (Davenport, Iowa: Bawden Bros., Inc., 1970), p. ii.
[24]*Ibid.*, p. 223.

We can give you no information because a claim takes from
six months to one year to process and it is very complicated.

We keep no records in this office. Anything could be
filed any place.

Fortunately, the needed data were made available somewhat later by the Commission's office in Detroit. However, if local residents receive the same degree of opaque treatment, which presents an image of a tedious, lumbering, and indifferent bureaucracy in which cases drop into unknown, unnamed, and possibly bottomless files, one can only speculate as to how many potential cases involving racial discrimination never reach the Commission's attention due to the attendant frustrations. Perhaps the level of efficiency in record keeping can be underscored by a telephone call I *received* in 1965 from the offices of the Michigan Civil Rights Commission, inquiring if *I* knew of instances of discrimination in Cass County. An interesting reversal of normal roles!

The United States Bureau of the Census and its outlets also eluded all early efforts to extract meaningful information. Sections of the manuscript collected dust for nearly a year pending necessary data from the Census. The bare minimum of information, namely the population count tabulated by race for minor civil divisions (townships), was issued between six months to a year behind original release dates of October 1970 to May 1971. The tabulations were received on November 21, 1971. A substantial amount of valuable data had been already stored on tape but, prior to January 1972, no university contacted over a series of months was able to decipher, extract, and supply the needed information in any usable form for Michigan.

The only other hindrances encountered in gathering data (in both the first and second studies) were of three types: first, individuals occupying visible (but unofficial) positions found that their memories had become very "cloudy" and their responses were consequently evasive when they were faced with questions which, if answered, could be potentially hazardous. Second, a number of individuals seemed to have plans for their own manuscripts at unspecified times in the future and they therefore perceived that the disclosure of any interesting data could represent a "cost" to themselves. To my knowledge, none of these manuscripts has appeared. Third, a very common source of inefficiency in data collection was attributable to the completely understandable lack of recognition, on the part of some of one's contacts, of what constituted usable data. One can hardly find fault with respondents who were relatively unsophisticated in "sniffing out" sociological data. For example, most of the local reports cited in the Bibliography to the Second Edition were initially mentioned offhandedly as having no bearing on my work or were found completely by accident. Clearly they did have applicability, as the pattern of footnotes in Chapters Eleven and Twelve will attest. In one case, it took over a year and one-half to acquire a copy of a report the existence of which everyone except one individual denied. Now, two known copies exist, one of them in my possession.

It should be clear to the reader that research of any type is not free from frustration, doubt, and uncertainty. Most of the situations that have been illustrated in this chapter are clearly not unique to research in Cass County. They have much wider application, which constitutes the essential reason for their presentation here.

eleven:

Race, segregation, and institutional participation

Alterations in localities and components of population

The United States Bureau of the Census formally issued the first printed data that would allow the tabulation of the racial composition of Michigan townships in August, 1971.[1] At a later date, printed tabulations for Cass County were extracted from the "first count tapes."[2] From these latter tabulations, many of which will never appear in printed form, it was possible to enrich our knowledge and to formulate a series of observations.

In most parts of the United States, the method of data collec-

---

[1] U.S., Bureau of the Census, *General Population Characteristics: Michigan.* Series PC(1), B24 (Washington: U.S. Government Printing Office, 1971).

[2] These data were processed by the Census Data Service, University of Michigan at Flint. "First count tapes" include data on population, race, age, sex, and housing characteristics. Unfortunately, they do not include any information on socio-economic characteristics, such as income or educational level. These variables will remain unavailable for some time—a time longer than it would have been reasonable to postpone the issuing of this second edition.

tion for the 1970 census differed from that used in 1960. In 1970, most census forms were mailed to individual households to be filled out and returned to a local census office for checking and processing. In 1960, every household had been visited in person by a local census enumerator. Fortunately, in Cass County and other rural areas the 1970 census was conducted on the *same* basis as it had been in 1960—face-to-face enumeration. This clearly controlled what could have been the interjection of major variation into the data. This is so because this research area is populated by many individuals of mixed or marginal racial identity. In such an area, the interviewer generally knows the race of the respondent as a result of local information gathered within the context of face-to-face enumeration.[3] However, using a mailed questionnaire, a respondent would have considerably more latitude in "choosing" or altering his identity. Such a change in procedure could have made 1960 and 1970 comparisons extremely unreliable.[4]

As an overview observation, the demographic profiles of Cass County in 1960 and 1970 suggest that most essential characteristics have remained nearly the same, although a series of interesting internal alterations has taken place and will be examined following the more general data. Regarding the county as the unit of analysis for the moment, the 1970 census reports a population increase from 36,932 to 43,312 (17.3 per cent). This is clearly higher than the 13.4 per cent increase for the state as a whole. However, this could be expected on the basis of the nationwide shifts

[3]Because the concept of race is not amenable to clear-cut delineation and categorization, but rather is subject to continuous variation and a multiplicity of admixtures, the data, regardless of how they are collected, will have the built-in subjectivity of individual interpretation. Ironically, it is our tenaciousness in clinging to the concept of race as a precise personal or social attribute that forces us to live with these ambiguities.

[4]The concept of race as now generally used by the Census Bureau does not denote clear-cut scientific definitions of biological stock. Rather, it reflects self-identification by respondents. The 1970 census obtained the information on race principally through such self-classification, although census takers rather than mailing procedures were still used in rural areas. For persons of mixed parentage who were in doubt as to their classification, the race of the father was used.

of population from central cities to the generalized metropolitan sprawl of sections of adjacent rural counties. The first edition proposed that the county could be expected slowly to increase in population and to evidence more and more "urban fringe" characteristics, such as an increasing proportion of the labor force commuting some distance to work.

On a county basis, the 17.3 percentage increase can be examined more closely to identify the components of the change and the ways in which these components might relate to racial composition. The white population of the county increased by 17.7 per cent, whereas the non-white segment increased by 13.6 per cent.[5] These differences are reflected in the fact that the percentage of persons in the county classified as "Negro" in 1960 was 10.4, compared to 10.1 in 1970. The only processes that can affect the size of a given population are fertility and mortality (natural increase or decrease) on the one hand, and migration on the other. Table 19 delineates the weight of these components.

Table 19: Components of population increase by race for Cass County: 1960-1970

Components of increase	White	Negro
Per cent change in natural increase	7.9	8.6
Per cent change in migration	9.7	5.0
Total per cent change	17.7	13.6

The increase in the Negro population is more directly attributable to natural increase than to migration. The increase in the white population, on the other hand, is due more to an increase

[5]As in the case of the first edition, the terms "Negro" and "non-white" are used synonymously for local comparisons. The reasons for this procedural decision are two-fold. First, the census data are inconsistent in reporting procedures; and second, in the case of the county, "other non-whites" (largely admixtures of Negro and Indian) constitute less than one per cent of the population. In the four-township area, "other non-whites" comprise a fraction of this fraction.

in migration than to natural factors. It must be pointed out that most of the growth in the white population is concentrated in the tier townships bordering the more urbanized and industrial sections of northern Indiana—not within the research area per se. (See maps on pp. 18-19.)

When focusing upon the four-township *research area*, one discovers different forces in operation. The localities of particular interest within this more limited area are Calvin Township, the village of Cassopolis, the unincorporated village of Vandalia, and finally, Paradise Lake (the latter having no direct census-related boundaries). Table 20 summarizes the percentage changes in racial composition for most of these localities.

Table 20: Negroes as a per cent of the population,
1960 and 1970: percentage alteration
by selected localities

Locality	1960	1970	Per cent change
Four-township research area	22%	24%	+ 9.1
Calvin Township	66	59	−10.6
Cassopolis	19	28	+47.4
Vandalia	70	80[a]	+14 (approx.)

[a]Because Vandalia is an unincorporated village, racial data are unavailable through normal census channels. These figures are estimated from several sources of information. I estimated (confirmed by respondents) that in 1960, 70 per cent of the residents were Negro. A door-to-door survey done by Wheeler and Brunn in 1968 indicated the percentage to be 75 per cent. (James O. Wheeler and Stanley D. Brunn, "Negro Migration into Rural Southwestern Michigan," *Geographical Review*, 58 [April 1968], 214-230.) Informants in a position to evaluate these percentages stated that, in their estimation, the Negro segment climbed to 90 per cent in 1969 but had "edged down" since that time due to some in-migration of Southern whites. These last observations are estimates, of course, but I believe them to be accurate and in accord with my personal observations in 1970 and 1971.

The numerical data for the *four-township research area* reveal that both the white and Negro segments of the population are growing, but at different rates. The white segment increased from

5,623 in 1960 to 6,353 in 1970, and the Negro segment from 1,647
to 2,070. These increases represent growth rates of 13 per cent
and 25.7 per cent for the white and Negro populations, respectively. The total population of the four-township area grew from
7,270 to 8,423. This rate of increase of 15.9 per cent is slightly
smaller than that of the county as a whole.[6]

The percentage of population residing in *Calvin Township* that
is classified as Negro has dropped from 66 per cent in 1960 to 59
per cent in 1970. Although a percentage is a convenient and efficient statistic to summarize numerical data, it can also lead to
misinterpretation. Namely, *is* Calvin Township losing Negro population? No, the actual number of Negro residents has remained
essentially stable—768 in 1960 and 797 in 1970. Whites have been
moving into the northwestern section of the township bordering
Diamond Lake, so that this population component has grown
from 403 in 1960 to 537 in 1970.

The data referring to *Cassopolis* reveal that a *substantial* change
in the racial composition of the population has taken place between 1960 and 1970. The Negro segment of the population has
grown from 19 per cent to 28 per cent (a percentage increase of
47.4). In this case, not only has the percentage composition
changed, but the numerical components have also changed quite
significantly. Between 1960 and 1970, the village of Cassopolis
gained Negro residents (from 303 to 583) and *lost* white residents
(from 1,724 to 1,508). A portion of this loss is explained by the
construction of a predominantly white subdivision just outside

---

[6]This more modest rate of growth led a research team from Western Michigan University to speculate:
Although specific data from the 1970 census are not yet available,
preliminary figures suggest that Cass County's economic growth is less
rapid than that for the Midwest generally. They also suggest that
while the population of Cass County has grown, that growth has occurred outside the Cassopolis school district, and that in-district
population growth rate has declined.

A Survey of Cassopolis Public Schools, A Report Prepared for the Casso-
polis Board of Education by the Department of Educational Leadership in
Cooperation with the Division of Continuing Education, Western Michigan
University (Kalamazoo, Mich.: May 1971), p. 4.

the boundaries of the village. The data suggest that a pattern of invasion and succession has been developing in which the older section of the village, in this case the south side, has become perceived as a "Negro area." As white residents either die or move, the homes are seen as attractive to, and are purchased by, Negro families. Although Cassopolis has experienced a fairly rapid gain in Negro population, no informant perceived this as presenting a threat to racial interaction. Nevertheless, the term "Negro area" *was* used.

The data on Vandalia present no particular surprises; the town continues to be characterized accurately as a "Negro area." Paradise Lake (labeled as "Mud Lake" in an earlier plat book) essentially adjoins the village of Vandalia and is also regarded as a "Negro area." Vandalia, located in Penn Township, contributes most of the township's Negro residents (326) reported in the 1970 census. Census tapes record the population of Vandalia as 427. Although no racial breakdown is provided by these tapes, one does find that the population of Vandalia *exceeds* the Negro population of Penn Township, which again would confirm that both Negroes and whites reside in the village.[7]

Alterations in economic institutions

As was observed in the first edition, patterns of family farming, tourism, and work-related commuting are the basic economic activities that have a series of important relationships to the nature of community life. The discussion to follow will give considera-

---

[7]The remaining variables for which data are available are intermarriage, age composition, and housing information. Information on the race of applicants for marriage licenses ceased to be collected, by law, on October 14, 1965. During the interval between 1963, when my collection of these data was initially completed, and October 1965, 763 marriage licenses were issued, 686 involving two white partners, 72 involving two Negro partners, and 5 of an interracial nature. Because these data span less than two years, their utility for the present analysis is extremely limited. Data relating to age composition and housing will be discussed at later, more appropriate points.

tion to these ties by focusing on the general economic conditions and more specific, but related, issues. The earlier study stated that the research area is not particularly prosperous. Little or nothing has changed in the intervening years in such a way as to warrant an alteration of that observation. Cass County, to the extent that it "suffers," does so not as a result of local peculiarities, but due to the pressures of economy of scale affecting "marginal" agriculture. To the extent, then, that the local villages serve as farming, trade, and gossip centers, their viability is increasingly tenuous. This marginal economic position is both measured by, and exacerbated by, increasing commuting to northern Indiana for industrial employment. Rural areas and small towns have not kept pace with the increasing levels of prosperity associated with the urban North. Although the following comment is concerned directly with the status of the aged, the implications of its message can be seen to relate to the present discussion as well:

The plight of the aging in Cass County is apparently not as bad as the worst pessimists would make it, nor as bright as the eternal optimists would have us believe. There appears [sic] to be definite pockets of poverty and need. "The life style" of the typical Cass County senior citizen does not include broad participation in the benefits and enrichments of late twentieth century life. On the other hand, the survey does not show that their's [sic] is widespread dissatisfaction with life as our senior citizens live it. The Council must be circumspect lest it be in the position of telling the senior citizens what they are missing. [Emphasis mine].[8]

Lack of "broad participation" was repeatedly suggested in the first edition. The problems that the community has had in the retention of its productive young—an inadequate industrial base,

[8]Cass County Council on the Aging, "Report of the Survey Committee." Donald Nepsted, Chairman, 1969.

low income levels, adequate but marginal housing, marginal agriculture—would tempt one to ask whether many of the non-senior citizens have been living lives including "enrichments of late twentieth century life."

In the earlier study I commented that "Most homes look weathered and somewhat obsolete" (p. 18). With the exception of a small subdivision on the eastern edge of Cassopolis, and some northern areas of the village, most homes in the county look more weathered and more than somewhat obsolete. This observation does not, however, rest solely on subjective appearance or personal reactions. A recent report found that 23 per cent of housing units show signs of some physical deterioration.[9] The fact that the figure is not significantly above state averages gives one only momentary comfort. In 1960 the median market value of a single family residential structure in the county was $8,500. In 1970 it rose to $12,500. During this same period of time, the median residential rent inched up from $66 to $76 per month.[10] Clearly there have been increases, but equally clearly the amounts are modest at both points in time. Additionally, the state of Michigan equalized valuation of real and personal property in the county was $2,940 per capita compared to $3,482 for the state and an average of $3,498 in the four surrounding counties. Although the data presented in Table 21 are collected through different sources with varying procedures, they still confirm the general image of modest evaluations and the additional fact that significant differences exist between white and Negro segments of the community. In short, both "subjective" and "objective" inputs of data point to the same general "reality."

As is the case with most data, these are subject to a variety of conditions and definitions. However, as the note following Table 21 points out, the value of a number of major categories of housing was unavailable and thus is not included in the census data presented. The effect of these deletions can be seen when one

[9]Williams and Works, *Cass County Michigan: Comprehensive Area-Wide Plan for Water and Sewer Services* (Grand Rapids, Michigan: 1967).
[10]*Cassopolis Vigilant*, March 11, 1971.

Table 21: Mean dollar value of owner-occupied housing
units by race for selected areas, 1970[a]

Area	White	Negro	Negro as a percentage of white
Calvin Township	7,200	4,325	60.1
Jefferson Township	7,125	6,725	94.4
La Grange Township (inc. Cassopolis)	10,975	9,300	84.7
Penn Township (inc. Vandalia)	12,950	6,300	48.6
Four-township area	10,300	6,275	60.9

[a]Comparable data for the county are not available due to the fact that several
townships have fewer than ten Negro owner-occupied units. In such cases,
it is standard procedure for the Bureau of the Census to suppress the data
in order to prevent individual, as opposed to group, comparisons from being
made. These data are tabulated from the University of Michigan tapes. They
exclude the values of rental, vacant, and mobile units (seasonal, permanent,
and for sale).

notes the types and values of housing in Cass County according
to census data reported in the Cassopolis Vigilant, March 11,
1971:

The 1970 census counted 17,276 housing units in Cass
County, 10,912 of them occupied by owners, 2,445 occupied
by tenants, and 3,919 stood vacant. These included vacant
units for seasonal use. The proportion occupied by owners
in 1970 was 63.2 percent, compared with 59.9 percent
in 1960.

Among year-round dwelling units there were 13,753 single
family houses, 786 housing units in multi-unit buildings and
912 mobile homes or trailers.

An additional deletion, which has not already been cited, is that
the definition of "single family homes" excludes those living

units on plots of land of ten acres or more upon which business is conducted. This means that prosperous households on larger farms are excluded from the analysis.

Finally, it should be noted that none of the above data received from local sources allowed race-related comparisons to be made. An additional measure, computed from University of Michigan census tapes, *does* allow such comparisons. This concerns the number of persons per household. It has already been seen, from Table 21, that the value of Negro-occupied housing tends to be considerably lower than that occupied by whites. Personal observation suggests that, as might be expected from the comparative values, the Negro-occupied units are often also considerably smaller. In the face of these conditions, however, Table 22 reveals that the number of Negroes per household is higher than that of whites.

Table 22: Persons per household unit: race by selected areas, 1970

Area	White	Negro
Four-township research area	3.18	3.34
Village of Cassopolis	3.12	3.61
Calvin Township	3.16	3.27

A pattern of obsolescence, deterioration, and slight overcrowding seems to affect Negro residents more directly. As a consequence, it can be quite difficult to acquire a mortgage or remodeling funds for obsolete structures in a tight money market. This is especially so when many of the individuals involved are Negro residents with non-local backgrounds who may have previously rented rather than owned living quarters, may be retired, or may present no current job information. Such factors can result in a lowered credit rating which might have no contemporary justification. However, the constellation of race, economic factors, migration patterns, subdivision construction, and lessening population growth can all be seen to militate against any resurgence in the market value of existing structures in areas tending to be populated by Negro residents.

As suggested earlier, a major explanation for the lack of economic boom, and perhaps the lack of prosperity as well, is functionally related to the decreasing economic value of the small or marginal family farm. As Williams and Works observe:

*Several areas in the county including numerous farm
communities that were once thriving farm trading centers are*

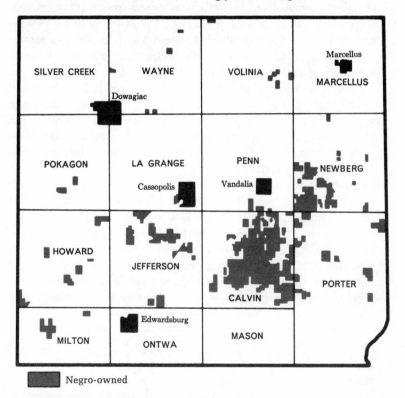

Figure 7: Negro-owned land: Cass County, 1968

experiencing a stagnation or loss of development, due to
the decline in the number of farmers and farm operators.[11]

This impact, too, is non-racial in origin but tends to strike the Negro community a stiffer blow, even though the preceding map, when compared to the one on p. 71, suggests that a lessening economic viability of farming has not resulted in an actual alteration of Negro-owned lands in Calvin Township.

Geographical contours do not, however, portray the essence of a complete perspective. Wheeler and Brunn report that in 1959 Negroes in Calvin Township operated 107 farms with an average size of 56 acres (compared to 189 whites with an average size of 75 acres). By 1968, the data reveal that the number of Negro farmers had grown to 164 but that the average unit size had decreased to 48 acres. (The number of white farmers had decreased to 176, with the average unit size remaining essentially unchanged at 72 acres.)[12] Thus, while the total Negro-owned acreage has grown from 6,000 acres to 7,900 acres, the modest average of 48 acres per farm unit makes capitalized farming virtually impossible given the technological demands of contemporary agriculture. A major exception to this condition will be discussed in the concluding chapter. The net result of similar processes throughout the nation is immediately apparent when one realizes that farmers averaged about $1.57 per hour for their labors in 1969 and that the average investment per farm required to support a family of four was $200,000 in land, buildings, and machinery.[13] Clearly, levels of subsistence such as these are not conducive to stimulating a revival of family farming in the research community or elsewhere.[14]

[11]Williams and Works, p. 34.

[12]James O. Wheeler and Stanley D. Brunn, "An Agricultural Ghetto: Negroes in Cass County, Michigan, 1845-1968," *Geographical Review*, 59 (July 1969), 323.

[13]*Cassopolis Vigilant*, May 15, 1971.

[14]*The New York Times* (November 21, 1971) introduced a humorous note into the discussion of the viability of marginal agriculture when it observed that "Cass County, one of Michigan's major farming areas, is also among the nation's largest marijuana producers, with 85 to 90 acres growing wild in the southwestern part of the county near the Indiana border."

Although the following comment is concerned primarily with Negro farmers in the South, Calvin Beale of the U.S. Department of Agriculture remarks:

To be optimistic about the future of Negro farmers would be to disregard almost every facet of their past and present status and of the factors that impinge upon them.[15]

The extent to which these forces have been felt locally can be seen in the following remark by Claspy:

With so little money in general farming now, the writer wondered if there were any real colored farmers left, but was assured by the Supervisor from Lagrange Township . . . that [the Calvin Township Supervisor] and at least two others are full-time farmers and many more, of course, are part-time or marginal farmers.[16]

Three full-time farmers are not enough to write about, but the lack of more might be of considerable import, as we shall see. The point of interest is that, although the land area remains, the incidence of rural non-farm labor force participation assumes a more and more important economic role. In addition, rural non-farm non-participation in the labor force as a result of retirement lends increasing support to the notion that the variable in common is "rural" and not "agricultural."

Housing and agricultural acreage are, of course, not the only types of real estate investments that Negroes control in the research area. A recent study reports that Negroes own or manage 15 retail and manufacturing facilities in the four-township area. The report comments that "this directory is the first comprehensive listing of black owned or managed business through the state

[15]Calvin L. Beale, "The Negro in American Agriculture," *The Negro American Reference Book*, ed. John P. Davis (Englewood Cliffs, N.J.: Prentice-Hall, 1966), p. 200.
[16]Claspy, p. 20.

[Michigan]."[17] Field research for this study uncovered at least another half-dozen such establishments—some of which are mentioned in the first edition. The enterprises include the following:
taverns (2), barber shops (2), construction companies (2), auto
repair shops (3), gasoline stations (2), trucking (1), manufacturing (2), taxi services (1), motels (3), and nursing homes (2). Some
of these operations are quite efficient and profitable; most, however, are marginal and unstable. In several cases they are temporarily combined with part-time farming to generate a sufficient
family income.

The Negro recreational establishments surrounding the north
shore of Paradise Lake seem to be in a particular state of visual
disrepair. Claspy, after visiting a similar Negro resort area in
Lake County, Michigan (referred to on pp. 11-12 and 86 above),
comments:

Houses and cottages are pretty scattered. It looked much like
Florida in 1927 after the collapse of the boom. Especially
dismal was the resort center called the Island. Everything
seemed closed but it was said that most of its taverns
and dance halls would be open in two weeks for the
Fourth of July.[18]

Having visited this area in Lake County the same summer (1965),
I concur with Claspy's description and further suggest that it
could be applied with equal accuracy to Paradise Lake. For example, during the final weeks of field research in the summer of
1971, there was not enough pedestrian traffic near several of the
lake motels to wear paths through knee-high grass at the picnic
grounds. I propose that this state of affairs (or, perhaps, lack of
affairs) was entirely predictable. In 1965 I commented:

One of the greatest attractions that Paradise Lake can offer
is an absence of embarrassment, harassment, or outright

---

[17]Donald Horning and Esau Jackson, *Directory of Black Businesses in Michigan* (Ann Arbor: University of Michigan Press, 1970), pp. v, 12.
[18]Claspy, p. 92.

*refusal typical of treatment of Negroes in most parts of the
United States. I rather suspect that this has been a major
factor in sustaining the Paradise Lake area over the years.*[19]

However, indications clearly suggest that the state of Michigan
is increasingly serious about enforcement of non-discrimination
statutes in public facilities. The message is clear: many black
businesses no longer can profit by offering a unique "backstage
service" and will either have to compete on an equal footing with
white businesses, receive subsidization, or face obsolescence and
further decay. It is crucial to keep in mind the conceptual differences between traditional Negro establishments that served an
avoidance function and newer types of Negro-owned enterprises
that are oriented to a larger market. The former are stepchildren of
white discrimination; the latter are increasingly products of (and
evidence of) Negro involvement in the mainstream economy. In
the case of Paradise Lake, relatively large amounts of capital
would be needed to insure a competitive stance. There is no externally evident data to suggest that such capital is or will be
forthcoming.[20]

This failing recreational establishment has economic implications
for Negroes in the Paradise Lake area. Far larger influences can
be discerned, however, when one contemplates the implications
for the more general role of tourism, especially its composition,
multiplier effect (introducing Cass County to successively larger
numbers of Negroes), and role in infusing the economy with "outside money" which the local economic base would, by definition,
not generate.

During the period of field work culminating in the first edition,
it was observed that the recreational establishments attracting
Negroes tended to alter the visible racial composition of the population on weekends: non-local Negroes were quite evident—in

[19]See p. 86.
[20]An additional factor that I do not think is substantial enough to provide an
alternative explanation for the seeming lessening of patronage is the existence of a recreation area near Lake Geneva, Wisconsin, which appears to
be attracting an increasing number of blacks from Milwaukee and Chicago.

the grocery stores, bars, on the lake, and so on. Local Negroes, who could have been identified as conservative Calvinites, tended to repair to their homes lest they be "caught" with those "Chicago niggers." This situation has changed. A check of traffic flows into Cass County on summer Fridays and Saturdays no longer reveals sizable numbers of out-of-state Negroes. The majority of those who do visit the county on weekends, however, continue to come from the Chicago area. Traffic is denser than on weekdays but its racial composition favors whites. Thus, while Diamond Lake is still heavily used by whites, particularly from northern Indiana, Paradise Lake seems to have lost much of its attraction and glitter. Moreover, Diamond Lake now has a "public access site" so that anyone who wishes to may use the lake—not just the owners of shoreline property, most of whom are white. Negroes are now frequently seen fishing or swimming in Diamond Lake, whereas they were definitely not seen doing so in 1965.

Although I predicted in the earlier edition that the influence of tourism should become greater, this does not seem to have been the case—at least for Negroes on a weekend basis. In addition to personal observation, retail sales tax receipts are another measure of "tourist area" activity:

An accurate indicator of the amount of retail sales attributed
to tourism can be determined from an examination of
monthly sales tax returns. The following illustration entitled
"Comparative Monthly Sales Tax Trends" points out that
counties with economies oriented to the tourist such as
Roscommon show a marked increase in sales tax collection
in the summer months and a substantial decrease in the
winter months. As can be observed, this trend is not
evidenced in Cass County.[21]

The second direct purpose of monitoring traffic flow relates to gathering data regarding daily commuting for employment. Once again, there are patterns that are discernably different for whites

[21]Williams and Works, p. 28.

and Negroes. In recent years there has not been a sufficient number of jobs for Negroes in the research area. Part of the "difficulty" was and is alleviated by the fact that a relatively low proportion of Negroes actually make full-time employment demands on the local economy, because many of them are not technically in the labor force.[22] Furthermore, many of those who are in the labor force are commuters.

The routes from Cassopolis to South Bend and Elkhart are heavily traveled by local residents commuting on a daily basis. Observation reveals that a large proportion of the cars bearing license prefixes GPC to GPV (Cass County) are driven by Negroes. Wheeler and Brunn report the same relationship between commuting and race when they observe that in Vandalia about half of the whites who work do so within the village, as compared with less than one-tenth of the Negroes. Moreover, among commuters the mean travel distance for whites is ten miles; for Negroes it is twenty miles. The result is that the cities of northern Indiana employ approximately 40 per cent of Vandalia's Negro labor force, as compared with only about 20 per cent of the white. A less obvious but important result is that Negroes spend over an hour a day driving to and from work, and whites about half this time.[23]

These patterns were observed in an earlier chapter. Knowledge of them led to speculation that Negroes may in fact have represented a *short-run* "profit" to the community, since earnings which a local economic base did not and could not generate were brought in from other areas. However, before we decide whether or not this situation is "profitable," a series of questions must be asked. First, what are its long-run implications? Second, are "externally generated" monies actually being spent in the research area? Third, is the tax structure capable of tapping these funds? The first question is perhaps the easiest to answer. There *may be* benefits in the *short run* analogous to the pattern of a family living beyond its income. In the long run, however, especially if tourism

---

[22]For example, marginal farmers, the retired or pensioned, female heads of broken homes receiving assistance, dependent children, or the unemployed no longer actually seeking work.

[23]Wheeler and Brunn, *Geographical Review* (1968), 229-230.

does not play a substantially greater role, one must contemplate the picture of a semi-rural area with more people than it can support due to changes in the larger economy—in this case, the lessening profitability of family farming. One need only look to Appalachia for a similar, although far more severe and advanced, set of circumstances. It is entirely possible that some of the deleterious effects of lessened employment prospects on a local level have structured the potential attractiveness of the area for components of the population in different economic positions (which are related to age). This can be seen, for example, in the proportion of the population (white and Negro) that is in its productive years (18 to 65, inclusive). Table 23 reports this information in the form of "dependency ratios" based on age composition

Table 23: Dependency ratio of the population by race for selected areas, 1970

	White	Negro
Calvin Township	1.00	1.16
Research area	.90	1.16

data. Any number larger than 1.00 indicates more dependents than producers. Differences which might appear modest in ratio form can have quite striking effects when comparative economic welfare is under consideration. If these high ratios continue, especially in the Negro population, we can hardly expect economic vitality.

Whether or not the monies derived from commuters circulate through the local community is an empirical question subject to examination in two ways. First, observation—that is, asking people where they shop—and second, checking sales tax receipts. Observation over the two periods of restudy suggests that at any one time about 10 to 15 per cent of the customers in most retail establishments are Negro. (The research area is 25 per cent Negro.) Wheeler and Brunn observe:

*Although there is less difference in the use of the urban
hierarchy for shopping, Negroes are again somewhat more
mobile than whites, both for lower-order goods such
as gasoline and groceries and for higher-order goods such as
clothing.*[24]

They then report that 22 per cent of the white minority in their
sample purchased groceries in Vandalia but only seven per cent
of the Negro majority did.[25] Neither figure is high, which suggests
that local enterprises are not able to capture much local business.
  Finally, in terms of the tax structure, Williams and Works
observe:

*The amount of retail sales tax collected per capita is con-
siderably less than state average. This indicates that the
county is not attracting a great deal of tourist trade and that
a large number of its residents are doing their shopping
out of the county in the larger [urban] areas.*[26]

Sales taxes, of course, are only one method used by governmental
authorities to secure funds for public needs. Although Negroes
do not provide sales tax "profits," they do own seasonal or vacation homes on which taxes must be paid. Moreover, whenever two
adjacent states have variant laws or tax structures, there is a
tendency toward "non-local" purchases. A classic example of this
in Cass County has been the "land-office" business done by liquor
outlets on Sunday, due in part to Indiana laws forbidding the sale
of alcoholic beverages on that day.
  It is perhaps a related phenomenon that merchants in the area
have not been employing a substantial proportion of Negroes. I
observed earlier that "Negroes are definitely under-represented
if not almost absent from the 'visible positions' on the main street
of Cassopolis."[27] While one may grant that a number of the retail

[24]*Ibid.*, p. 227.
[25]*Ibid.*, pp. 227-228.
[26]Williams and Works, p. 27.
[27]See p. 80.

establishments are family-owned and do not "employ" *any* workers, it is revealing that on two different canvasses of the twenty-
one white-operated shops (twenty-three including taverns), not a
single Negro employee was seen.[28] It is entirely possible that my
canvassing was done on their days off. (This is not totally fa-
cetious because I know of at least two Negro employees—a check-
er and a teller.) However, one can safely conclude that Negroes
are still "under-represented." An explanation which may have
some validity, but one which I do *not* share, has been offered by
Claspy:

> There has been great pressure in the cities to give Negroes
> jobs in stores, especially in cases where they compose a
> substantial proportion of the customers. In Cass County,
> however, there is hardly a store that makes a special bid for
> their business, for they might be insulted at any such
> efforts. The old residents would fear that it was a move
> toward segregation and many of the new people moved here
> in order that they could buy things at the same stores as
> the white man and might resent Negro clerks.[29]

In general, then, the evidence seems to indicate that Negroes do
not present the community with "unearned" profits in terms of
either tourism or "hometown shopping."[30] It is therefore important
to note that Negroes do not present themselves as an economic
power to be taken into account. Two immediately obvious reasons
for this can be cited. First, Negroes have less money to spend, and
second, as has been noted, much of what they do have is spent
outside the community. A case can be made for the statement that

[28]It is also interesting that in 1971 one would find it impossible to purchase a
Negro doll in the middle of an area with a 25 per cent Negro minority, although a large variety of white dolls was available.

[29]Claspy, p. 39.

[30]One additional "profit" that Negroes might present would be found in the
collection of the real estate tax on structures that might otherwise be abandoned. Although there is a distinct possibility that this might occur, especially in Vandalia, there is no direct way to approach the issue with
certainty.

having a dollar to spend is like having a vote to cast. That is, this buying power marks one as a person or part of a group to be taken into account if purchasing decisions are related to attempts to secure other "benefits" and rights. In earlier stages of the "civil rights movement," the phrase "double-duty dollar" was used. The point was that spendable dollars are able to purchase goods and build political power or leverage at the same time. If this is the case, the political power that Negroes possess in Cass County does not seem to rest on their economic power to spend or withhold spending.

Political institutions and voting behavior

As in the first edition, the term "political institution" is defined in a broad fashion to include the following types of considerations: 1) to what extent has the residential concentration of Negroes in the county affected, or does it now affect, their ability to acquire political power?; 2) how do Negroes fare in the attainment of offices or positions, elected or appointed, in the formal political structure?; 3) more subtly, to what extent are Negroes able to wield power or influence through informal channels?; 4) finally, what do recent patterns of voting behavior suggest regarding the influence of the traditional Republican establishment?

It seemed clear from data presented in the first edition that Negroes controlled the political institutions in Calvin Township. While whites were found in township offices, the key position of supervisor was filled by a Negro. The township supervisor, in addition to possessing the ultimate authority on the township level, was also guaranteed a position of proportionate influence in the county's governmental affairs. This was so because the county government was composed of the 15 township supervisors plus representatives from Dowagiac's three wards. (The four villages in the county were represented on the Board only indirectly— through their township officers.) Additionally, the supervisors constituted the membership of various county committees concerned with such important functions as appointments, assess-

ments, budget, education, zoning, and so on. Thus, the single act
of electing a Negro to the post of township supervisor guaranteed
political representation at three levels: township, county administration, and county committees. This voice was obviously strong
on the township level and quite weak on the county level—unless
the "Negro voice" was combined with others in a coalition for
political action. In the earlier study, the Negro supervisor of
Calvin Township was a member of the Civil Claims, Insurance
and Bonds, Veterans' Affairs, and Zoning Committees.

In the middle 1960's, the state ruled that such a pattern violated
the Constitutional concept of one-man one-vote. Why this was so
can be easily seen from the populations of the townships in 1960,
which varied between 815 and 4,622. The resulting court-directed
change split the functions of township supervisor and county
governmental supervision so that the township supervisors lost
their former power at the county level. A new 21-member Board
of County Commissioners contains no township supervisors. The
potentially negative results for Negroes' political power can be
immediately discerned. At the very least, equalizing the representation between districts on the basis of population means a larger
board with no necessary increase in Negro representation, in that
Negroes constitute a majority only in Calvin Township. Moreover,
Calvin Township is not heavily populated and, as the preceding
demographic data suggest, the areas of the county that are increasing most rapidly in population are those townships bordering
northern Indiana. With one exception, these townships have the
fewest Negroes of any in the county. Finally, if in the future voting for the county board is altered to an at-large basis, as has been
done in other states, Negroes would not *automatically* control *any*
seats. These statements artificially assume, of course, that voting
behavior is completely predicated on racial identity. Because this
is not so and racial concentrations and political units do not present an automatic fit (for example, approximately 40 per cent of
Calvin Township residents are white), it is impossible to predict
what eventual effect the court-ordered alterations may have. However, voting behavior data indicate that Negroes generally do not
get elected in areas where they do not constitute a substantial pro-

portion of the population. This has been true in other townships and, particularly, in county-wide races. Thus, the potential for Negro political power or at least Negro representation has historically been a function of area concentration, but this correlation is less strong than it once was.

Inasmuch as the changes discussed above are recent, they have not stimulated an attrition of Negro office holders. While Calvin Township is now represented on the county board by a white man, the new 21-member board still has two Negroes—one from the heavily Negro ward in Dowagiac, the other from the township just east of Vandalia. A majority of Calvin Township offices are still controlled by Negroes (including the supervisor, clerk, treasurer, and constables). Cassopolis has one Negro trustee, who led the ticket in number of votes cast. Dowagiac's police chief is a Negro, as is one of three commissioners. Numerous county offices have Negroes employed in a variety of capacities—most notably, perhaps, the sheriff's department, which has a Negro undersheriff (second in command) as well as a sergeant and deputy. The postmaster in Vandalia is Negro. The Cassopolis Board of Education now has a Negro member. It is suggested, then, as a general observation, that Negroes play a quite visible role in the formal political affairs of the county. Two situations, however, should be cited to suggest that some inconsistency can be found in the above pattern. First, Vandalia no longer has a Negro mayor. A number of informants saw this change as having more than passing meaning.

———— *was the last of the Negro presidents of Vandalia.*
They felt an all-black government wouldn't be good. Many
of the Negroes felt this way too. [WI]

We didn't think it was wise to turn Vandalia into a Negro
town. It is holding its own now and that is just fine. [NI]

The whites were getting scared—you know, feeling like
they weren't wanted around. [NI]

You have to be careful with some of these Southern whites.

They are interested in letting you alone and you can't
push them too far. Many of them are a lower class of
people. [WI]

The second political event from which many local informants
were quite willing to draw negative racial implications involved
the 1968 Republican primary race for county treasurer. In this
instance, a very well known, active, respected Negro and former
supervisor of Calvin Township was defeated by a lesser-known
white woman (who later won the general election and appointed
a Negro woman as deputy treasurer). The Negro candidate carried
Calvin Township with a 78 per cent majority and the four-township area with 52 per cent, but received only 42 per cent support
county-wide.

Informants observed:

That is the first time since the early 1900's that a Negro
tried to win a county election, and you see what it got
him. [NI]

You can't get a Negro elected to county-wide office. [WI]

Whatever support he gets around here [the research area]
will just be wiped out by the rest of the county. [WI]

I observed in the first edition that participation in the formal
political structure was only the "tip of the iceberg." Whereas
Negroes still hold a significant number of appointed positions, the
"behind-the-scenes" role played by them at the party level has
not improved, and in all probability it has suffered significantly.
Although only scattered data relating to this point can be collected
(for example, the choosing of county convention delegates,[31] at-

---

[31]Mimeographed documents entitled "Delegates to Democratic (Republican)
County Convention Elected Aug. 4, 1970" showed that no delegate from
either party came from Calvin Township. However, a number of Negroes
were elected from other townships to the Democratic convention. The Republican convention projected a solidly white character with respect to the
21 delegates from the four-township area.

tendance at Lincoln Day dinners, party caucuses, etc.), the issue
of *informal* power vis-à-vis the white community intricately involves the structure of the internal leadership of the Negro community and the way in which it relates to the larger community.
The major emphasis in Chapter Twelve will be on changes occurring *within* the Negro community as the power and prestige
possessed by Calvinites erode. Generally speaking, as this erosion
proceeds, the value to the white power structure of having Calvinites in the traditional "spokesman" role also recedes, in that
newcomers no longer accept the automatic elevation of Calvinites
to the ascendant position of representing the interests of the entire Negro community.

The 1964 election gave Calvinites the opportunity to repair their
crumbling power base through a different set of tactical moves.
The Republican ticket, headed by Barry Goldwater, drove Calvinites to switch their political allegiance to a significant degree.
Their departure from predictable and consistent conservatism was
generally considered to be a temporary situation which resulted
from the Calvinite perception of Goldwater as an unreconstructed
racist. By doing nothing to dispel the notion that Goldwater was
the sole issue, Calvinites did not reveal the fact that whites' enthusiastic response to Goldwater had laid the groundwork of
deep suspicion, concern, and distrust throughout the township.
Thus, whites were inadvertently led to assume that the Calvinites'
voting behavior signified nothing beyond a "temporary deviation"
and they therefore saw no compelling reason not to hold fast to
the notion that Calvinites would again faithfully support the
straight Republican ticket. As a result, white Republicans assumed
that little or no effort need be spent in attempting to insure the
resurgence of century-old allegiances. However, since 1964, although Democrats have undertaken only modest recruiting efforts
and proposed few patronage possibilities to attract the vote, Calvinites continue to turn in Democratic pluralities in most national
and state contests. Thus, they have not kept whites of either
political persuasion "off balance." As a direct result, they have
lost the advantage inherent in the position of being able to force
whites to "court" them. A potentially strong political edge has

thus been blunted. In this sense, they have again become "predictable" and are not seen to be a swing group to be "won over." Republicans tend to see Calvinites as lost *and* unnecessary; Democrats tend to feel that they are safely "in the bag." Compare this
contemporary state of affairs with the comment below, which
illustrates the traditional stance of unfailing Republican loyalty
projected by the Calvinites:

*I think my grandfather began voting in 1872 and he never
missed an election. We have been Republican. Up until
30 years ago there were only six Democrats in the township.
For years and years, anyone who was nominated for office
in Cass County was sure of 200 straight Republican votes
from Calvin Township. That continued until after Roosevelt
came.*[32]

Carefully regarding more contemporary events, the Negro informant observed:

*I had never heard much about the Muslims until they started
coming in here but their ideas are different from mine
and the majority of my people. We have lived here for generations. In 1916, Booker T. Washington visited this community and you will find an article of his in the Outlook
Magazine sometime around 1912 or 1915, "Three Generations Under Freedom." Now there have been five or six generations who have lived here and got along fine with
the people.*[33]

Despite the impression gleaned from the preceding quotes, the
disenchantment with the national Republican leadership, which
sent the percentage of Calvin voters favoring the Republican
standard-bearer skidding from 57 per cent for Nixon in 1960 to 23

---

[32]Comments reported by Welch, p. xxx, and taken from a taped interview in
1968 with an old Negro resident.
[33]*Ibid.*

per cent for Goldwater in 1964, does not seem to have terminated. As Table 24 demonstrates, voters in Calvin Township were not able to muster much enthusiasm for Nixon in 1968 or the Republican state candidates in 1970. In 1966, however, Republican Governor George W. Romney was able to carry the township while Republican Senator Robert P. Griffin, running against Democrat G. Mennen Williams, was not. The Republican candidate for secretary of state, *a black*, received 50 per cent of the votes in Calvin and slightly more in the county.

Politics on the *local level* continues to be dominated by the Republican party. However, the pattern of vote-splitting in national and state as opposed to local races was detected during the period of initial field work—dramatically so in the 1964 election. It continues. Calvinites have shown that they are no longer in the hands of Abe Lincoln's party. They resent the 1964 Goldwater race and their traditional Republican moorings have been badly shaken. On county, state, and national levels they continue to favor the Democrats. The old automatic "delivery system" of Republican votes in Calvin Township has been seriously weakened, and, I suspect, permanently.

Table 24: Percentage of votes cast for the Republican candidate by area: 1966 through 1970

	1966			1968[a]	1970	
	Gov.	Sen.	Secy.	Pres.	Gov.	Sen.
Calvin	58	45	50	33	42	35
Research area	66	60	55	46	55	44
County	62	58	52	47	52	43

[a]Governor George C. Wallace of Alabama received a low of 6 per cent of the votes cast (in Calvin Township) to maximums of 22 and 27 per cent (in tier townships bordering northern Indiana). The four-township research area produced an 11 per cent vote for him, and the county 15 per cent. These figures, while substantial, are not out of range for the rural Midwest. The unavailability of data by race makes it impossible to discern whether these patterns are caused by white backlash in the areas bordering the research area, Negro population concentration within the research area, or a combination of both.

Education and race

The original analysis pointed to the significant role played by the local school system in three diverse ways. First, the "research community" was (and is) comprised of the four townships surrounding the village of Cassopolis. The district school system roughly paralleled this geographical area. Second, the boundaries of the school system also functioned as a symbolic delineation for patterns of activity such as shopping, church attendance, some employment, newspaper subscriptions, etc. Finally, the school was seen to serve an integrative function in the life of the community. For example, sports events were followed with intense interest and pride, thus fulfilling some of the "central locality" identity functions that a community center might have fulfilled had there been one. Based on a substantial input from the literature, I maintained that the existence of a functioning bi-racial school system could serve as a particularly sensitive indicator of community sentiments on racial issues. Latent animosities that could easily lie dormant in other institutional spheres of community life might well emerge and cluster about the school system, its activities, etc.

The restudy confirms the critical role that the school can assume in a small, rural community. However, this "confirmation" came to the surface in an unanticipated fashion, namely in the form of an increase in fears regarding racial friction. Moreover, I discovered what I had perceived to be a model interracial school system staggering as financial difficulties came close to causing fiscal strangulation. The incidents—and the rumors—of racial tension in the schools have an interest in themselves, as well as a considerably broader applicability for the nature of patterns of interracial contact in the community. For this reason, they will be mentioned here but will be discussed in greater detail in the following chapter, where I endeavor to present a more macroscopic and inclusive view.

Three issues will be reviewed and compared with the earlier work. These are: first, the system's racial composition, including its relationship to interracial interaction and participation in school activities; second, an examination of the system's facilities and services in relation to the community it serves, as contrasted with the financial and moral support provided; and third, the relationship between the boundaries of the system and any possible patterns of de facto racial segregation. In connection with this final topic, the function of both external boundaries, that is the limits of the entire system, and internal boundaries, namely the distribution of children within elementary schools, will be examined.

Twenty-eight per cent of the system's students are Negro. The proportion in the school system bears a relation both to the overall racial composition of the area (25 per cent) and to the racial composition by age. Thus, when one discovers a higher proportion of the population in the "non-productive" years (under 18 or over 65) within the Negro sector, one might expect a larger proportion in the schools.

Casual observation would detect no dramatic changes in the role Negroes play in the schools. However, a closer examination points to several alterations that do have implications for the way in which the larger community may view the school and its function. Negroes participate even more than previously in the highly visible extra-curricular events of the system—essentially sports. Each of the teams has substantial participation by Negroes—generally at least one-half of the members. In the case of the basketball team, an informant observed:

They have a basketball team that is almost all Negroes.
There are only about two whites on the team. The whites
have given up—they feel inferior. [NI]

In less obvious but more academic forms of participation, Negroes are under-represented. Most of the recent debate and forensic teams have been either white or predominantly so. In addition, all of the senior honor students in the past several years have been white. Informants familiar with the regional junior college observe that relatively few Negro students from the research community attend. The proportion going on to any form of higher education is not precisely known, but it is generally considered to be fairly low. This pattern of differing student behavior by race (sports for Negroes and academic pursuits for whites) bears a striking resemblance to national stereotypes regarding the types of activities in which each racial category excels.

On the social level, informants perceive the situation to be similar in character to that seen in the first study.

There comes a time when the kids just separate. [NI]

Another informant went a bit farther with the following comment:

Segregation? No! Oh hell, they date all the time but there are no really mixed parties. [NI]

Still another informant was even more explicit on the type, and source, of attitudes underlying what could be described as the community version of "kids will be kids, but later it's different." I would maintain that this informant describes the situation accurately in the following comment:

The kids had started an interracial sort of club [on the high school level]. Some white parents threatened the kids to stop it. It's the same deal as before, but it used to be covered up better. The kids are going to have to act as a bridge between the communities. [NI]

Whether or not the "kids" can build such a "bridge" is obviously dependent on the existence of a gap. If such can be found, and I suspect that it can, it then becomes a question of whether the "communities" wish a bridge to be built and would devote a sustained interest to the effort, and whether the "kids" intend to stay in the community. It is on these points that I feel deep suspicions. The reader will, I believe, sense some of these same suspicions when remembering the lack of local attractions for young adults and will again sense them in Chapter Twelve, where I report the manner in which a recent "racial incident" was "managed."

The second broad consideration concerns what the school system is in terms of its functions—what it does and what it attempts to do—and how its actions have been received by the community. On a descriptive level, the system serves approximately 2,000 students, almost all of whom live in the four-township research area. [34] The superintendent is described as "a sociologist and educational administrator."[35] He and other staff members with whom I have had contact seem particularly sensitive to the challenge and potential difficulties of administering or teaching in a bi-racial system. The system employs 85 teachers, six of whom are Negroes, and recently appointed a Negro assistant high school principal. The number of Negro teachers is lower than that found in the initial study: seven of 63.

Local administrators express their concerns regarding this situation, and I take them to be genuine. The competition for Negro professional personnel has become so acute that the local schools simply cannot compete with wealthier systems wishing to provide the contribution and perspectives which it is felt that Negro teachers can impart. An even more difficult and insidious form of competition comes from systems suddenly becoming aware that this is indeed an interracial society and rushing out to hire an "Exhibit A" Negro teacher to prove it at any price. "At any price" does not refer to differences of a few hundred dollars, but as much as $10,000. Despite local efforts to retain Negro staff, it is my prediction that the Cassopolis school system, while maintaining a high proportion of Negro students, will have little success in attracting more Negro professional personnel and may well lose some of those whom it now has. General salaries are low (1970 median was $7,850) and turnover is high. A recent survey observed:

There are 85 faculty members in the Cassopolis Public
Schools and of these 36 (42 per cent) are new to the school

[34]Small sections of the system extend into fragmentary segments of five additional townships, but the borders retain their essential contours.
[35]*Dowagiac Daily News,* June 18, 1969.

*system this year. Nineteen of the 85, representing 22
per cent, are beginning teachers.*[36]

The same report commented that "central administration offices
are in a timber-framed brick-veneered building built in 1918. . . .
The entire building is a firetrap and a hazard to the newer structure [the high school] that surrounds it."[37] Finally, Claspy observed that "the school system . . . may well be the best integrated in the United States despite the fact that the High School
building is so overcrowded."[38]

Overcrowding is only one manifestation of difficulty. It is obvious that the school system has fairly severe troubles. However,
it is difficult to seek out the culprit, assuming that one exists,
within the system. Rather, the level of support, essentially financial, that the system receives from the residents it serves is something less than abundant, resulting in, or compounding, many of
the problems briefly mentioned above.

I base my less than enthusiastic assessments on the belief that
the school system operates on the very edge of financial catas-
trophe. This fiscal strangulation comes about through a taxation
system that seems too outmoded to provide sufficient supporting
resources for a modern and well-equipped educational plant. Insufficient monies are granted to the schools to carry on their activities, even on a bare-bones basis. Thus, they must constantly
seek additional funds in special bond elections just to keep even
or, in some cases, to prevent further slippage. The schools, then,
seem to be the victims of fiscal conservativeness and "normal"
taxpayer resistance, as well as of a tight money market. They are,
therefore, placed in the nearly constant defensive position of going
to the voters to seek funds and simultaneously attempting to
justify these requests on the basis of past successes. In a moment
of populist sentiment, one might argue that this is exactly the way
public institutions *should* operate; they should outline the job,

[36]*A Survey of Cassopolis Public Schools*, p. 73.
[37]*Ibid.*, pp. 41-42.
[38]Claspy, p. 34.

seek the funds, and be held accountable if their performance is inadequate. However, after years of fiscal stringency, the schools do have problems and cannot rest upon a bed of well-earned merit points. Thus, segments of the community see the school literally in the beggar role and many school personnel see the community's behavior as indifferent, shortsighted, and even vindictive. This difficulty has in the past been economic, with no detectable racial overtones, but the future may well witness a joining of these two forces.

The school, *as a collective entity*, has responded with a variety of informational tactics that can be perceived as thinly disguised public relations activities. For example, the superintendent has begun to write a "What the school is doing"-type column in the local newspaper.[39] However, the community, *as a collective entity*, has consistently refused to vote necessary funds. In this case, "necessary" means sufficient funds to reopen existing schools and to take children off half-day sessions. The degree of seriousness of the situation can be seen in the following passage:

Cassopolis School District voters will go to the polls April 16 [1970], the fourth time in the past year, to vote on extra millage [increases in the rate of taxation] to operate the schools. The other attempts were defeated.

Presently there are 400 children on half-day sessions and other cuts have been made in the Cassopolis school program.

School officials say more is at stake this time—the Cassopolis schools are threatened with the loss of accreditation by the North Central Association. The district has been accredited since 1924. . . .

[39]For example, the March 19, 1970, *Cassopolis Vigilant* published a picture of the superintendent speaking to the Mothers Study Club. The caption under the picture reads "Superintendent of Cassopolis Schools . . . exploded a lot of myths, tensions and t'aint so's about the Cassopolis school system at the meeting of the Mothers Study Club last week." He went on to justify the system's teaching, spending of money, and so on.

*A lack of community support for the entire school system,
as evidenced by the failure of three millage elections, was
one of the deficiencies listed in the local system, according to
————. Others were deficiencies in the school library, teaching staff, and lack of an assistant high school principal, he
said.*

*———— told the board that once a school loses accreditation with the association it is almost impossible to regain
it, particularly with a small school.*[40]

The grimness of the situation is reflected further in the following commentary by members of the school board:

*... This year marks the first time in the memory of the
school district oldtimers that hundreds of children attend
classes on half-day schedules. As one board member
recalled: "Our schools here operated full time in the darkest
days of the depression. Things can't be that bad," he said.*

*"The half-day sessions will have their effect when the
students enter the job world and are not prepared properly
for their jobs."*[41]

Dark days, however, did not begin or end in 1970. In 1969 the
voters refused in *four* separate elections to vote the necessary
operational funds. In 1970, after it became obvious that half-day
sessions were unsatisfactory, support grew for some additional
monies. As a result, a request for additional funds in that year
finally passed, but only after one more defeat. The now-familiar
pattern was repeated in 1971. An election was held to seek funds
in June. It failed. Two more elections failed in August. Finally,
in the fourth election in three months, on August 28, 1971, the
schools received sufficient funds to open for the fall. In this last
election, the measure carried by 143 votes out of 2,040 cast.

[40]*Dowagiac Daily News*, February 27, 1970.
[41]*Cassopolis Vigilant*, January 29, 1970.

On an individual level, school personnel react to the situation in predictable ways: some take the community's response as a rejection of their efforts and become embittered; others "vote with their feet" and leave the community. Individuals in the community, after viewing the system that has failed to secure an adequate budget, realize that such features as half-day sessions, high teacher turnover, teachers lacking in experience, lack of student discipline, and the quality of education are not to their liking. However, they also express concern over high taxes. It should be no great surprise that a community is often unable to have both low tax rates and quality education simultaneously.

The preceding remarks did not maintain that race-related issues were of immediate relevance to the discussion. I do not believe that they were. Unfortunately, however, the system's racial composition brought points of contention into the educational process of the community. In most communities, this is seen to result in a pattern of "accidental" de facto segregation. This brings us to the last of the three concerns related to the school system.

The avoidance of such de facto segregation is quite difficult and the issues become complex in view of the ecological characteristics of this unique bi-racial community, which has identifiable racial concentrations yet wishes to remain desegregated.

The first formal indication that a series of racially related events had been taking place with respect to the educational structure was found in the following comment authored by Claspy three years after my initial field work:

The tourist will look in vain for a school which might serve as a community center. None exists and that is the way the community wanted it to be. Calvin was happy to escape the tensions that existed in Vandalia, Volinia, and Silver Creek [nearby villages] in connection with the consolidation of the schools. After consultation with educators, including a Community Development Team at Michigan State University, it was realized that such a school would be 70% colored and involve problems that the area had been able to escape for one hundred years. The elementary

students [from Calvin Township] are taken by bus to
the school in Cassopolis, to the elementary school in Van-
dalia, or across the Jefferson Township line to Brick School.[42]

After the publication of Claspy's materials, I spent several years attempting to document the existence of such a study. Neither contacts with local residents nor with related universities succeeded in securing a copy of the alleged report, or even recognition of its existence. Although the document was written in 1958, I finally managed to secure a copy in October of 1971. The report effectively substantiates Claspy's reference. The documentation rests on a 98-page report entitled "Cassopolis Area School Study" and two pages of attached commentary by a former school official. He states:

Since I was the Superintendent of the Cassopolis Public
Schools during the consolidation and construction of new
facilities, I can testify that his [Claspy's] statement, based on
recall, is correct in every detail.[43]

This is quite important because the possibility of consolidating rural school districts into the Cassopolis unified system, which involved the construction of additional facilities, gave the Board of Education a perfect opportunity to place in Calvin Township a school which would, for all intents and purposes, be a Negro one. The former superintendent's letter to me concurs with this assessment:

After considering the report and the logical attendance areas,
. . . the Board of Education decided to hold hearings in
each of the areas indicated in an effort to determine the de-
sires of citizens in the specific area.

[42]Claspy, p. 18.
[43]Letter from a former superintendent of the Cassopolis school system, October 6, 1971.

*Upon evaluating the response in Calvin Township, it seemed
clear that the predominance of Negroes and whites believed
it would be unwise to build an elementary school in the
center of the township since it would be predominantly
Negro in its student population. Further, they argued that
while the current School Board might equitably support the
school, future boards might not.*[44]

The end result was that Calvin Township "lost" a community
center, though the Board of Education and the community had succeeded, through bond issues, in preventing the creation of a de
facto segregated elementary school. The course of events that
prevented a segregated school was taken openly. In the main,
the effort was accomplished by expanding or constructing facilities on the edges of Calvin Township that would effectively distribute the Negro population in several elementary schools, and
by consolidating grades seven and eight and the high school into
central facilities in Cassopolis. It is important to note both the
actions taken and the awareness of the implications of these
actions for school racial composition.

These actions were consistent with those taken over the past century on a number of different issues relating to the undesirability
of creating a "rural Negro ghetto." The first edition cited a comment by my oldest respondent that "mixing up" of the races was
commonplace in the schools, referring to the period in the late
1800's. On a wider scope, Katzman refers to the historical influence that the concentration of Negroes in Calvin Township had
on state law:

*Although blacks were not enfranchised in Michigan until the
Fifteenth Amendment nullified the Michigan constitution's
ban on black suffrage in 1870, Negroes had been permitted to vote in school elections since 1855. That year
the legislature had passed a bill removing the ban on non-
white suffrage in school districts. The statute was passed in*

44Ibid.

response to the organization of schools in Calvin Township. *Since the township was predominantly black, exclusion of the Afro-Americans from voting and paying taxes would have effectively barred the organization of the rural schools. [Emphasis mine.]*[45]

Calvin Beale, Research Director of the U.S. Department of Agriculture, recently wrote:

The establishment of separate schools for the racial isolates was a major factor in maintaining group identity. Typically, the mixed bloods were denied enrollment in white schools and declined to attend Negro schools. In some States, separate public schools were provided for them. . . . So long as segregated public schools were permitted, and so long as small rural elementary schools were common and high school education was not often sought, the separate school pattern was feasible. But in recent decades, the school situation of the mixed-blood communities has changed rapidly, sometimes through law suits, sometimes without. Most of the mission schools have been closed or made a part of the public system. Most of the rural one and two room schools have been consolidated into larger integrated schools.[46]

Solely on the basis of the data already presented, one might be led to assume that little besides a spirit of brotherly goodwill has been operating in all historical and contemporary events. However, a series of actions came into full public view following a number of local court actions in the late 1960's. It then became obvious to many local informants that the *lack* of local segregation was of such significant interest to a small group of *white* parents that they were motivated to transport *their own* children by bus

[45]Katzman, p. 31.
[46]Calvin L. Beale, "An Overview of the Phenomenon of Mixed Racial Isolates in the United States," prepared for presentation at the annual meetings of the Southern Anthropology Society, Athens, Georgia, April 8, 1970.

to a less integrated system in contiguous portions of northern Indiana.

Prior to this incident, the village of Vandalia, predominantly Negro, was having increasing fiscal problems in the maintenance of its school system. Finally, in late 1964, village residents voted to annex their system to the Cassopolis school district. However, Claspy introduces a sobering note when he reports:

Vandalia finally voted October 17, 1964 to join the Casso-
polis School District, but the famous Bonine Elk Farm was de-
tached and permitted to become part of the wealthy
Geneva district, which includes the beautiful Diamond Lake
area consisting of lovely summer homes and few children.
This biggest lake in the county is a good example of how
all-white areas have survived in this part of Michigan.
The fact that there is almost no commercial activity in con-
nection with this resort has made it easier to avoid trouble,
and both races have made efforts to avoid offending
the other.[47]

A knowledgeable Negro informant added to my understanding of these events when he commented:

The Geneva School served Diamond Lake and the area to the
North [between Vandalia and Cassopolis]. Parents in
Geneva were able to bus their students to Penn Township in
Indiana. The Court in 1968 ruled that they had to affiliate
with a K-12 nearby [a district offering instruction from
kindergarten through twelfth grade—namely, Cassopolis].
[NI]

As a result of this decision, students in the Geneva district could no longer take the daily round-trip bus ride of more than 50 miles. Their parents were "instructed" to send them to the school system operating almost in their own front yards. The original rationale

[47]Claspy, p. 28.

for sending students such long distances to avoid local schools must certainly interest the reader by this time. A variety of informants have some sage but not always kind observations to make on the subject.

Lots of those people over there [in the Geneva school area] are Quakers and bigots. Those two can come together, you know. [WI]

I wouldn't say that any prejudice was involved. It was simply that the school in Indiana had a better class of people. [WI]

They didn't want their kids in the Cassopolis schools because there were too many Negroes in the schools. [NI]

Every time some of the people around here get the chance, they vote down millage. This is a simple retaliation vote. There are too many Negroes in the schools. [NI]

It should be remembered that the persistent refusal to pass additional taxes for school support came *after* the white children who were bused out of the district were returned by court order. If whites had removed their children from the local district and then refused to provide sufficient support, one could argue a lack of interest based at least in part on a backlash reaction to Negroes. However, parents of either race who refuse to educate their children adequately are frustrating their own goals. Any number of informants mentioned that their children have grown up, married, and migrated. Consequently these informants have little or no personal interest in the system. Many of them live on fixed incomes. The term "taxpayer revolt" would be too dramatic a term for this phenomenon because one does not find an overburdened community finally saying that taxes are oppressive and that enough is enough. Rather, one finds poor people becoming poorer due to inflation and trying to conserve almost regardless of the consequences.

Once again, we are presented with renditions of facts and events which individuals or groups of individuals have linked to motives or sets of attitudes. In a study such as this one, it is particularly important to distinguish between the interpretations of individuals and collective or community actions. These are on two quite different "levels." The analysis has presented both as having importance.

The compound influence of residence: an overview

When dealing with a unique bi-racial settlement, conceptual frameworks oriented to more normal patterns of interracial interaction are not necessarily appropriate to, or capable of encompassing, local reality. This was certainly observed in the first edition, where it was pointed out that such labels as "Uncle Tom" did not present a close fit with the available data. This same phenomenon can be observed in each social institution examined in the second edition.

I urge the reader to avoid "quick and tidy" categorizations or assessments of cause-and-effect relationships. I contend that such terms as "racism," "discrimination," and "ghetto" must be used with the utmost care in a uniquely derived situation. For example, one can easily find evidence to suggest that "segregation" exists. The first edition repeatedly noted such evidence. However, it does not logically follow that segregation per se, especially segregation generated in the main by rural land purchase patterns begun over a century ago, can be taken as conclusive evidence of "discrimination" or "racism." The fact that Calvin Township and the Negro-related term "Calvinite" represents, respectively, a "community" or "neighborhood" and a resident is clear and has important sociological ramifications. In a somewhat different context, I commented:

Neighborhood, initially an areal referent but increasingly a nameable status "cue," functions as one of the most pervasive, visible, and scarce aspects of symbolic status. The neighborhood, once established, named, and symbolized, can

perpetuate a status level and have status functions for
later occupants. It should be noted, in this context, that the
upwardly mobile individual, rather than being permanently
ensconced at his hearth, will often change neighborhoods
rather than alter his house.[48]

I clearly cannot claim to be the originator of such notions. For
example, Ross, looking at communities in terms of survey research
techniques, comments that his study

. . . supports the local community conception of the city by
demonstrating that named units with "natural" boundaries
are recognized by residents of an urban area. It further
suggests that named areas have a status-ascriptive
function.[49]

In recent years the word "neighborhood" as an adjective has become emotionally charged, especially when combined with the
noun "school" or the verb "control," to the extent that one finds
a form of mental shorthand taking place (segregation in the first
case and black power in the second). One again becomes imbued
with a sense of caution in attempting to address the question of
whether or not the Negro settlement centered in Calvin Township
represents a ghetto with walls held up by external (white) forces
of discrimination and fear. Some say yes, others no. *Generally,*
I concur with the latter, although at least one other recent investigation of the community disagrees. Wheeler and Brunn term the
Negro settlement in Calvin Township an "agricultural ghetto." In a
footnote elaborating on the meaning of this term, they state:

The term agricultural ghetto suggests itself because of the
spatial similarities of the Negro-owned land to residential
ghettos in cities. We are using the word ghetto to denote

[48]George K. Hesslink, "The Function of Neighborhood in Ecological Stratification," *Sociology and Social Research*, 54 (July 1970), 442.
[49]H. Laurence Ross, "The Local Community: A Survey Approach," *American
Sociological Review*, 27 (February 1962), 318.

residential segregation; that is, spatial concentration
that has been fostered in large part by discriminatory
attitudes.[50]

Later in the article the authors repeat their position:

The fundamental similarities relate to spatial structure and
change. The processes of residential filtering, invasion, and
succession are applicable to the expansion of the agricultural ghetto. However, filtering, where a few Negro families locate within a white area, leading to a new influx
of Negroes (invasion) and a subsequent take over (succession) has been rather limited in Cass County until recently.
Even today the ghetto is largely contained by a ring of
white ownership, and the filtering process is taking place in
areas outside Calvin Township. The lack of white ownership within the ghetto, especially at present, reflects
white aversion to, and Negro preference for, Negro neighbors. Even though physical distance is different in the rural
and urban residential environments, social distance appears
to be similar. [Emphasis mine].[51]

Perhaps the clearest statement of their ghetto hypothesis is reflected in the following comment:

Discrimination still plays a part in explaining recent changes
in ownership. Changes from white to Negro have taken
place primarily in areas either encircled by land already in
Negro ownership or adjacent to it. Parts of the township
continue to remain white, especially in the northwest,
which has been white owned from the earliest period.
Rumors persist that Negro farmers are unable to obtain
land, even when the offer is more than the normal market
value. Other complaints of discrimination concern
financing for land, farm buildings, and equipment.[52]

[50]Wheeler and Brunn, Geographical Review (1969), 318.
[51]Ibid., p. 329.
[52]Ibid., p. 326.

What does not seem to be given extensive consideration is the fact that resident Negroes are not expanding their agricultural holdings because increasingly they are not in the capitalized farming business. *Rural non-farm* Negroes, as defined by the census, are not apt to "push" the ghetto walls (if they indeed exist) aggressively in order to purchase more land, even if they had the resources. The *essence* of Calvin Township is a century of tradition and meaningfulness. Figure 8, reproduced from Wheeler and Brunn's work, clearly documents the historical continuity of land ownership over the last century. Also, capitalized white farmers are not aggressively attempting to purchase acreage in the center of Calvin Township because the land is not highly productive and is clearly not adjacent to their presently existing plots. Finally, the area has not attracted new independent Negro farmers in any substantial numbers. In fact, the only Negro "outsiders" to purchase major plots of land in the township recently have been the Black Muslims. They have bought land from *Negroes in* the township, from *Negroes* in *adjacent* townships, from whites on the *fringes* of the settlement and, reportedly, from whites in adjacent townships. Perhaps Wheeler and Brunn inadvertently touched the core of the issue when they wrote:

Discrimination in the sale of land was of a subtle kind; most
of the Negroes, from "old families," were accepted by the
whites and had little outward desire to purchase land
in white areas. Lacking both aggressive attempts by Negroes
to purchase such property and vocal racism among the
whites, the mixed community lived in relative tranquillity.
[Emphasis mine.][53]

Clearly the concept of de jure (legally based and enforced) segregation is totally inapplicable. Additionally, given the historical origins and relatively slow nature of residential change, one is tempted to ask whether de facto segregation as it is currently conceived is relevant either. "De facto" means "in fact" and

[53]*Ibid.*, p. 325.

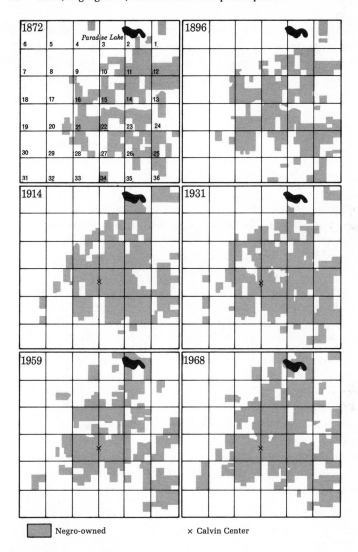

Figure 8: Changing Negro land ownership:
Calvin Township

implies that "it just happened." Nearly any adult American knows that a large proportion of de facto segregation didn't "just happen," but that it is the predictable outgrowth of whites fleeing the problems of the central city, one of the major "problems" being blacks per se. Even though the research area has concentrations of Negroes and whites, and Chapter Nine perceived them as forming the basis of overlapping but distinct patterns of interaction, is the symbolism of an impoverished ghetto (city) ringed by affluent whites (suburbs) an accurate reflection of reality? I think not.

The recent school survey comments:

A number of ethnic or social concentrations are represented in the school district. The Diamond Lake area is a recreational and vacation center; consequently, the land-owning residents tend to share a common philosophy on school issues. The Calvin Center-Paradise area was settled by long-time black residents who also share a common history and concerns. The town of Penn was a Friends settlement, with its own heritage and social interests. Such social and ethnic concentrations must be considered in school planning.

In spite of the diversity of population centers, a sound community spirit seems to allow for sensible dialogue on community issues. The informal communication and power structures appear to function well. Community events are well attended and the community recreation program sponsored by the schools seems to be well used, although there seems to be some division along racial lines. People seem to know their neighbors and desire mutual understanding between families. . . .

A basic value structure seems to have been propagated and maintained through the church as well as through the family and the school. The churches are historically committed to integration of the races. Churches frequently exchange pastors, choirs or services across racial and denominational lines. While one cannot isolate a basic community moral standard or theological belief, there does

260

seem to be a pervasive religious under-pinning upon which many personal judgments are made. A rural-type honesty and respect for others is reflected in community cooperation.[54]

The major instance of "segregation" is found in the following brief passage:

The American Legion has posts in both Calvin Center and Cassopolis, and one of the few instances of racial segregation reported to the survey team was in connection with these clubs. Apparently by mutual consent, blacks attend the former and whites the latter. There is a Yacht Club at Diamond Lake, although most members are not year-round residents.[55]

The message is clear: there may well be prejudice between segments of the community (as one would, incidentally, find in an all-white community) and individual discriminatory acts, but one cannot leap from these circumstances to the assertion that there is institutionalized racism supported by the community as a collectivity or to the automatic equating of population concentration with discrimination in this community. To attempt to do so reminds one of the old adage about a beautiful theory being murdered by a brutal gang of facts.

[54]A Survey of Cassopolis Public Schools, pp. 5-6.
[55]Ibid., p. 10.

twelve:

Race and

community status:

an altering

equation

"The traditional checkmate"

Traditionally, the basic sources of community status for the Calvinite Negro were essentially three-fold: stability of residence, predictability of behavior, and an assumable political alliance. These were delineated in Chapter Eight and will be serially re-examined in the light of developments during the past five years.

Stability

The Calvinite community can clearly be viewed as a stable and integral part of the total community. A strong indication of this is that status is conferred not on the basis of *objective* attributes such as income, occupation, or education, but rather on *reputational* attributes—ones which are clearly localistic. Reputational status obviously could be assumed to be a "catch-all" phrase for land tenure, Republican conservatism, and, in general, abiding by "local understandings." Patterns of behavior that generate rewards are predominantly "localistic" rather than "cosmopolitan."[1] Stability of residence can be seen in the fact that individuals tend to be known as "the son of" rather than "the husband of." Those occupational roles that might generally be associated with cosmopolitan patterns—for example, professional ones—are not generally filled by "newcomers," but by "hometown boys coming back." In short, geographical mobility, per se, is taken as indicative of a lowered commitment to the community, hence, a lowered level of predictability. Thus, in this situation one finds an unusual pattern in which geographical mobility and social mobility or prestige are *inversely* related.

A number of studies, drawing on quite diverse sources of data, have provided confirmatory evidence of the general importance of the 'old-timer – newcomer" distinction. Certainly Vidich and Bensman's very important work suggests this when they observe that "the old families serve to emphasize the symbols of continuity and the degree of 'Americanization' of the town," or when they state that the existence of an old aristocracy "confers a sense of continuity to a nonexpanding town which is as a whole as committed to the past as it is to the present and the future."[2] Barber also observes that

> *... this folk distinction, which is nonetheless sociologically*
> *significant, between "oldtimers" and "newcomers" also*
> *turns up in survey research studies of social stratification*
> *when the respondents are freely allowed to suggest their*

---

[1]The term "localistic" is drawn from Robert K. Merton's *Social Theory and Social Structure* (New York: The Free Press, 1957), primarily Chapter 10, "Patterns of Influence: Local and Cosmopolitan Influentials." It is used to designate the type of status which is gained from an increasingly wide network of community relationships rather than from objective criteria of status, such as advanced training, that a migrant "cosmopolitan" might bring into the community.

[2]Arthur J. Vidich and Joseph Bensman, *Small Town in Mass Society: Class, Power and Religion in a Rural Community* (Princeton: Princeton University Press, 1958), p. 67.

*own views in response to the question "What different
kinds of people would you say live around here?"*[3]

In the present study, the reverence for the status quo must not
be underestimated. Welch, a local author, comments:

*The life-style of the residents of Cass County has remained
essentially the same over the past century and a half. This,
despite remarkable strides in technology, especially in
areas of communication and transportation. The landlocked
nature of the County which beleaguered the early settlers
had become, in effect, the saving grace of an area where
progress keeps pace with the nation, but not at the expense
of personal turmoil.*[4]

It is perhaps difficult to determine whether this "traditional" area
has in fact had the "best of both worlds"—namely change with no
change and secure tradition with revered progress. The preceding
chapter would certainly subject the logic and empirical under-
pinnings of this optimistic perception to some strong questions
and careful scrutiny.

Predictability

It has been stressed that stability is valued, but not only for its
own sake. Stability leads to and supports predictability, the second "prop" of the "traditional checkmate." Patterns of interaction
and expectations between Calvinites and tenure whites were predictable. They both had been "playing the game" and "using the
same rules" for some time. It can, of course, be argued that this
framework labels Calvinites' behavior as reflexive or adaptive in
nature and thus predictable by demands placed on the relation-

[3]Bernard Barber, *Social Stratification* (New York: Harcourt, Brace & Co.,
1957), p. 194.
[4]Welch, p. 222.

ship. This is essentially true, *as is the reverse.* That is, whites' behavior can be predicted from Calvinites' behavior. Such predictions would be expected to flow, *by definition,* from any enduring,
interactive relationship. In this case, should the "rules" be violated, the entire localistic edifice could collapse. Should this
eventuality come to pass, Calvinites would have far more to lose
simply because the "subcultural tradition" has served to shield
them from the worst aspects of what it means to be Negro in
American society.

One can, of course, view the relationship between whites and
Calvinites as nothing more than the instrumental interaction of
white paternalism and Uncle Tomism. I reject this stance because
it tends to extract certain traits out of an interaction set and to
remove the others from further consideration. Ideological labels
function as filters, blinding one to nuances and hindering objective
analysis. One need only be reminded of the function of name calling during the grade school recess. It did not "win" the argument
but *did* preclude any further discussion.

The term "white paternalism" is an ideologically based label that
can be, and often is, misapplied to nearly any behavior in which
whites may engage short of sullen noncompliance with inadequately enforced laws. The issue of white paternalism is not to be
decided on the basis of whether or not whites and Calvinites derive benefits from interacting with one another. Of course they do.
The essential questions should be: are the Calvinites and whites
able to interact on an equal footing with a mutual recognition of
human dignity?; and do both derive "profits" from the relationship? The answer to each question is a conditional "yes." I say
"conditional" because one must assess the degree to which acceptance of Calvinites would predict acceptance of non-local
Negroes. The data clearly suggest that Calvinites are accepted not
as racial objects but as community residents in spite of their racial
identification. This is further reflected in attitudes toward migrant
Negroes which tend to be far from gracious.

The first edition vacillated on the way to conceptualize the interactive relationships between whites and Calvinites. I recognized
this "intellectual tug of war," and I still do. I have no intention of

drawing a set of firm conclusions because my field research and observations do not uncover definitive data which would lead one to such conclusions. Furthermore, there is no academically sound reason to "tidy up" issues based on inconsistent data. As Professor Street observes in the Foreword, "The ordinarily amicable relations between them carried an undertone that the Negroes were present on their good behavior—at the sufferance of the whites." Of course! But it is exceedingly difficult to define induced "good behavior" in a century-old, bi-racial community that rewards acquiescence to the lessons of the past and punishes nonconformity, regardless of the racial identity of the nonconformist. One must recall that white migrants, especially those from the South, are present in the community on *their* good behavior. As long as they don't "rock the boat," white newcomers are tolerated.

The reciprocal half of the white paternalism interaction set is normally labeled "Uncle Tomism." Are Calvinites Uncle Toms? That, again, obviously depends upon how broadly one wishes to apply the term. If by the label one means that Calvinites "shuffle and grin" for crumbs off the table—definitely not! However, if one means that Calvinites perceive that it is in their best interests to cooperate with the dominant community ethos—the ethos that they joined in formulating and the ethos to which whites subscribe —most definitely yes.

What is happening here is that the "labeling process" either obfuscates or obliterates distinctions that must be kept sharply separated. The term "Uncle Toming it" is usually used to refer to a pattern of *behavior—of action*. One should ask if the *essence* of "Tomism" is *not* an action pattern at all, but rather a combination of motivational or attitudinal patterns. The "true" Tom first sold his body, then sold his dignity, and, more critically, finally came to believe in his own act. That is, Tom did not stand up to "the man" because playing the role of the inferior being began to function as an internal behavioral control. Tom *did not* stand up because Tom *could not* stand up. Compare this to the "overseer" or "broker" role. The external pattern of behavior was the same, or at least similar. The overseer did not stand up either—but why? He could not—but for a different set of reasons. It was not wise, it was not smart, it was not politic. In short, he would jeopardize the privilege of position. Both Tom and overseer played the game on the surface, but Tom accepted the rules as legitimate ascriptions of status. The overseer or broker, on the other hand, accepted the rules as procedural mechanisms to gain advantage. In contemporary terms, who wins this game? Tom is beaten literally and figuratively. The broker is "playing the man" and may or may not be beaten depending on the shrewdness of his act, the demands for his services, and so on.

This is far more than a game of words. The sociological concepts of dominant-minority relations *definitionally* indicate a differential access to power—to prestige. They also describe and define the ground rules for deferential behavior. Do Calvinites defer to whites? Yes. Does this "guarantee" that the interaction will generate conditions of mutual and equitable benefit? No! This is so, if for no other reason than that Calvinites and whites do not come to the "bargaining table" with equal numbers of chips, with equal arrays of options. If and when all the "chips are played," whites are seen as whites, and Calvinites are seen as Negroes. This fact of life has not escaped the attention of any segment in the community. These are not gracious conditions—but the contemporary state of American race relations is not based on tea-and-biscuits niceties. That one wishes that this were not so does not change the issue. One is not talking about integration and soft music. We are, I assume, opting for a situation in which, at some level in the social structure, whites and blacks can find a relationship other than conflict to be mutually advantageous. This has occurred in the research community.

One finds a broad-based agreement which functions to retard the influx and potentially disruptive influence of newcomers. Racial dignity per se, or even racial identity, is secondary. In a community of individuals, both white and Negro, who formally and publicly defend the notion of racial equality, in a community that is localist and traditional, and in a community which is small and informal, one would expect exactly this type of "operating agreements." Again one returns not to Brotherhood Week admonitions to love one's neighbor, or to integration, but to the concept of a just and honorable, bi-racial stability.

Political alliances

The preceding discussion should not imply that Calvinites are basking, motionless, in well-earned accolades of community respect. As the following analysis indicates, Calvinites' political power is slipping because one of their traditional functions has been disrupted—namely, the spokesman role. They have not, however, become "niggers." This must be noted very carefully.

Political alliances have been strained primarily because the "operating agreements" no longer produce equal degrees of social profits to both constituencies. Calvinites had come to assume a "power broker" role between local whites and Negro newcomers. As elaborated in Chapter Eight, one aspect of this role involved inadvertent or deliberate ostracization of the Negro newcomer. Consequently, many whites, soothed into the belief that race relations were perfect, came to see "militancy" as a bankrupt social policy characteristic of urban centers and clearly unlikely to gain any foothold in this historically Quaker-influenced, Underground Railroad community. In their pacific attitudes and actions, it is clear that Calvinites played a role similar to that played by the broker or overseer in the traditional South. They had a communication service to offer and there was a price ("subcultural acceptance") attached. There was also a risk: filtering reality for whites (and themselves).

During the original study, the *perceived local* militants of the day were an unlikely lot to harbor radical values, namely retired postal workers, marginal farmers, industrial workers fleeing Chicago's decaying South and West Side ghettos, people belonging to the NAACP, etc. As suggested then, the definition of what constituted a "militant" in Cass County was not quite what would be considered a proper definition elsewhere. One must keep in mind that many of the respondents, both Negro and white, were seeing such organizations as the NAACP as a vague and blurred catch-all category for militancy, at the same time that the NAACP was being faulted nationally for its legalistic, non-militant, and conciliatory stances on a variety of issues. Organizations such as the Black Muslims (and later the Black Panthers) simply could not be contemplated even at a distance, to say nothing of next door.

Black Muslims "discovered"

Beginning in 1968, individuals and a corporation reputedly linked with Black Muslim interests began making land purchases in Cass County—primarily in Calvin Township. One can easily speculate as to why Cass County was selected as a site for these purchases: the historical existence of Negro farmers, reasonable soil productivity, proximity to Chicago and Detroit, and the fact that the Muslims already owned "large farms in Michigan."[5] Additionally, it has been known for some time that the Muslims have sought agricultural enterprises. For example, Black Muslim publications have shown consistent interest in rural land purchases.[6] Prior to recent Muslim activity, Calvin Beale of the United States Department of Agriculture commented:

Today the largest number of Negro farmers in the North and West is in Michigan. The largest settlement is in Cass and Berrien Counties, Michigan, not far from South Bend, Indiana. This is perhaps the most persistent of the

---

[5]C. Eric Lincoln, *The Black Muslims in America* (Boston: Beacon Press, 1961), p. 93.

[6]See, for example, *Muhammad Speaks*, December 16, 1966, which contains the following advertisement: "TEMPLE OF ISLAM WANTS large farm and land, preferred location South or Southwest. We will buy fully equipped 1,000 to 10,000 acres and will lease up to 100,000 (small plots not wanted). Payment in cash or ½ down in cash." Or see *Muhammad Speaks*, May 24, 1968, which contains a large notice stating: "WANTED FARMERS AND FARM WORKERS EXPERIENCED IN: corn, wheat, rye, vegetables, fruits, milk cows and general dairy knowledge, poultry raising." The January 16, 1972, issue of the *Los Angeles Times* (p. 1) contains an article entitled "Internal Turmoil Mars Black Muslim Facade." This article mentions Muslim acquisitions of farm land in Michigan (as well as a cannery).

Northern areas developed by free Negroes in the generation
before the Civil War. After a period of some decline as a
commercial farming area, it has begun to grow again as a
part-time farming and residential area.[7]

These land purchases have a variety of relationships to the Black
Muslim organization, both as an entity and in terms of individuals
identified with it. These relationships vary, but tend to cluster into
three categories: Elijah Muhammad and his family; a land development corporation; and local residents consistently identified as
members of the Black Muslim organization or pursuing actions
suggesting sympathy with its goals.

An early purchaser was Elijah Muhammad, the recognized leader of the Black Muslims. As C. Eric Lincoln observes:

Muhammad is known not only as "Messenger" and
"Prophet" but also as "Spiritual Head of the Muslims in the
West," "Divine Leader" and "The Reformer." His minis-
ters most often refer to him as "The Honorable Elijah
Muhammad" or as "The Messenger of Allah to the Lost-
Found Nation of Islam in the Wilderness of North
America."[8]

To my knowledge, he has made only one direct purchase. This
parcel of about 100 acres is registered as belonging to "Elijah
Muhammad Sr., and Sons."[9]

Second, far more substantial holdings have been acquired by
a firm named the Progressive Land Corporation.[10] Between February and April of 1968, this corporation acquired at least four

[7]Beale in Davis, p. 174.

[8]Lincoln, p. 183.

[9]Official records of Cass County, Michigan. (Section 9, Tract 7, Range 14.)

[10]Many of the comments in this section can also be substantiated by an excellent piece of journalistic "detective" work by Arthur Sills, a staff writer
for the *Kalamazoo Gazette*. He wrote "Black Muslims Linked to Cass Land,"
which was published in that paper on June 2, 1968, and was later reprinted
in a number of other regional papers.

plots of land totaling approximately 550 acres, or nearly a square mile. The amount paid for this acreage was $155,000.[11] Thus the average price per acre was just under $300—certainly not an excessive amount. A number of sources reveal that the Progressive Land Corporation is a Chicago-based firm which filed papers of incorporation in 1963 with the secretary of state of Illinois.[12] In these papers, Raymond Sharrieff is identified as the corporate president. C. Eric Lincoln states that Raymond Sharrieff has had a long, intimate, and powerful role within the Black Muslim organization. Lincoln comments:

Apart from Muhammad, no one has an inherent claim in any
office. Malcolm serves as Muhammad's aide at the Mes-
senger's pleasure; by the same token, Muhammad could
summarily banish him to outer darkness. Presumably the
same is true of Raymond Sharrieff, who is Muhammad's
son-in-law and the Supreme Captain of the secret paramili-
tary organization, the Fruit of Islam [FOI]. Sharrieff has
long been a Muslim, but he is hardly known outside of
the organization. Even the Muslims know little about him
expect that he is Muhammad's chief aide in managing
the sect's commercial enterprises and overseeing the FOI.
Some police authorities suggest that Sharrieff also
collects tithes from delinquent members and, through a
hand-picked corps of lieutenants, effectively silences any
defectors from the movement who may wish to cooperate
with the police in exposing its secrets. The Muslims say
only that Sharrieff "sees that the wishes of the Messenger
are carried out." [Emphasis mine.][13]

Lincoln also speculates that "The two leading contenders [then

[11]Official records of Cass County, Michigan. (Sections 10 and 15, Tract 7, Range 14; Section 14, Tract 7, Range 14; Sections 23, 26, 35, and so on.)
[12]See, for example, Sills in *Kalamazoo Gazette*, June 2, 1968.
[13]Lincoln, pp. 192-193.

seen as successors to Muhammad] would logically be Malcolm X
and Raymond Sharrieff."[14]

The third relationship between the Muslims and Cass County involves at least one local resident, who has been playing a very
active role in the real estate market. Numerous informants, realiz-
ing the amount of money necessary for these sizable land purchases, attribute a direct relationship. A regional newspaper reported the following concerning this individual:

Contacted by The Truth *about the land buying, [the local
resident] said he intended to farm his newly-acquired
property. Asked about the possibility that the Black Muslims were behind the activity, [he] said he could not say and
that he would give out more information in about six
weeks or sooner if certain things developed. [He] declined
to answer if he is a member of the Muslim organization.*[15]

Other recent and varied sources reveal additional evidence. First,
the man in question was featured as a "Black Muslim leader"
during a televised broadcast of "Black Journal."[16] Second, I interviewed him in an informant-type relationship during the restudy
field work at his farm in Calvin Township on August 19, 1970.
There ensued an enlightening discussion, the contents of which
I agreed to regard as confidential. However, the decorations in the
home could be observed by any visitor. I sat in his living room
under a picture of Elijah Muhammad, amid piles of *Muhammad*

[14]*Ibid.,* p. 195. As recently as January 16, 1972, the *Los Angeles Times* reported the following relevant information on the leadership of the Muslim
organization: "Just under him [Elijah Muhammad] are members of his immediate family—five of his six sons, two daughters and son-in-law Raymond
Sharrieff, 52, considered to be the most powerful. He is supreme captain of
the karate trained Fruit of Islam, the Muslim security force."

[15]*The Truth* (Elkhart, Indiana), March 29, 1968.

[16]National Educational Television Network. Broadcast April 27, 1970, on
KCET, Channel 28, Community Television of Southern California, Los
Angeles.

Speaks, and next to a carpet with the inscription *AS SALAAM ALAIKIM.*[17]

Finally, nearly all other informants identified this man as a "Muslim leader" and viewed his actions with this ascription in mind. The *exact* nature of his relationship to the Black Muslim hierarchy is not extremely significant. What *is* important is that Muslim interests have arrived—both in actuality and, more importantly, symbolically. There is, indeed, a difference between these two types of "arrival." The fact that the Black Muslims have made substantial investments in land, buildings, and equipment is overshadowed by their *potential* symbolic role in the race-related "tug of war" for local legitimation and respectability now and power in the future.

The initial study in no way predicted the entrance of Black Muslim interests. I must admit my surprise. However, to say that the several racial sectors of the community were surprised would be a drastic understatement. Definitions of reality, following either actual or perceived sudden social change, proceeded in a fairly predictable fashion. First, there is an initial panic-type reaction characterized by the circulation of rumors, uncertainties, exaggerations, and fears. Second, a period of "normalization" follows in which less threatening alternative explanations are sought and expounded. Finally, an emotional diffusion and accommodation restores order and tranquillity. Informants and secondary sources confirmed this sequence of community reactions to Black Muslim acquisitions. A Muslim informant observed:

Whites reacted in fear originally. Now there is more respect.
But the old-timers don't care for our presence. If they
say they were calm from the beginning they are lying to
you. [NI]

I inquired of this informant: "Do the whites around here know what Black Muslims are?" After I suggested that I thought more

[17]The traditional Arabic Muslim greeting, meaning "Peace be unto you."

was involved than raising chickens or corn—such as the building
of black identity—he replied:

*Very few whites knew originally what it meant but they are
learning more and more what it means. Initially they
just thought it was some strange sort of religion.*

Other Negro informants commented:

*They [whites] seem to have gotten used to them
[Black Muslims] but it took a while. [NI]*

They have had to learn to respect them. [NI]

White informants were quite a bit more graphic in their accounts:

*They threw the white community into a state of shock.
They were alarmed. These blacks couldn't care less about
the white community. They came here to make a living.
They contribute nothing to the community and take nothing.
Some of the whites around here read about the radical one
—Malcolm, I think it was. The rest are not like that. [WI]*

Another commented:

*There was a lot of resistance originally from other blacks.
They found out that they were good people—just because their religion is a bit different is no reason to discriminate. Among whites there is no resistance as long as
they stay where they are. Their morals are better than
ours are. [WI]*

Arthur Sills commented in the *Kalamazoo Gazette:*

*The string of purchases by Progressive [Land Corporation]
and ——— has started speculation that is making virtually
every resident a retailer in rumor.*

*These rumors, hawked from the county courthouse and the
neighborhood bar, range from a reputed $1-million offer
for a 1,200 acre farm to plans that would turn the
countryside into a training ground for a black militia.*

"I don't know what people are getting upset about," ———
*says. "A white man could buy a lot more property than
that and nobody would pay a bit of attention."* [18]

The Truth reported:

*The purchase of land in Cass County by a Chicago developer
has touched off speculation that the Black Muslims are
trying to set up a black community or training center in
Calvin Township.*

*———— , Calvin Township supervisor, a Negro, said he is
looking into reports that the Black Muslims are associated
with the land buying.* ——— *said, however, that he knows of
only three Muslims in the area and that he has been
unable to verify the reports.* [19]

After the reactions were normalized, the initially tense situation
was diffused through attitudes consistent with community value
orientations. Namely: 1) the Muslims are good capitalistic farmers; 2) the Muslims have traditional and conservative morals; and
3) the Muslims could be expected to "mind their own business"
—they keep to themselves.

Each of these three perceptions is a perfectly accurate assessment of the situation in Cass County. First, the holdings identified
as being Muslim-related are a modern agricultural establishment
that appears to be impeccably managed. C. Eric Lincoln observed
in 1961:

[18]*Kalamazoo Gazette*, June 2, 1968.
[19]*The Truth* (Elkhart, Indiana), March 29, 1968.

The Muslims themselves maintain a number of small businesses and other enterprises. In Chicago they operate department stores, groceries, bakeries, restaurants and various kinds of service establishments. They own large farms in Michigan and near Atlanta. . . . All are run with efficiency and aplomb.[20]

Lincoln's earlier observations are quite consistent with a number of recent scholarly analyses of the surprising similarity between recently espoused Muslim economic values and traditional concepts normally associated with Max Weber's notions of the Protestant Ethic and economically related asceticism. For example, Laue suggests "viewing the Muslims in Weberian terms as a twentieth-century case of this worldly activism motivated by religiously sanctioned asceticism."[21] Tyler, writing in Current, concurs with this position:

In contemporary American society, the Black Muslims constitute one of the most vigorous and obvious dissents by a minority religion. And as the earlier asceticism was strongly appealing to the merchant, so is this contemporary asceticism attractive to a certain Negro element. . . .

By such a definition the religious ethic of the Black Muslims does indeed qualify as the manifestation of asceticism. The Black Muslim ethic both in its demands upon its adherents and in its practical effect upon their lives ironically parallels Weber's "Protestant ethic," which so greatly facilitated the economic inequality that the Muslims are retaliating against.[22]

[20]Lincoln, p. 93.

[21]James H. Laue, "A Contemporary Revitalization Movement in American Race Relations: The Black Muslims," Social Forces, 42 (1964), 315. In these observations, Laue recognizes the related research of A. F. Wallace, "Revitalization Movements," American Anthropologist, 58 (April 1956).

[22]Lawrence L. Tyler, "Black Nationalism in the U.S.," Current (September 1966), 35-36.

Finally, Howard and a number of other sociologists have become interested in what is perceived to be a bifurcation of the Muslim membership. The terms used in various studies vary but they can be distilled down to the militant versus the Protestant ascetic.[23] It is the latter type that has been drawn to Cass County and it is partially this Weberian work ethic which provides grounds for the détente, mainly with white residents of the community. (Negro residents do not evidence much enthusiasm for yet another "black" segment to—potentially—"complicate local understandings.")

The second perception regarding Muslim behavior centered on the issue of traditional morals and is clearly related to the preceding observations. One should recall that the stereotypical image of the Negro newcomer included such comments as "chip on the shoulder," "rowdy," "disorderly transients," "touchy," "mouthy and crude." In the restudy, no informant was willing to apply such epithets to the Muslims. Their behavior had been sufficiently observed for informants to be satisfied that, in addition to subscribing to capitalistic values, the Muslims were "just a funny little religion similar to the Amish or Mennonites." Informants were quick to point out that "Muslims don't drink, smoke, go out at night, get divorced, or waste money." The women dress modestly in long-skirted dresses and keep to themselves. In a traditional area that confers status reputationally, these traits are obviously all highly valued.

The third Muslim characteristic generally perceived to be positive was that "they mind their own business." The implications of this perception are considerably more complex and profound than informants realize or would choose to realize. The components of minding one's own business include the following: a complete lack of visible racial hostility, a professed belief in racial separatism, the pattern of purchasing land in or near areas already heavily populated by Negroes, and no apparent inclination to upset the apple carts of previous racial "understandings."

[23]John Howard, "The Making of a Black Muslim," *Trans-action*, 4 (December 1966), 15-21.

The Muslims whom I contacted were polite but stiffly correct. My questions were met with a professed lack of knowledge or mild rhetoric rather than with refusals to answer. Social movement groups such as the Black Muslims are often known for the flamboyance of their rhetoric, but this was certainly not the case here. Aspects of Black Muslim ideology or behavior that might be expected to threaten the community have been sublimated or assiduously avoided. Here, for example, "X's" are not publicly used as last names (though occasionally "X" is used as a middle initial); whites are not publicly referred to as racist devils; and the doom of the white race is not predicted. Local Muslims seem not only to avoid antagonism, but even on occasion to express public admiration for "white" economic prowess and ability. A local Muslim observed:

Our leader teaches us that we shouldn't tear down what
you have but rather we should build our own and by building
our own, we have and respect what you have at the
same time. The Muslims are good for both races. [NI]

As one might well expect, the Muslim belief in racial separatism does not bother the white community very much—in fact, a number of informants saw this as an essential difference between the Muslims and "pushy newcomers." One immediate result of this separatism is an extremely low level of visibility. Although the Muslims are active in the economic sector, they keep quite to themselves on the social level. Lincoln observes:

The Black Muslims do not pretend to love the white man, but
they avoid overt antagonism. They shun the white com-
munity entirely, except for the requisites of work or
business, and they do not seek the white man's social
acceptance.[24]

The initial study devoted considerable attention to the precar-

[24]Lincoln, p. 172.

ious "balances" upon which local race relations pivoted. The Muslims give the appearance of being quite willing to let the other segments of the community play whatever "racial games" they wish. If the Muslims are undertaking any substantial recruiting efforts, this fact has not come to the attention of the local community—especially the white sector. For example, a Muslim "membership enhancing tactic" elsewhere has been to pass out leaflets in front of black Christian churches inviting the recipients to come and "learn the truth." This has not been seen to happen. *The Truth* comments:

Reports that Muslims have been recruiting members through threats in the small Calvin Center community apparently are unfounded. One long-time resident said he has not been approached nor does he know of anyone who has. A prominent Cassopolis businessman said the Negro people of Calvin Center are proud and are hard workers "who through thrift and hard work have been able to buy homes and small amounts of land."[25]

The Muslims with whom I spoke did not seem to be particularly concerned with Calvinites and whites or the relationship between them:

The word Negro is a neutral word. The Calvinites are in neutral and the Black Muslims are in gear. [NI]

The old-timers certainly don't care for our presence here. The Negro is a tool—you use it—and the Calvinites have been used for many, many years. [NI]

When I spoke with you five years ago, I mentioned that I could not get financing. This has changed. I changed banks but now both banks will lend me money and I know the reason why. When I went in the first time, I went in as

a Negro. This time I came in as a Black Muslim, and that
makes all the difference in the world. [NI]

In addition to these informant comments, the *Dowagiac Daily
News* reports:

[A local resident] was outspoken in his views of the
racial situation in general. "You say the Negro has had it
pretty good in Michigan, especially in this area. Do you
know why? Because he has allowed the white man to
dominate him and call him 'boy.'

"Well, I'm not a boy and all I want is the right to be a man
like anybody else. People have got the cart before the
horse when they talk about civil rights for the Negro. Before he can have civil rights, he has to have human rights.
That's all I'm asking for—the right to be treated as a human
being like anybody else. I've never been in trouble and
I don't want to cause trouble."[26]

The reader may very well be doubting the degree to which peace
and brotherly love prevail between the whites and Black Muslims. I think this doubt would be well founded. However, they
have found ground for a détente—for an accommodation. One
must be reminded of the analogous set of conditions existing between whites and Calvinites. It is this communality of interest that
allows each to function without friction or harassment. As an
example, I inquired of an informant identified as a Black Muslim
leader whether Muslims had anticipated or experienced any political or economic repression through such practices as increasing
land assessment values and thus raising taxes. He replied:

Oh no, of course there is none of that. They just wouldn't
do that. There has been no problem in becoming a
Muslim in Cass County. [NI]

[26]*Dowagiac Daily News*, May 8, 1968.

I asked what the reactions were to whites who sold land to Muslims.

They have helped us in every way and have not suffered in
the white community either. [NI]

Several whites gave their reactions to this Black Muslim leader: e.g.

He was an ambitious person who wanted to be a successful
businessman. This he has accomplished. This was the
only way. [WI]

We have given [him] a lot of help. We have had specialists
in sheep, poultry, and beef. He calls for this help. [WI]

The following item drawn from a regional newspaper underscores the way in which interracial accommodation between part of the white community and the Muslims is manifested:

The Cass, Berrien, and St. Joseph County Dairy Tour will be
Thursday, March 4, this year. . . . The second stop at
11:30 will be at the [Muslim] farm in Cass Co., 3½ miles
east of Cassopolis and 3½ miles south on Calvin Center
Road. Here dairy farmers will see a 3 year old 100-cow
enclosed housing unit.[27]

Finally, Wheeler and Brunn observe:

The immediate repercussions of increased Negro-owned land
in Cass County are difficult to evaluate because of the
diversity of views held by the area's residents. Recent farm
purchases by Black Muslims have occasioned some
tensions,* and a few apparently believe that a black mili-
tarist state may be in the process of forming in southern

[27]*Ibid.*, February 27, 1971.

Michigan or that a black militia may be trained in the
area with the aim of invading Southern states. Thus far
these scattered land purchases have been equivalent to
slightly more than one square mile of land, on which, however, considerable expenditure has been made for farm
buildings and equipment.** Most whites in the area show
interest in, but little alarm over, the purchases, and
Negro-white relations continue without discernible hostility, in contrast to other parts of southern Michigan.

*The Progressive Land Corporation in Chicago, an organization
closely linked with the Black Muslims, has made recent purchases,
from both Negroes and whites, of plots of good quality land.
**Elijah Muhammad: Muhammad's Aims for Black People in
America: Setting Up Farms, Muhammad Speaks, July 5, 1968, pp. 16-17.
Muhammad mentions that in addition to land in Michigan the Black
Muslims have nearly 1800 acres in Georgia. They expect to expand to 100,000 acres soon in order to help Negroes become self-
sufficient in cooperative agriculture.[28]

The total amount of acreage (about 1,000 acres) and the economic investment (estimates range from $200,000 to $500,000) are
not overwhelming. A number of informants feel that the level
of capitalization is more than is needed—thus enhancing symbolic
presence. For example, a regional newspaper summarizes some
of these perceptions:

Another source, however, said that the amount of his investment in both the poultry and the dairy operations is
such that it is hard to believe that [he] can operate
economically.

"Apparently he has access to all the money he needs to
make this a real showplace," the source said, adding
that both the chicken house and the barn could be built at
much less expense and still be as modern as any in the
state.[29]

[28]Wheeler and Brunn, Geographical Review (1969), 327-328.
[29]Dowagiac Daily News, May 8, 1968.

Nor is the number of people involved large. However, the implications for alterations in the previous racial relations of the community *are* symbolically staggering, and the reasons for this can be pinpointed by recalling the bases of status and the power structure prior to the Muslim arrival.

Waning Calvin

A community is obviously more than a physical place or a collection of structures. It is a symbol, a sentiment, a network of functions. When one speaks of waning, the implied reference may be to physical deterioration, to the weakening of the bonds of solidarity, or to a shift in the power structure. These separate aspects may well vary independently of one another. The broad contours of the physical component seem to have remained quite similar over the years.[30] Yet, moods have changed; feelings have changed. It is in these latter, subjective—perhaps psychological—perspectives that the social and political fortunes of the Negro residents of Calvin Township will be analyzed.

The *potential* for disruption related to Black Muslim in-migration has reached deeply into the relative status positions of whites, Calvinites, and newcomers. Neither white nor Negro newcomers had been able to penetrate the relationship between locally established whites and Negroes. In fact, the traditional structure of deference within the Negro community and the broker-type role that Calvinites assumed led to greater solidarity on an in-group–out-group basis as long as two conditions prevailed: first, that the Calvinites were able to maintain their capacity for influence over the newer Negro community; and second, that established whites kept their part of the bargain—to accept the legitimacy of this broker-type role and thus include Calvinites as an integral part

---

[30]In 1964, I undertook a photographic study of physical aspects of the community in order to make comparisons in any future restudy. I retook the same series of photographs in 1971 and found that few "objective" changes had taken place, although some buildings showed more deterioration. Vandalia, for example, appeared less sound.

of the "community." Clearly these two conditions are so inextricably woven together that *any* significant change in either condition would unbalance the equation and thus cause repercussions throughout the system. The Muslims, by their *symbolic* presence, have provided the groundwork which is capable of triggering change.

Calvinites have not seemed to fare well in the past decade. I sensed this during the first period of field research when I likened their position to that of a holding action. The reasons for this instability are several and complex. On a very general level, "subcultural" communities have been faced with the homogenizing forces of an increasing "industrialization" of agriculture. As Beale points out:

> *The history of Negro farm communities outside of the*
> *South is often of great interest. But with few exceptions*
> *these communities have been disintegrating in modern*
> *times. The people who have grown up in them have usually*
> *assimilated well the characteristics and aspirations of the*
> *local culture. But they are not staying in agriculture.*
> *Their stable Northern background and higher than average*
> *education have made it easier for them to succeed in*
> *the cities than for their Southern cousins, and it is to the*
> *cities that they are going.*[31]

Beale goes on to discuss the direct implications for the economic viability of Negro farming:

> *Negro farm owners have about 4.7 million acres of land,*
> *but 2.0 million acres of it is in the hands of elderly and*
> *part-time noncommercial farmers, who are cultivating only*
> *half of their crop land. If more of this decidedly underused*
> *2.0 million acres were channeled into the hands of as-*
> piring tenants or commercial owners, as many as 10,000 addi-

[31]Beale in Davis, p. 174.

tional commercial Negro farmers might have a reasonable
chance for survival. *But the trend has been for a decline in
Negro-owned farm land, while the total of land in white-
owned farms has been stable. [Emphasis mine.]*[32]

The preceding comment should underscore the striking implications for both the increasingly marginal farming in Calvin Township on one hand and the coordinated agricultural acquisitions of
the Black Muslims on the other. Nearly any recent issue of
Muhammad Speaks lists as one of the organization's prime goals
the acquisition of land and the need for agricultural labor to farm
"commercial" farms.[33]
As American society has moved gradually from the family farm
to "agri-business," technological advances have been inflating
the size of what constitutes a "viable" versus a "marginal" farm.
The small, family-owned farms of past generations often have
gradually slipped into weeds or have been consolidated into
larger units because marginal farming does not produce sufficient
capital to expand operations and usually does not even produce
enough to maintain the status quo. In the early 1970's, no more
than one or two full-time, capitalized, Negro farmers in Calvin
Township can be characterized as "Calvinites." These circumstances have stimulated the gradual shift to a "rural non-farm"
status. Backyard farming, commuting, or retirement present an
agricultural attrition to the Calvinite community. Although the
causes of such trends are related to alterations in national, economic conditions, they still reflect race-related status situations
which are quite meaningful at the local level.
Indicators of an "aging" agricultural community abound. "Township news" columns in the local newspaper seem to be allotting
more and more space to the "recently departed" (dead), to ill-

[32]*Ibid.*, p. 201.

[33]In this regard, Calvin Hernton observes that "the Black Muslim Movement
is one expression of an historical necessity for the black man in America,
just as Zionism was a movement designed to 'deliver' the Jews out of bondage and alienation. The white liberal should understand this." (*Negro Digest*
[October 1963], p. 6.)

nesses and sick calls, to visits by grandchildren (many of whom are themselves adults), and to the intricate patterns of who visited whom among the elderly.[34]

Thus, the waning of Calvin is the waning of a viable community power structure once related to political and economic assets. Negroes who do locate in the community, perhaps with income, occupation, and education commensurate with those of the white community, are nevertheless newcomers. Merton's analysis of the local-cosmopolitan pattern would predict this state of affairs. Calvinites who remain do so as trusted old-timers, having to depend more and more on their local reputation than on economic viability to retain community status. It is in this light that one might be led to conclude that the youth of the community have made a sound and rational economic decision to migrate, either on a daily basis to nearby industrial centers or on a permanent basis. This attrition of human resources comes at the very time when more effort is required from traditional Calvinites to function as "filters" and "brokers of respectability." The spokesman role also falters as free-floating fears of "outside agitators," symbolized in the extreme by groups such as the Black Muslims, become diffused through day-to-day peaceful reality. Muslims are no longer a symbolic threat to the status quo. One can easily perceive how power status alliances and power balances could be disrupted in the process. Certainly some white residents must be wondering at this point exactly what the vague, distant, and sinister threat to community stability really was. One cannot, however, exempt whites from their own "social construction of reality." Perhaps what had been feared all along was the actual manifestation of localistic latent racial anxieties.

It is clear that informants perceive the wide range of implications in the emerging status of Calvinites and the forms of behavior that can be expected as appropriate. The following comments indicate the range of these perceptions encountered during the restudy periods:

[34]A recent report found that 76 per cent of the elderly residents of Calvin Township reported contact with relatives once a week or more. (Cass County Council on the Aging, 1969)

You don't hear that much [about the issue] any more. The
old-timers certainly don't think much of the newer ones,
especially the Muslims. [WI]

The Muslims don't vote. They could be a powerful bloc of
votes, but they are a negative group in the community.
Some of the Calvin kids are joining them. They join because
they are frustrated. The downfall of the natives is that
they could never get together to do anything. [WI]

The Calvin people are slowly losing their power. The old
ones could have assumed leadership at one time, but they
didn't push it. Now it is too late. [NI]

You have a lot of trouble with the elderly blacks around
here. They have the Alabama complex. They won't stand up
and come out. [WI]

These Negroes didn't know what was going on—they just
listen to the white people. [Local Muslim during interview
on "Black Journal" television presentation.]

Whatever assessment one wishes to place on the behavior of
the Calvinites, there is fairly uniform agreement that their power
has been eroding. This can be detected most directly in their cooperative arrangements with whites. Whites' perceptions of the
Calvinites and Black Muslims are remarkably similar at base.
Yet, it should be noted that the reader is probably not of a mind
to equate Black Muslims with Calvinites, although the similarity
of their behavior is quite interesting.

To a great extent, one can understand the behavior of any member of an interactive relationship only after perceiving that behavior as a part of a response set. As Dollard observed many
years ago:

In this discussion of gains we must always remember that
the gains are not exclusively on the side of the white caste.
It will be urged, as Southern white people do urge, that
the Negroes also gain from the situation, and in ways

which are inaccessible to white caste members. This is a
matter of fact. . . . The gains concept is a mere instrument of
analysis and not a battle slogan; it is used because it serves
to clarify the social mechanisms of class and caste re-
lationships which otherwise seem mere outline forms
of action.[35]

It is reasonable to observe that the "new-old" dichotomous fence
running through the middle of the Negro community was an acceptable state of affairs for both Calvinites and whites. Moreover,
the pervasive structure of racial deference in this society suggests
that minority groups are most often cast in the role of *reacting*
to the demands placed on them—demands for conformity, for
agreement, for deference. It is clear that Calvinites were able to
extract "gains" from the "bargain." What about whites?

It has been proposed that, prior to the actuality of finding Black
Muslims as neighbors, the anxiety that newcomers traditionally
generated in whites could have been magnified one-hundred fold.
Black Muslims had been labeled as extremists, racists, gun-toting
militants. But they arrive in the community and, lo and behold,
what happens? Absolutely nothing. The symbolic "enemy" settles
down, purchases land, pursues farming, stays in his place, and
generally presents no threat to white interests. Moreover, his value
orientations appear as conservative and traditional as those of the
Calvinites. Clearly whites have not lost anything. However, just
as clearly, Calvinites have. As white fears of the incursion of
race-related external conditions recede, so does the power and
prestige that was accorded the Calvinites. In a very real sense, it
was whites who, in the clinch, violated the bargain. Tradition
becomes less and less of a motivating force. Whites have succeeded in demonstrating their ability to "co-exist" with "outside
Negroes"—in this case, Muslims. The Calvinites, therefore, should
be quite able to see that a new group, symbolizing everything des-
picable and fearful in past abstraction, has "leapfrogged" over

[35]John Dollard, *Caste and Class in a Southern Town* (New Haven: Yale University Press, 1937), p. 252.

the newcomers with no visible retaliation. Although the power-broker role is threatened, it could, of course, be buoyed up by whites' latent fears of "Chicago types," kept quite alive by racial polarization on both national and regional levels. This could be so even if local conditions are not immediately threatened.

The role of external influences

The years between the initial study and the restudy were marked nationally by ominous conditions clearly not conducive to racial tranquillity. Disorders had occurred during the initial field work but they had yet to involve the predictability and intensity of the "long hot summer" pattern of the following years. As the Kerner Commission reported, "the summer of 1967 was not the beginning of the [then] current wave of disorders."[36] This report traces the crisscrossing threads of disorders in 1963 and 1964 from Philadelphia, Pennsylvania, to Philadelphia, Mississippi, from Chicago to St. Augustine, Florida. The year 1965 marked the mass demonstrations in Selma, Alabama, and the riot (or rebellion) in the Watts district of south-central Los Angeles. The latter inflicted injuries on hundreds and resulted in death to 34 persons, 4,000 arrests, and $33 million in property damage. The Commission observes that "the events of 1966 made it appear that domestic turmoil had become a part of the American scene."[37] The cinematic "Long Hot Summer" with the sweet scent of magnolia had been replaced by the "long hot summer" of the acrid smell of burning tenements and the spectacle of ghetto residents and armed National Guard troops "interacting" with bricks, bottles, and bullets.

The race-related violence which followed in 1967 both strained and dulled the imagination. The senseless had blended into and given way to the absurd. The names, places, "body counts," and arrest figures fuse into a dreary litany: the Tampa, Florida "riot,"

[36]*Report of the National Advisory Commission on Civil Disorders* (Washington: U.S. Government Printing Office, March 1, 1968), p. 19. Hereafter referred to as "Kerner Commission Report."
[37]*Ibid.*, p. 20.

the Cincinnati, Ohio "disorder," the Atlanta, Georgia "violence," the Newark, New Jersey "hysteria," the northern New Jersey "outbreaks," the Plainfield, New Jersey "clash," the New Brunswick, New Jersey "random vandalism," the Detroit, Michigan "carefree nihilism," and so on. The words change, the pattern remains: the encirclement of poverty-stricken blacks by walls of white affluence had generated despair and hostility on one side of the ghetto walls and fear and hatred on the other. It has been repeatedly observed that the "ghetto walls" are maintained by the reactions on "both sides."

However, the incidence of street violence (either "police violence" or "mass violence") is not the only "external influence" which could affect race relations in the research community. Concepts such as "Black Power," in both their actual and rhetorical forms, were being proposed, distilled, and disseminated. Additionally, the assassinations of John F. Kennedy, Martin Luther King, Robert F. Kennedy, and Malcolm X stand as monuments to the volatility of the era. The terms "black militant" and "white racist" had become catch-all labels for people with whom one disagreed. Although these years were marked by minor improvements in the socio-economic status of blacks, they were also marked by increased disillusionment. This was stimulated by the gap between buoyed aspirations and the grinding sameness of reality. Finally, the brutalizing war in Vietnam, inflation, and increasing unemployment can all be seen to have contributed to the growing race-related polarization in American society. Clearly these years have been a time of turmoil and searching. The implications for Cass County are clear if, as Leonard Reissman maintains, "We are totally in and of the city. We are engulfed by the very phenomena we seek to study and to understand."[38] The analogy to the alleged "subcultural isolation" should be clear.

Mass media influences do penetrate the research area to a substantial degree. No man is an island, nor is any community able to remain quarantined from reality. The county is within the

[38]Leonard Reissman, *The Urban Process: Cities in Industrial Societies* (New York: The Free Press, 1964), p. 4.

broadcast area of all major television networks. Although the local weekly newspaper features local events to the virtual exclusion of all else, this narrowed focus has slight influence in muting race-related issues. Claspy maintains:

Most of the people of Calvin probably prefer that difficult problems such as race not be mentioned. Outside papers, however, sometimes discuss such things with more freedom, but people in the area concerned may not even know about the articles.[39]

The issues which Claspy addresses are both allusive and sensitive, with little empirical evidence. My research suggests that Calvinites are considerably more aware of Negro events than they might wish one to believe. Additionally, the research by Wheeler and Brunn suggests, for Vandalia at least, that the exposure to metropolitan dailies is indeed related to race:

Newspaper subscriptions by city of publication also revealed differences in Negro-white preferences. Metropolitan newspapers enable Negroes to maintain closer contact with events in Chicago, with which they are often more concerned than with the local news in the community newspapers. The Cassopolis newspaper, the chief community paper serving Vandalia, is taken by more than 30 per cent of the Vandalia whites who subscribe to a newspaper, but only 11 per cent of Negro subscribers; however, the most popular paper in Vandalia among both whites and Negroes is the South Bend Tribune.[40]

One should not search only on the national level for external influences pervading the local community. Nearby urban centers become psychologically closer as commuting workers bring back external information, values, concerns, and perspectives. Cass

[39]Claspy, p. 41.
[40]Wheeler and Brunn, *Geographical Review* (1968), 228.

County is within thirty minutes driving distance of these centers,
nearly all of which have had recent race-related tensions, and in
some cases explosive situations. In fact, one finds three of these
among the 45 communities cited in 1967 by the Kerner Commission Report as centers of "minor disorders" (South Bend, Benton
Harbor, and Kalamazoo.)[41]

South Bend has had difficulties between its West Side black and
Polish-American populations resulting in injury and death; Benton
Harbor and Kalamazoo have both been marked by violence in the
schools. Informants report that in at least one of these communities Civil Defense officers and sheriff's deputies were on regular
patrol inside the high schools.

In addition, Dowagiac has had a series of "disorders," most of
which have been described locally as "youth-oriented disturbances" and "curfew violations." Furthermore, segments of the
Negro community in Dowagiac seem to be engaging in active
forms of in-fighting. ("Passive in-fighting" has been, of course,
quite common in the area.) Some Negroes feel, for example, that
the city's Negro police chief is too moderate, others that he is too
radical. Informants perceive the issue in the following fashion:

Dowagiac Negroes demonstrated against him. He can't win.
The old-timers don't like him because he doesn't go to
church enough and the radicals feel that he is out to get
them. [The "radicals" generally seem to be identified as
"members of that SCLC (Southern Christian Leadership
Conference) bunch."]   [WI]

Recently the SCLC has been sponsoring a recall campaign to
remove the elected Negro council representative (a relative of
the Negro police chief).

The SCLC spokesman said the efforts to remove [him] were

---

[41]The Kerner Commission Report characterizes a "minor disorder" as "(1)
a few fires or broken windows; (2) violence lasting generally less than a day;
(3) participation by only small numbers of people; and (4) use, in most cases,
only of local police or police from a neighboring community" (p. 65).

*caused by what he described as [his] attempt to control
all Blacks in the community through his son. [The
chapter president] accused [him] of trying "to build up a
dictatorship and trying to take over the city government."*[42]

In-fighting among segments of the Dowagiac Negro population
does not appear to be the total explanation for charges of excessive police action, when the Michigan Civil Rights Commission
dismisses one police officer, demotes a second, and clears a third
as a result of charges of brutality brought against the police.[43]
One must be reminded of the "external" definitions of "reality"
which have been brought in by migrating whites from Midwestern
and Southern states. The effect of these white newcomers, as
suggested in Chapter Nine, has been a continued source of local
anxiety. Additionally, constant "temporary" migration brings both
whites and Negroes into the area for recreational purposes. The
presumptive effects of all these sets of commuting patterns (both
outbound for employment and inbound for recreation) and different patterns of mass media exposure are that many area residents
are put in day-to-day contact with sets of understandings and conditions variant from local tradition. Given the levels of tension
in the surrounding, more urban areas, the results could well be
unsettling. As the report by Williams and Works dramatically
suggests:

*It can be said that regional factors outside the limits
of the county will have a more profound effect on the
growth and development of the county than will internal
county factors. . . . [The shortened work week] coupled
with an efficient transportation system could make Cass
County literally a suburb of Chicago, Kalamazoo, Benton Harbor, St. Joseph, Mishawaka, Elkhart, and South
Bend.*[44]

[42]*Dowagiac Daily News*, August 26, 1970.
[43]*Ibid.*, August 18, 1970.
[44]Williams and Works, pp. 5-6.

The potential for emerging tension

One could postulate that some of these external inputs would function to enhance in-group cohesion of area residents. However, the nearness of threat plus differential exposure to that threat is seen to generate a situation in which polarization is a more likely result than is a reaffirmation of subcultural uniqueness.

It would do an injustice to reality to suggest that local race relations were entirely placid up to a given point and then suddenly collapsed in a battle of recriminations. The immediately preceding analysis has suggested a series of conditions, events, and processes that could be seen to contribute to growing racial animosities, fears, and divisions within the community. It is not the purpose of this section to look for *explanations* of why such polarization might occur, but rather, to seek evidence that it has occurred, is occurring, or will occur. The tone of most of the comments which follow is no more inflammatory or negative than that of many of the comments found in Chapter Eight. However, in the initial study *respondents* were *exceedingly* careful to preface their observations with the old-timer – newcomer caveat. As the line between these latter groups has receded (primarily as a function of altered power equations), it appears that *informants* have become increasingly willing either to make blanket racial comments or to lapse into such vagueness as to make it impossible to determine their real attitude patterns.

The term "polarization" carries the psychological implication that *perceived* conditions may or may not be found in actions or empirical social reality. I will first survey these perceptions and then present data on the allied empirical conditions. It should be noted that there is a direct parallel between the present remarks and the earlier distinction between prejudice and discrimination, the former being psychological sets and the latter actions likely to be induced by these sets, but tempered by social control or inflamed by the absence of restraints.

Informants in the restudy generally expressed some apprehension, which was not oriented directly to anything that *had* hap-

pened but rather to what might happen. This apprehension came
to the surface in such vague references as "things may be getting
worse."

*Things are certainly no better now than five years ago—
in fact, I think we are backsliding a good bit. [NI]*

*In the old days, the colored and the rich used to get
together. They don't any more. [WI]*

*There are problems in Vandalia. Some Negroes resent whites.
One woman resented white migrants hanging their wash
in the front yard. [NI]*

*The power people really don't care what happens any more.
They can be a bunch of bigots. [WI]*

Perhaps the most classic example of the changed mood can be
seen in the following comparison of two quotes from the *same
individual*—the first in 1964 and the second in 1970:

*My daughter does not realize that there are white and
Negro. I am trying to tell her that she is a part of these
demonstrations on TV. She watches the demonstrations on
TV, and she might as well be watching a fairy tale as
far as she is concerned. [NR-31 in 1964, p. 138]*

*Yes, there is more separation and fear now. My daughter
lives in two different worlds—the one being a Negro in Cass
County and the other being a black in America. [NI in 1970]*

These impressionistic comments tend to be supported by a recent written account of race relations in the area:

*Almost everyone this writer talked to expressed the opinion
that the racial situation in Cass is worsening. Last se-
mester [Fall 1969] the Dowagiac High School was closed
for the first time due to racial strife, and it was learned*

*that several families have begun to send their children to
school in Mishawaka and South Band.*[45]

Kundtz also observes:

*The County continued in this manner [white paternalism]
until the 1940's and early 1950's when an influx of Southern poor whites and a renewed immigration of urban,
ghetto dwelling blacks (most from Chicago) caused a further change in attitude. This change is one to increased
intolerance on the part of whites and a heightening of
militancy among blacks. It is my contention, then, that Cass
has run the gamut of racism in 130 years along the
spectrum from no racism to volatile race relations.*[46]

The surfacing of such attitude patterns has already been noted
in Chapter Ten, where I observed that the initial study had found
respondents willing to volunteer information, willing to engage
in "backstage behavior." The restudy detected and reflects a
great deal more caution and reserve. It might be reasonable to
assume that the results of increased national polarization, combined with interview effect, might be the explanation. However,
a series of local events and conditions provides more direct empirical evidence that some tranquillity has been lost.[47] These are,

[45]Kundtz, pp. 42-43.

[46]*Ibid.*, p. 2.

[47]Although one election does not establish a pattern, it is interesting to note
the appeal that Governor George C. Wallace had in the 1968 Presidential
election (running on the American Independent Party ticket). During the
field work for the initial study, respondents occasionally referred to Wallace,
but only in the context of discussions regarding racial extremism. Yet Wallace was able to garner 2,257 votes of the 14,906 cast in the county, or 15%
of the total. The distribution of these votes within the county reveals
that he did especially well in those townships that both border the four-
township research area *and* have a lower Negro population. Calvin Township reported six per cent of its votes cast for Wallace, a heavily Negro
ward in Dowagiac nine per cent, the four-township research area 11 per
cent, the city of Dowagiac 12 per cent, and, finally, the townships bordering the research area 17 per cent.

first, a growing awareness of civil rights and racial identity; second, a shift in population characteristics; and third, rumors of racial disturbances, primarily in the streets and schools.

In a less unusual bi-racial community, one would hardly be tempted to assert that increasing awareness of the civil rights movement or of racial identity could necessarily be taken as indicative of racial polarization. In the research area, however, it can be so asserted. One need only be reminded that race relations were not topics of general conversation—especially when old-timers were involved. The term "Calvinite" was used to avoid direct reference to racial identity. "Race" per se was an issue supposedly "injected" into local understandings by "newcomers." Increasingly, the youth especially do not seem to be enthusiastic supporters of the political games of their parents.

In 1965 the word "black" was an adjective to be attached to the "newcomer" or a noun to be used interchangeably with "nigger." In 1970 some informants exhibited an inconsistent use of racial terms, including black, Negro, and colored (or colored folk). In 1965 an Afro haircut was prima facie evidence of a Chicagoan in the area for the weekend. In 1970 Afros were quite common among the local youth. For example, a substantial proportion of the schools' athletic team members now wear them. The Cassopolis High School has an Afro-American Club; the regional junior college schedules not only a Martin Luther King Week but also a Malcolm X Week, and a Black Culture Association has been formed there. "Black is Beautiful" buttons appear here and there —again worn by the young. These manifestations of identity have not gone unnoticed. For example, the superintendent of schools reported in one of his weekly newspaper columns:

This week on Friday you will have the opportunity to see
the special film documentary of the life of Dr. Martin
Luther King. This movie has been voted as one of the finest
documentary films produced. It traces the life of Dr. King
and his struggle to attain equal rights for all citizens in
the United States. You owe it to yourself to see this fine

production. Profits from the ticket sale will be used by the
Afro American Club for a local scholarship.[48]

None of these activities appears to generate any *visible* backlash
reaction in the white community, but they cannot help but suggest
that "their Negroes" *are in fact* Negroes. Furthermore, they cannot help but suggest that national and regional conditions may be
having an effect on how local Negroes now perceive themselves
and their role in the community. The reciprocal of this situation
is that the white population seems to be more aware that race
is an issue that must be dealt with as an *internal* matter by means
other than simply moulding newcomers into scapegoats.

A second alteration also implies "disturbing tendencies." In the
first study, the only locales in the research area that respondents
were willing to label as "Negro areas" were the village of Vandalia (then estimated at 70 per cent Negro), Calvin Township (65
per cent Negro), and Paradise Lake. By 1970 the proportion of the
Vandalia population classified as Negro had risen to about 80 per
cent. Informants, white and Negro, maintain that the figure may
be higher. Calvin Township retains a balanced population which
favors Negroes and Paradise Lake is still all-Negro.

In 1970, informants used the term "the Negro section" to refer
to the south side of Cassopolis. This is new. The area *does* have
an increasing Negro population, and the term "Negro area" may
well be applicable, provided, of course, that one realizes that it is
perceptual in origin and not a precise statistical construct. It is
clearly a much more heavily integrated area than the newer section of town, but no section is exclusively Negro or white. One
should be reminded that, as noted in Chapter Eleven, Cassopolis
has *lost* white population at the same time that a substantial Negro
increase has occurred. In addition, informants now use the term
"Negro slums" to refer to portions of Dowagiac.

The symbolically polarizing influence of these changes is found
in the fact that, as recently as five years ago, patterns of population distribution were directly related to historical land settlement

---

[48]*Cassopolis Vigilant,* superintendent's column, May 13, 1971.

patterns. In the case of Calvin Township, the contours of the Negro settlement were laid down a century ago; in the case of Vandalia, the concentration of Negroes was attributable to a 35-year attrition of old white families. By 1970 an invasion-succession process may have been operating in some parts of the research area, primarily in Cassopolis. Informants saw a changing population distribution as a reaction to an increasing proportion of Negro residents (which is not the case overall). The data in Chapter Eleven show a quite stable situation in the racial composition of the research area taken as a whole. However, the *perceived* change is substantial. For example, the population of Vandalia has not been that volatile in terms of racial composition, but it does seem to be growing. Wheeler and Brunn report that 47 per cent of Negro residents feel that the community is growing whereas only six per cent of whites perceive that to be the case.[49] The census figures presented in Chapter Eleven document the assertion that Vandalia is growing (from 360 to 427 in ten years).

The third and most serious set of conditions indicating increased local racial tensions concerns rumors of events in the school system. The word "rumors" must be stressed because segments of the community seem quite primed to believe that potentially inflammable, race-related tensions are increasing in the school system.

In the early spring of 1971, an incident involving several girls occurred. The actual facts of the matter may have been submerged and wrapped in mythology. All that is really known is the following. A girl or girls of one race allegedly attempted to use an automobile to "run down" a girl or girls of the other race. This "incident" resulted in fights (face slapping) between several girls in the school halls. In April, after a series of intermittent slapping episodes, the school administration received a bomb threat. At this point a search of the building, including student lockers, was undertaken. As the search was underway, informants report that a Negro student visited a counselor to inform her that his locker contained a shotgun that had been used as a prop in a school play

---

[49]Wheeler and Brunn, *Geographical Review* (1968), 225.

earlier in the year. The student was rightly concerned about what might be assumed if the weapon were found in his locker, even though it was not functioning. The counselor agreed to open the locker and take possession of the "weapon." As the gun was being taken to the counselor's office, a group of white parents entered the building and observed part of the sequence of events.

Within a day or two, rumors circulated that the racial situation had become so inflamed that female teachers were patrolling the halls armed with shotguns for their own protection, that several students and staff lay dying (conveniently of stab wounds) in the county medical care facility, and that some deaths had occurred. A meeting was held to take the predictable action—to form a human relations commission. Approximately 60 persons attended. The next night another meeting attracted about 150 people, some of whom shouted unpleasantries at one another about the "riot."

Had there been a riot? Informants close to the scene maintain that nothing had happened beyond the initial slappings, the bomb scare, and the subsequent removal of the prop from the locker— no armed patrols, no attacks on teachers, no fires, no stab wounds, no deaths. During this period, the superintendent requested that the community "cool it":

We ask the cooperation of the students, the parents and the entire community to work to insure a climate of under- standing that will result in positive action and growth for the Cassopolis school system. While the school is not perfect, it is still the only school system this community has and it is frightening to contemplate what this com- munity would be like if it had no school system at all.[50]

By the time the final period of field research began in May of 1971, informants had managed to put the incident in its proper perspective both for me and *possibly* for themselves.

You know how it goes—kids will be kids. [NI]

[50]*Cassopolis Vigilant*, April 8, 1971.

That sort of thing happens all over, you know. [WI]

It was just a little race riot—you know how easily those things get started. [Emphasis mine.] [WI]

Retrospect

One cannot help but speculate as to what types of residual fears and doubts remain. Informants simply preferred not to discuss the situation except in the most abstract terms, indicating that such "riots" are a normal part of everyday life. One can hardly accept this perception as a reflection of the bonds of "community." As a sociologist with nearly a decade of contact, professional interest and direct access to information in this community, I am deeply troubled by the types of "alleged" incidents that are able to send segments of the community "to the wall." Rumor thrives on volatile situations—on deep-felt anxieties and tensions. It was surprising to me that neither internal nor community controls were sufficiently strong to prevent the susceptibility to rumor. It also troubles me that incidents have been wallpapered over so neatly, quickly, and quietly with "boys will be boys" statements.

Perhaps informants were so embarrassed by their own behavior and that of some of their neighbors that they would prefer to forget and build anew. However, on the broad panorama of race relations, such instances are rarely found. Crisis situations drive people to crisis-type reactions; calmness *may* smooth over some or all of the wounds. In the case of the research area, I find little or no evidence of any attempt to understand what happened, why it happened, and how to prevent its recurrence.

What about the future? It seems clear that the years to come will not be a replay of the years of subcultural tranquillity. Both whites and Negroes have had to come to grips slowly with race as fact in the structure of community affairs. They have not totally accepted the fact that the community is truly bi-racial and not composed of magnanimous whites and "Calvinites." Negroes and whites live and will continue to live in the area. I expect a slow accommodation to this fact without the frictions found in the

late 1960's and early 1970's. The Negro community is not growing substantially, so no particular threat can be found from this
source. Those that do live in the area have seen much of their
economic and political power dissipated either by their own actions or the changed attitudes of whites. One stimulant to continued change could occur if a substantially increased Muslim
establishment were to center in the county and to reveal the level
of militance which it seems capable of expressing where such
behavior is unlikely to damage its organizational interests.

One would have to conclude that the characterization of the
community as "stably bi-racial" is justified. How stable are the
varying sets of definitions and emotions that weave the fabric of
community? One must be cautious, though not necessarily cyni-
cal, in answering this question. However, human rights commis-
sions that operate only in an ex post facto fashion following an
incident remind one of fire fighters, not of students of prevention.

As the reader might well imagine, I have given the situations described throughout this book a great deal of penetrating thought,
leading, I hope, in the direction of addressing the questions: what
does it all mean?; where does it all lead? In his preface to a recent book already generally regarded as a classic, Lewis Killian
interrupts himself to ask what he might *really* be saying. Although
his message is more somber than mine, I think the emotive tone
and content are well worth observing:

> The sociologist, no matter how gloomy his predictions, is
> usually inclined to end his discourse with recommendations
> for avoiding catastrophe. There are times, however, when
> his task becomes that of describing the situation as it
> appears without the consolation of a desirable alter-
> native. There is no requirement in social science that the
> prognosis must always be favorable; there may be social ills
> for which there is no cure. Therefore, this book has no
> happy ending.[51]

[51]Lewis M. Killian, *The Impossible Revolution* (New York: Random House,
1968), p. xv.

Appendix

to the

First Edition:

The respondent

One of the major sources of data for the present research was intensive interviews with local residents. Seventy-one individuals served in this capacity. Reported here are some relevant biographical materials on each respondent so that their textual comments might be placed in a more meaningful framework. No information has been deliberately altered, but the descriptions must of necessity be vague to insure anonymity—especially of those respondents who might have a readily identifiable position in the community. See Table 17, p. 305 for biographical information on Negro respondents; see Table 18, p. 306 for material on white respondents.

Remarks relevant to Negro respondents

Code number

Because of the stress placed on the "old-timer—newcomer" distinction, code numbers with asterisks (*) indicate respondents considered to be "old-timers," usually Calvinites. As this distinction is more applicable for Negro respondents, these data will be reserved for them only.

Sub-area

Because of the small size of the Paradise Lake settlement, respondents living there have been classified as "Vandalia"—the village one mile to the north.

Color

Although I am aware that designations of skin color are subjective and relative, nevertheless these gradations serve as an important variable to many respondents. This indicates the desirability of attempting to make a rudimentary assessment of skin color an item of biographical identification. For this purpose, four categories are defined as follows:

Pass. Those people in the community who are recognized as "Negro" because of ancestral ties. They are, in a sense, voluntary Negroes for by remaining in this small community they are known as Negro. However, there is little or nothing in their appearance to suggest nonwhite parentage.

Fair. This category includes respondents that would be considered marginal in appearance. They probably could pass in a situation where race is not a salient element in the culture. However, most people could probably identify them as Negro, Mexican, Puerto Rican, or American Indian should the issue arise.

Medium. This designation is used for a respondent who is obviously "Negro" in appearance but yet clearly "mulatto," that is, of mixed parentage.

Dark. Those respondents who exhibit little or no mixed parentage were classified as dark in appearance.

Based on these data, the following summarization, shown in Table 16, can be derived. The data tend to substantiate assertions from respondents in Chapter Eight that old-timers are generally lighter in color.

Table 16: Negro respondents: color by
community tenure

Community tenure	Color				Total
	Pass	Fair	Medium	Dark	
Old-timer	8	7	0	0	15
Newcomer and unclassified	1	8	8	3	20
Total	9	15	8	3	35

Table 17: Selected biographical information
on Negro respondents

Code number	Residency sub-area	Color	Code number	Residency sub-area	Color
a*NR-1	Calvin	Fair	NR-19	Vandalia	Medium
NR-2	Cassopolis	Medium	NR-20	Vandalia	Dark
*NR-3	Vandalia	Fair	*NR-21	Cassopolis	Fair
*NR-4	Vandalia	Pass	NR-22	Vandalia	Medium
*NR-5	Cassopolis	Fair	*NR-23	Dowagiac	Pass
*NR-6	Calvin	Pass	NR-24	Niles	Dark
*NR-7	Calvin	Pass	NR-25	Cassopolis	Fair
*NR-8	Calvin	Pass	*NR-26	Calvin	Pass
NR-9	Vandalia	Medium	NR-27	Cassopolis	Fair
NR-10	Calvin	Medium	NR-28	Cassopolis	Fair
*NR-11	Calvin	Pass	NR-29	Dowagiac	Medium
*NR-12	Calvin	Fair	NR-30	Dowagiac	Fair
*NR-13	Cassopolis	Fair	NR-31	Cassopolis	Fair
NR-14	Vandalia	Fair	NR-32	Calvin	Fair
NR-15	Cassopolis	Dark	NR-33	Vandalia	Medium
NR-16	Vandalia	Pass	*NR-34	Cassopolis	Pass
*NR-17	Vandalia	Fair	NR-35	Calvin	Fair
NR-18	Cassopolis	Medium			

a Asterisks (*) indicate respondents considered to be "old-timers," usually
Calvinites.

*Table 18: Selected biographical information
on white respondents*

Code number	Residency sub-area	Code number	Residency sub-area
WR-1	Cassopolis	WR-19	Vandalia
WR-2	Cassopolis	WR-20	Cassopolis
WR-3	Cassopolis	WR-21	Cassopolis
WR-4	Cassopolis	WR-22	Vandalia
WR-5	Cassopolis	WR-23	Cassopolis
WR-6	Cassopolis	WR-24	Cassopolis
WR-7	Cassopolis	WR-25	Calvin
WR-8	Cassopolis	WR-26	Cassopolis
WR-9	Cassopolis	WR-27	Dowagiac
WR-10	Cassopolis	WR-28	Vandalia
WR-11	Cassopolis	WR-29	Cassopolis
WR-12	Dowagiac	WR-30	Cassopolis
WR-13	Calvin	WR-31	Dowagiac
WR-14	Cassopolis	WR-32	Calvin
WR-15	Calvin	WR-33	Cassopolis
WR-16	Cassopolis	WR-34	Cassopolis
WR-17	Calvin	WR-35	Cassopolis
WR-18	Cassopolis	WR-36	Cassopolis

Bibliography
to the
First Edition

Public documents

U.S. Bureau of the Census. *County and City Data Book: 1962.*

U.S. Bureau of the Census. *Negroes in the United States: 1920–1932.*

U.S. Bureau of the Census. *Negro Population: 1790–1915.*

U.S. Bureau of the Census. *Seventh Census of the United States: 1850.* [And all subsequent decennial censuses terminating in 1960.]

U.S. Bureau of the Census. *U.S. Census of the Population: 1960. Characteristics of the Population.* Vol. I.

Books

Allport, Gordon. *The Nature of Prejudice.* Garden City, N.Y.: Doubleday & Co., 1958.

Baker, Ray Stannard. *Following the Color Line.* 2d ed. revised. New York: Harper and Row, 1964.

Barron, Milton L. *People Who Intermarry*. Syracuse, N.Y.: Syracuse University Press, 1948.

Beegle, Allan, *et al*. *Michigan Population: 1960. Selected Characteristics and Changes*. (Special Bulletin 438.) East Lansing: Michigan State University Agricultural Experimental Station, 1962.

Bettelheim, Bruno, and Morris Janowitz. *Social Change and Prejudice*. New York: The Free Press of Glencoe, 1964.

Booker, Simeon. *Black Man's America*. Englewood Cliffs, N.J.: Prentice-Hall, 1964.

Clark, Kenneth B. *Dark Ghetto: Dilemmas of Social Power*. New York: Harper and Row, 1965.

Coffin, Levi. *Reminiscences of Levi Coffin*. Cincinnati: Western Tract Society, 1876.

Corrothers, James D. *In Spite of the Handicap*. New York: George H. Doran Co., 1916.

Dollard, John. *Caste and Class in a Southern Town*. New Haven: Yale University Press, 1937.

Dorson, Richard M. *Negro Folk Tales in Michigan*. Cambridge: Harvard University Press, 1956.

Drake, St. Clair, and Horace Cayton. *Black Metropolis: A Study of Negro Life in a Northern City*. New York: Harper and Row, 1962.

Embree, Edwin R. *Brown Americans: The Story of a Tenth of the Nation*. New York: Viking Press, 1945.

The Fifty States Report. Submitted to the Commission on Civil Rights by the State Advisory Committees, 1961. Washington: U.S. Government Printing Office, 1961.

Franklin, John Hope. *From Slavery to Freedom: A History of American Negroes*. New York: Alfred A. Knopf, 1948.

Frazier, E. Franklin. *The Negro Family in the United States*. Chicago: The University of Chicago Press, 1939.

————. *The Negro in the United States*. New York: The Macmillan Company, 1949.

Furnas, J. C. *Goodbye to Uncle Tom*. New York: William Sloane Associates, 1956.

Gordon, Milton M. *Assimilation in American Life*. New York: Oxford University Press, 1964.

Grodzins, Morton. *The Metropolitan Area as a Racial Problem*. Pittsburgh: University of Pittsburgh Press, 1958.

Gysin, Brion. *To Master—A Long Goodnight: The Story of Uncle Tom, A Historical Narrative*. New York: Creative Age Press, 1946.

Herskovits, Melville J. *The Myth of the Negro Past*. Boston: Beacon Press, 1958.

Homans, George C. *The Human Group*. New York: Harcourt Brace & Co., 1950.

Hunter, Floyd. *Community Power Structure*. Chapel Hill: University of North Carolina Press, 1953.

Johnson, Charles S. *Patterns of Negro Segregation*. New York: Harper and Bros., 1948.

Killian, Lewis, and Charles Grigg. *Racial Crisis in America: Leadership in Conflict*. Englewood Cliffs, N.J.: Prentice-Hall, 1964.

Lauriston, Victor. *Romantic Kent: The Story of a County 1626 to 1952*. Chatham, Ont.: Shephard Printing Co., 1952.

Lee, Frank F. *Negro and White in Connecticut Town*, New Haven, Conn.: College and University Press, 1961.

Lomax, Louis E. *The Negro Revolt*. New York: The New American Library, 1963.

Masuoko, Jitsuichi, and Preston Valien, eds. *Race Relations: Problems and Theory*. Chapel Hill: University of North Carolina Press, 1961.

Mathews, Alfred. *History of Cass County, Michigan*. Chicago: Waterman, Watkins, and Co., 1882.

Michigan: A Guide to the Wolverine State. Compiled by Workers of the Writers' Program of the Work Projects Administration in the State of Michigan. New York: Oxford University Press, 1941.

Myrdal, Gunnar. *An American Dilemma*. New York: Harper and Bros., 1944.

Park, Robert E., Ernest W. Burgess, and R. D. McKenzie. *The City.* Chicago: The University of Chicago Press, 1925.

Parsons, Talcott. *Structure and Process in Modern Societies.* New York: The Free Press of Glencoe, 1960.

Pease, William H., and Jane H. Pease. *Black Utopia: Negro Communal Experiments in America.* Madison: The State Historical Society of Wisconsin, 1963.

Putnam, Carleton. *Race and Reason: A Yankee View.* Washington: Public Affairs Press, 1961.

Roberson, Jno. *Michigan in the War.* revised ed. Lansing: W. S. George and Co., State Printers and Binders, 1882.

Rogers, Howard S. *History of Cass County from 1825 to 1875.* Cassopolis, Mich.: W. H. Mansfield, Vigilant Book and Job Printer, 1875.

Rose, Arnold. *The Negro in America.* Boston: Beacon Press, 1956.

Rose, Peter I. *They and We: Racial and Ethnic Relations in the United States.* New York: Random House, 1964.

Schoelzow, Mae R. *A Brief History of Cass County.* Marcellus, Mich.: *The Marcellus News,* 1935.

Simpson, George E., and J. Milton Yinger. *Racial and Cultural Minorities: An Analysis of Prejudice and Discrimination.* 2d ed. revised. New York: Harper and Row, 1958.

Smith, T. Lynn. *The Sociology of Rural Life.* New York: Harper and Bros., 1947.

Still, William. *The Underground Rail Road.* Philadelphia: Porter and Coates, 1872.

Vander Zanden, James W. *American Minority Relations: The Sociology of Race and Ethnic Groups.* New York: Ronald Press, 1963.

Vidich, Arthur J., and Joseph Bensman. *Small Town in Mass Society: Class, Power and Religion in a Rural Community.* Princeton: Princeton University Press, 1958.

Washington, Booker T. *The Story of the Negro: The Rise of the Race from Slavery.* Vol. I. New York: Doubleday, Page and Co., 1909.

Williams, Robin M., Jr. *The Reduction of Intergroup Tensions: A Survey of Research on Problems of Ethnic, Racial, and Religious Group Relations.* (Bulletin 57.) New York: Social Science Research Council, 1947.

————. *Strangers Next Door: Ethnic Relations in American Communities.* Englewood Cliffs, N.J.: Prentice-Hall, 1964.

Woodson, Carter G. *A Century of Negro Migration.* Washington: The Association for the Study of Negro Life and History, 1918.

Woodward, C. Vann. *The Strange Career of Jim Crow.* New York: Oxford University Press, 1957.

Articles and periodicals

Aptheker, Herbert. "The Quakers and Negro Slavery," *Journal of Negro History,* 25 (1940), 331–363.

Cassopolis Vigilant. 1888–1965.

Dancy, John C. "The Negro People in Michigan," *Michigan History Magazine,* Vol. 24 (1940).

Gans, Herbert J. "Park Forest: Birth of a Jewish Community," *Commentary,* 2 (April 1951), 330–339.

"Historic Calvin: A Cass County Village and a Township That Defied Kentucky Raiders," *Journal* (Detroit), January 6, 1896.

Hughes, Everett C. "Race Relations and the Sociological Imagination," *American Sociological Review,* 28, No. 6 (December 1963), 879–890. (Presidential address.)

Landon, Fred. *Journal of Negro History,* 3, No. 3 (1918), 366.

Lewis, Hylan, and Mozell Hill. "Desegregation, Integration, and the Negro Community," *The Annals of the American Academy of Political and Social Science,* 304 (March 1956), 116–123.

Mayo, Selz C., and Robert McD. Bobbitt. "Biracial Identity of Rural Locality Groups in Wake County, North Carolina," *Rural Sociology,* 15 (1950), 365–366.

Michigan in Books, 5, No. 3 (Winter 1963), 127–128.

Michigan Chronicle. 1964.

The Niles [Michigan] *Daily Star.* 1963.

Ontario History, No. 4 (1949), p. 195.

South Bend Tribune. 1963–1965.

Washington, Booker T. "Two Generations Under Freedom," *The Outlook,* 73 (February 7, 1903), 292–305.

Weatherspoon, Lee. "Cass County News," *Pittsburgh Courier* (Detroit edition), 1955–1959.

Other sources

Cass County, Michigan. Pamphlet of Historical Information Compiled by the Cass County Historical Society, 1960.

Directory of Cass County: Issue of 1963–1964. Compiled and Arranged by Kenneth M. Poe, County Clerk, for the Cass County Board of Supervisors.

Looking Ahead. Cass County Conservation Needs Committee. Cassopolis, Mich., April 10, 1962.

"Program of Cass County: Soil Conservation District, State of Michigan, December 1947." (Typewritten.)

Windle, Helen Hibberd. "The Underground Railroad in Northern Indiana, Based on Personal Narratives and Famous Incidents." South Bend, Ind., 1939. (Mimeographed.)

Bibliography

to the

Second Edition

Barber, Bernard. *Social Stratification.* New York: Harcourt, Brace & Co., 1957.

Beale, Calvin L. "The Negro in American Agriculture," *The Negro American Reference Book,* ed. John P. Davis. Englewood Cliffs, N.J.: Prentice-Hall, 1966.

————. "An Overview of the Phenomenon of Mixed Racial Isolates in the United States." Prepared for presentation at the annual meetings of the Southern Anthropology Society, Athens, Georgia, April 8, 1970.

"Black Journal." "Report on Black Muslim Leaders, Organizations, and Industries," National Educational Television Network. Broadcast April 27, 1970, on KCET, Channel 28, Community Television of Southern California, Los Angeles.

Cass County Council on the Aging. "Report of the Survey Committee." Donald Nepsted, Chairman, 1969.

Cass County, Michigan. Official records of the county.

Cassopolis Vigilant.

Claspy, Everett. *The Negro in Southwestern Michigan.* Dowagiac, Michigan: By the author, 1967.

Dobriner, William. *Class in Suburbia.* Englewood Cliffs, N.J.: Prentice-Hall, 1963.

Dollard, John. *Caste and Class in a Southern Town.* New Haven: Yale University Press, 1937.

Dorson, Richard M. *Negro Folk Tales in Michigan.* Cambridge: Harvard University Press, 1956.

Dowagiac [Michigan] *Daily News.*

Hawley, Willis, and Frederick M. Wirt, eds. *The Search for Community Power.* Englewood Cliffs, N.J.: Prentice-Hall, 1968.

Hernton, Calvin. *Negro Digest* (October 1963).

Hesslink, George K. "The Function of Neighborhood in Ecological Stratification," *Sociology and Social Research,* 54 (July 1970).

Horning, Donald, and Esau Jackson. *Directory of Black Businesses in Michigan.* Ann Arbor: University of Michigan Press, 1970.

Howard, John. "The Making of a Black Muslim," *Trans-action,* 4 (December 1966).

Kalamazoo [Michigan] *Gazette.*

Katzman, David M. "Early Settlers in Michigan," *Michigan Challenge,* June, 1968.

Killian, Lewis M. *The Impossible Revolution.* New York: Random House, 1968.

Kundtz, Robert J. "A Short History of Cass County, Michigan, and the Development of Racial Tension Through Demographic Shift." Unpublished senior honors thesis, Department of History, University of Notre Dame, 1970.

Lasswell, Thomas E. *Class and Stratum.* Boston: Houghton Mifflin Co., 1965.

Laue, James H. "A Contemporary Revitalization Movement in American Race Relations: The Black Muslims," *Social Forces,* 42 (1964).

Lincoln, C. Eric. *The Black Muslims in America.* Boston: Beacon Press, 1961.

Los Angeles Times.

Lowry, Ritchie P. "Who's Running This Town?" *Trans-action*, 3 (November-December 1965).

Merton, Robert K. *Social Theory and Social Structure.* New York: The Free Press, 1957.

Muhammad Speaks.

The New York Times.

Reissman, Leonard. *The Urban Process: Cities in Industrial Societies.* New York: The Free Press, 1964.

Report of the National Advisory Commission on Civil Disorders. Washington: U.S. Government Printing Office, March 1, 1968.

Ross, H. Laurence. "The Local Community: A Survey Approach," *American Sociological Review*, 27 (February 1962).

A Survey of Cassopolis Public Schools. A Report Prepared for the Cassopolis Board of Education by the Department of Educational Leadership in Cooperation with the Division of Continuing Education, Western Michigan University, Kalamazoo, Michigan, May, 1971.

Thernstrom, Stephan. " 'Yankee City' Revisited: The Perils of Historical Naiveté," *American Sociological Review*, 30 (April 1965).

The Truth (Elkhart, Indiana).

Tyler, Lawrence L. "Black Nationalism in the U.S.," *Current*, no. 75 (September 1966).

U.S. Bureau of the Census. *General Population Characteristics: Michigan.* Series PC(1), B24. Washington: U.S. Government Printing Office, 1971.

Vidich, Arthur J., and Joseph Bensman. *Small Town in Mass Society: Class, Power and Religion in a Rural Community.* Princeton: Princeton University Press, 1958.

Vidich, Arthur J., Joseph Bensman, and Maurice R. Stein. *Reflections on Community Studies.* New York: John Wiley and Sons, 1964.

Wallace, A. F. "Revitalization Movements," *American Anthropologist*, 58 (April 1956).

Warner, W. Lloyd. *Democracy in Jonesville: A Study in Quality and Inequality*. New York: Harper & Row, 1964.

Welch, Lois Webster. *A Diamond Sparkles: The Facets Of Diamond Lake*. Davenport, Iowa. Bawden Bros., Inc., 1970.

Wheeler, James O., and Stanley D. Brunn. "An Agricultural Ghetto: Negroes in Cass County, Michigan, 1845-1968," *Geographical Review*, 59 (July 1969), 317-329.

————. "Negro Migration into Rural Southwestern Michigan," *Geographical Review*, 58 (April 1968), 214-230.

Williams and Works. *Cass County Michigan: Comprehensive Area-Wide Plan for Water and Sewer Services*. Grand Rapids, Michigan: 1967.

Related research on
Cass County, Michigan:
an annotated
bibliography

As the Introduction to Part Five states, unnecessary work could
be avoided if barriers were overcome among varying sources of
information—both among academicians pursuing various discipli-
nary interests and among resources found within the research
community. This forms the rationale for attempting to inform the
reader about the types of information that we now have, so that
future research efforts may build upon one another and cumulate
rather than merely discover the same data time and time again.

The entries to follow are quite variant in terms of orientation,
coverage, and applicability to specific issues. Some summarize the
efforts of professional articles and academic works. Others serve
to direct the reader to valuable sources of information located
within the community. Often the latter sources are the more
difficult to uncover but they can also be more productive. I have
made no attempt to evaluate these several contributions in terms
of scientific merit. The reader must assume this obligation. My
remarks are confined to indicating the types of information that

can be found and their *applicability* to the issues that have been raised in both the first and second editions of my work.

Beale, Calvin L. "The Negro in American Agriculture," *The Negro American Reference Book*, ed. John P. Davis. Englewood Cliffs, N.J.: Prentice-Hall, 1966.

Beale briefly sketches the history and character of Negro involvement in farming from pre–Civil War years through the Emancipation, Reconstruction era, Northern urbanization, World Wars, and Great Depression to the present. He provides data concerning the number, distribution, and concentration of Negro farmers. Additional information is given concerning the type of farming, amount of Negro-owned acreage, land tenure (other than ownership), value of land and crops, etc. The author notes that the number of Negro farm operators is decreasing due to conditions adverse to their continued survival. Among these is the minimum amount of acreage necessary for profitable farming, given advances in agricultural technology. However, increases in Negro "rural non-farm" population are offsetting losses in the farm operator category. Although Beale does not discuss problems within the research area per se, his observations have very germain and direct implications.

"Black Journal." "Report on Black Muslim Leaders, Organizations, and Industries," National Educational Television Network. Broadcast April 27, 1970, on KCET, Channel 28, Community Television of Southern California, Los Angeles.

Although a video-tape print of this program is unavailable upon simple request, the program does provide important documentation of the Black Muslim activities in Cass County, Michigan. Thus, it constitutes a completely independent source of such information. The fact that the Black Muslim operations in Cass County are featured on network television may also suggest their importance, if only symbolically. (I have stressed their symbolic importance repeatedly in the text.) The nature of the content of the broadcast is discussed particularly in Chapter Twelve of *Black Neighbors*. The concerned scholar may wish to contact his local NET outlet regarding possible plans for rebroadcasts of the program.

Blackwell, Edward. "Blacks Enjoy Life on Lake," *The Milwaukee Journal*, July 28, 1968.

This article traces the development of Lake Ivanhoe, Wisconsin, a community of 200 Negroes, from a place of summer recreation and residence for Negro families from Chicago to a Negro community in which about half the population are permanent residents. The distances to major population centers, the similarity to the Paradise Lake area, and the employment problems faced by Negro residents provide close parallels with Cass County.

Cass County Council on the Aging. "Report of the Survey Committee." Donald Nepsted, Chairman, 1969.

A sample survey of Cass County's elderly citizens (fifty-five and over) was undertaken in an effort to determine the size, condition, and outstanding needs of that population. High visitation rates by relatives and friends in Calvin Township and the county as a whole indicate a lower level of social isolation than was anticipated. However, the report does not portray an optimistic economic picture.

"Cassopolis Area Schools Study: A Study Conducted Through the Cooperation of Fifty-four Citizens in the Cassopolis Service Area." May 13, 1958. (Mimeographed.)

This study was produced locally and it proved quite difficult to find. Its most important feature is the raising of the issue of de facto segregation, at least by implication. The Board of Education resisted moves toward such segregation and reasserted the principle of the integrated school system (at the cost of "neighborhood school-centers"). The study includes additional valuable data that can be compared with later documents and reports concerning the same issues.

Claspy, Everett. *The Negro in Southwestern Michigan*. Dowagiac, Michigan: By the author, 1967.

Claspy depicts the southwestern portion of Michigan as an area where "the two races dwell in considerable harmony." He deals heavily with descriptions of Negro residents, particularly such details as family histories, length of residence, land tenure, occupations, prominence in the community, and positions held in various voluntary organizations. A considerable portion of his study concentrates on Cass County, particularly the townships that make up the Cassopolis School District and thus the research area for *Black Neighbors*. A history of Calvin Township is briefly sketched. This work contains a wealth of information. Anyone interested in this unique area would be well advised to obtain a copy of Claspy's work.

Fields, Harold B. "Free Negroes in Cass County Before the Civil War," *Michigan History,* 44 (December 1960).

After examining census data, histories of Cass county, tax assessment rolls, and property deeds, Fields concludes that early Negro settlers were not runaway slaves but "free colored persons." Therefore, in his view, the Underground Railroad did not substantially contribute to an increase in the permanent Negro population. A search of records pinpointing the origins of families founding the Calvin "colony" reveals much evidence to support Field's contention. Evidence and analysis that some construe as contradictory can be found in *Black Neighbors* and a number of the sources cited by Fields. The important point is that the reader realize the diverse origins of the original population and that he be made aware of the various interpretations.

Hart, John Fraser. "A Rural Retreat for Northern Negroes," *Geographical Review,* 50 (April 1960).

Hart describes Lake County, Michigan, the isolated rural county in the northern portion of lower Michigan referred to in *Black Neighbors* as having an extremely high percentage of Negro residents. The article explains how Lake County became a Negro resort and retirement area. The subject matter is particularly relevant because both Lake and Cass

321 Related research on Cass County

Counties have developed Negro recreation areas, although each area grew as a function of a differing set of historical circumstances.

Katzman, David M. "Early Settlers in Michigan," *Michigan Challenge,* June, 1968.

The participation of Negroes in the development of the state of Michigan, from its pre-settlement, fur-trapping days to the decade of the Civil War, is discussed in an abbreviated form. The origins of Calvin Township's pre—Civil War population are noted.

————. "Rural Blacks in Michigan," *Michigan Challenge,* June, 1969.

This brief but quite informative article deals with the history, settlement, and dispersion of Negro farmers in Cass and, to a lesser extent, several other counties in Michigan. Both of Katzman's articles are useful for gaining a brief overview of materials difficult to find in more detailed form.

Kundtz, Robert J. "A Short History of Cass County, Michigan, and the Development of Racial Tension Through Demographic Shift." Unpublished senior honors thesis, Department of History, University of Notre Dame, 1970.

This essay asserts the thesis that increased racial tensions are occurring in Cass County and attributes them directly to an influx of prejudice-carrying migrants, both Negro and white. Emphasis on this causal factor distinguishes the work from others in the literature. One finds in this essay a recognition of other literature dealing with the area. The reader may wish to examine the assertion regarding increased tension, as well as the causative relations, quite carefully.

Sills, Arthur. "Black Muslims Linked to Cass Land," *Kalamazoo* [Michigan] *Gazette,* June 2, 1968.

This very important article examines the reputed relationship between the Muslim-controlled Progressive Land Development Corporation (a Chicago-based firm) and the purchase of farmland in and near Calvin Township. These land purchases are substantial, symbolically important, and possibly predictive of future cooperative developments. Specific purchases and purchase prices are cited and are recorded as public information in the county clerk's office in the courthouse in Cassopolis. The development of a 10,000-chicken egg-production plant and the construction of a dairy are revealed and plans for future construction are intimated. Raymond Sharrieff, son-in-law of Elijah Muhammad, is identified as president of the land corporation. The interested reader is urged to seek out this excellent example of journalistic research and writing.

A Survey of Cassopolis Public Schools. A Report Prepared for the Cassopolis Board of Education by the Department of Educational Leadership in Cooperation with the Division of Continuing Education, Western Michigan University, Kalamazoo, Michigan, May, 1971.

This management-consultant type study of the Cassopolis school system is devoted to an in-depth analysis of the various components of the district. Recommendations are made regarding improvements in each component, including suggested courses of action on specific problems. Concerning community awareness of school-related programs, the study points out that minority groups (Negroes, the aged, widows, etc.) receive less information than the majority group. This finding is consistent with those in other studies, which suggest that Negroes, in the main in Vandalia, are less likely to depend on local newspapers than on metropolitan dailies. However, about equal percentages of Negroes and whites were found lacking in *any* knowledge whatsoever regarding the community school program. This fact can be seen to be one of the root causes for continued failure of the community to support district programs with adequate funds. One could also suggest that lack of knowledge regarding the school and its programs contributed to the volatility of the rumors concerning racial tensions in the schools.

Warner, R. Stephen, David T. Wellman, and Lenore J. Weitzman. "The Hero, the Sambo, and the Operator." Prepared for presentation at the 66th annual meetings of the American Sociological Association, Denver, Colorado, August 31, 1971.

This paper reviews two conceptions of the character of the oppressed, the "Hero" and the "Sambo," and argues for the conceptual superiority of a third, the "Operator." The "Operator" is not presented as a character stereotype, as are the other two, but as a capacity for calculation and manipulation to one's advantage in role relationships, while occupying an inferior social status imposed by the dominant group. The authors assert that the primary value of the "Operator" strategy is that it allows the individual to maintain personal integrity. This type of conceptual approach is particularly relevant when one considers the delicate balances of interpersonal-interracial interaction among the communities in Cass County—whites, Calvinites, newcomers, and Black Muslims.

Welch, Lois Webster. *A Diamond Sparkles: The Facets of Diamond Lake.* Davenport, Iowa: Bawden Bros., Inc., 1970.

In this work, Welch imparts to the reader an appreciation for the history of a particular area—Diamond Lake. Her fond sentiments for the lake, family traditions, and rich history are such that they present a fine source of background information, especially for local residents who can share many of the events with her. There are few observations regarding race relations, except for references to the historical continuity of the Negro settlement near the lake. A serious researcher with an interest in family lineages may wish to examine this book—especially because the resident author presents information from the local news sources that might otherwise be unavailable.

Wheeler, James O., and Stanley D. Brunn. "An Agricultural Ghetto: Negroes in Cass County, Michigan, 1845-1968," *Geographical Review,* 59 (July 1969), 317-329.

The authors state the objectives of their study as follows: "To illustrate the areal changes in Negro land ownership in Calvin Township, Cass County, from the earliest purchase, in 1845, to the present; to examine salient differences and changes in size-number relationships of farms of Negroes and whites; and to investigate current and future patterns of ownership in the light of social and economic changes." Recent increased Negro land ownership is partially attributed to the historical existence of a Negro farm community, availability of land in and near Calvin Township as whites migrate from the area, and proximity to metropolitan areas. Recent Black Muslim farmland acquisitions are cited. The effect of Muslim purchases and farming activities on Negro-white relations is described as occurring "without discernible hostility." Increased land purchases and agricultural undertakings by externally based Negro corporations, with consequent increasing employment opportunities, are predicted.

————. "Negro Migration into Rural Southwestern Michigan," *Geographical Review*, 58 (April 1968), 214-230.

It is suggested in this paper that recent Negro migration into rural southwestern Michigan represents a trend to "suburb skipping" by ghetto dwellers seeking to escape ghetto life, but barred by prejudice from suburban migration. The study utilizes census data as well as data obtained from household interviews in selected communities (in the main, Vandalia) to document the "suburb skipping" hypothesis. It also compares Negro-white demographic composition and traces Negro in-migration patterns. The research uncovers significant race-related contrasts in age structure, work and shopping travel patterns, type and place of employment, home ownership, assessments of problems associated with living in small communities, and perceptions about whether the community is growing or declining. Many of these findings are noted in the second edition. The reader may want to consider the relationship between the trend to "suburb skipping" proposed by Wheeler and Brunn and the remarks by Grodzins quoted in Chapter Nine.

Williams and Works. *Cass County Michigan: Comprehensive Area-Wide Plan for Water and Sewer Services.* Grand Rapids, Michigan: 1967.

This document is interesting to the general researcher for several reasons. In addition to the valuable information brought to the analysis, it points to a feature of community research that should be stressed. Namely, bits and pieces of information can be found in most unlikely sources. A researcher with an interest in Cass County might be tempted to pass by such a document in a library, assuming that it dealt with technical aspects of public utilities. However, as chapters in the second edition demonstrate, the report uncovers a number of interesting types of data and presents them in a comprehensive and meaningful fashion.

BLACK NEIGHBORS

NEGROES IN A NORTHERN RURAL COMMUNITY
SECOND EDITION
GEORGE K. HESSLINK
WITH THE CONTRIBUTION OF JOANNE M. HESSLINK

Cases of stable and egalitarian communities of whites and Negroes in the United States are so rare that the discovery of a clear-cut instance is like finding a gold mine. George Hesslink has written a fascinating historical and sociological account of the development, persistence, and problems of a rural northern community that has remained bi-racial in character for more than a century.

—from the Foreword by David Street

First published in 1968, *Black Neighbors* was hailed as a path-breaking sociological study of a uniquely enduring community of blacks and whites in America today. Based on extensive field work in Cass County, Michigan, in the mid-1960's, this pioneering effort in community studies research contributes greatly to our understanding of the manner in which genuine racial integration can actually work.

The second edition now offers a re-study of the same community made five years later, during separate visits in 1970 and 1971. Not surprisingly, the author found that many noteworthy changes had occurred in the study area during the elapsed years—the nature of race relations in the community reflected in significant ways, in fact, the pace of similar developments in the United States in general.

The three new chapters added for the second edition discuss the nature of community reactions to the first edition, the methodological difficulties this awareness generated, and the consequent alterations in field procedures. In addition, the author reviews emerging trends

(Continued on back flap)